Between Two Cultures

An Introduction to Economic History

Also by Carlo Cipolla

Before the Industrial Revolution: European Economy and Society, 1000–1700

Clocks and Culture, 1300–1700

Faith, Reason, and the Plague in Seventeenth Century Tuscany

Between Two Cultures
An Introduction to Economic History

Carlo M. Cipolla

Translated by Christopher Woodall

W • W • Norton & Company
New York   London

To Ora with love

Published in Great Britain under the title, *Between History and Economics:
An Introduction to Economic History.*

Originally published in Italian as *Tra Due Culture*.

This publication was made possible through the cooperation of *Biblioteca
Italia,* a Giovanni Agnelli programme for the diffusion of Italian culture.

Printed in the United States of America
Manufacturing by The Maple-Vail Manufacturing Group.

Library of Congress Cataloging-in-Publication Data

Cipolla, Carlo M.
[Tra due culture. English]
Between two cultures / by Carlo M. Cipolla; translated by
Christopher Woodall.—1st American ed.
p.   cm.
Translation of: Tra due culture.
Includes bibliographical references and index.
1. Economic history.   I. Title.
HC21.C5313   1991
330.9—dc20   90–22994
ISBN 0-393-02977-8

W.W. Norton & Company, Inc.,
500 Fifth Avenue, New York, N.Y. 10110
W.W. Norton & Company, Ltd.,
10 Coptic Street, London WC1A 1PU

1 2 3 4 5 6 7 8 9 0

Contents

List of Figures

List of Plates

Preface

We usually watch a theatrical spectacle from a seat in the auditorium. If everything runs smoothly, we see only what we are meant to see and fall under the spell of the unfolding story; sound, lights, sets and action all help to perfect the illustration and enhance the performance. But a production can also be viewed from the wings – and then the show is transformed. The focus is no longer on the plot: it is the production itself, the work going on behind the scenes that grips our attention. We see ropes and pulleys, electric cables, spotlights, stage sets and machinery, actors who have just come off, panting from the effort of performance, their make-up smudged and their faces running with sweat. Waiting their turn, others, visibly nervous, can be seen adjusting their costumes, trying out the facial expressions needed for their roles. There is a hushed coming-and-going of actors, managers and stage-hands, whispering and gesturing, while everything appears to proceed in the utmost confusion.

The work of historians too is generally enjoyed from the 'auditorium'. The historian's audience is invited to yield to the spell of the events narrated, without worrying about what is happening in the wings – that is, the actual making of the historical narrative: the business of searching out, gathering, interpreting and piecing together the materials that go to make up that great puzzle (Paul Veyne has called it *une intrigue*) that we call history.

This book, by contrast, invites its audience to leave their seats and to come behind the scenes, to observe economic historians putting the 'show' together. Things are not as neatly arranged, as streamlined or as glittering as they appear from the auditorium. But, if the observer remains undeterred by this, he or she will eventually gain an insight into the internal structure and logic of the spectacle, and will feel, I hope, that the effort was worth making. It is indeed worth the trouble to get behind immediate appearances, to take a look at a world that is normally hidden by screens that only professional training enables one to penetrate, and to catch a glimpse of a fascinating form of inquiry.

In particular, a glance behind the scenes of economic history raises peculiar and interesting questions. Economic history is an eminently interdisciplinary subject: it occupies an area of human knowledge at the crossroads of two other disciplines, history and economics, and cannot afford to ignore either of them. If it yields ground on either front, it becomes distorted and runs the risk of losing its identity. The problem is that the two disciplines that underpin economic history belong to two quite different cultures. History has always been the humane discipline *par excellence*. Economics, ever since Ricardo, has progressively distanced itself from both history and the humane sciences. For, while remaining as weak as ever as a basis for prediction, economics stubbornly clings to its foothold in the so-called exact sciences, through the use and misuse of mathematical logic as its fundamental analytical tool. As a result, economic history has come to occupy an awkward position from which it has to mediate between two cultures and two ways of thinking that regrettably remain quite foreign to one another.

Humanist culture originated in ancient Greece. Scientific culture came into being in seventeenth-century Europe and gained strength by adopting a position of polemical opposition and critical hostility towards traditional humanist culture. A bitter conflict arose between the 'moderns' and the 'ancients' (Jones, 1936). The stage of open warfare ended long ago, but an intractable dualism persists. The methodological issues that economic history raises provide an opportunity for taking a long hard look at certain aspects and implications of the distressing dispute that continues to separate these two cultures.

This book is in two parts. Part I, which consists of six chapters, including a would-be conclusion, asks what economic history is and how it is constructed. Part II discusses the principal sources of European economic history from Mycenaean times to the present day, within the framework of the cultural, political and economic developments that gave rise to the documents described and on which the documents themselves throw light. In the original draft, this discussion formed part of chapter 3, which as a result was disproportionately long. Worse, it interrupted the logical thread that binds together the chapters that now form Part I. Since it does in fact represent a separate and logically independent unit, that has been recognized in the final structure of the book. Part II is itself now divided into eight chapters.

It remains for me to thank all those who so generously helped me with the preparation of this book, especially Franco Amatori, Vittore Branca, K. N. Chaudhuri, Luigi De Rosa, Giorgio Doria, Giuseppe Felloni, Emilio Gabba, Gregory Grossman, Keith Hopkins, Takashi Hotta, M. Levy-Leboyer, Massimo Livi Bacci, Jordi Nadal, Antonia Pasi Testa, Vicente Perez Moreda, Raphael Sealey, Marco Spallanzani, Giovanni Vigo, Dante Zanetti, and my students D. H. Fado, E. E. Ruddick and D. W. Wirt.

Carlo Maria Cipolla

Part I

Economic History:
Nature and Method

1   What is Economic History?

The discipline known as 'economic history' (*histoire économique* in French, *Wirtschaftsgeschichte* in German, *storia economica* in Italian, *historia económica* in Spanish and Portuguese, *ekonomicheskaia istoriia* in Russian, *jinji shi* in Chinese, *keizái shi* in Japanese) is the history of facts and of economic events, as they relate to individuals, firms or communities. As such, it differs from the 'history of theories', i.e. the history of economic doctrine. The definition of economic history just given needs to be both narrowed and extended. It needs to be narrowed by pointing out that 'economic history' is to be taken as meaning the economic history of people. One might after all imagine economic histories of ant-hills or of bee societies. Indeed, the natural world itself possesses an economy of its own, the history of which certainly deserves to be written. Yet we normally restrict the term 'economic history' to the history of human beings, be they white, yellow, black or brown, palaeolithic, neolithic or members of an industrial society. This point, which at first sight seems trite, means that economic history must take account of the physiological and psychological characteristics specific to humans, of their rationality and irrationality, and of their mental, social and cultural characteristics, as these appear in both individuals and communities.

On the other hand, the above definition of economic history also needs to be interpreted broadly. The term should refer not only to the chronicling of economic events but also to the analysis of their close and inextricable relations and interactions with social, political and cultural events and institutions.

Economic history is a relatively young discipline. There existed a kind of proto economic history as early as the seventeenth century, but it was not until the second half of the nineteenth century, and, more decisively, the start of the twentieth century, that economic history emerged as a fully-fledged and academically respectable discipline. In a polemical and colourful vein, Henry Hauser wrote that

> Grand History traditionally left such scraps disdainfully to one side. Interrupt a
> tale of glorious exploits to note the price of wheat; replace an eloquent harangue

3

with the history of the candle, of sugar or of coffee; retell the story of spices and spice-traders? That would never do! To relate the life of Master Jourdain the Draper, of Master Josse the Goldsmith and of Master Dimanche the Taylor, of this journeyman capmaker or that mason's apprentice, of tradespeople and riff-raff: that would spell the downfall of History.

Between 1846 and 1856, George Grote, one of the most distinguished Hellenists of his time, managed to publish a monumental *History of Greece* which, where it touched on economic and social life, did so only in passing. Nowadays, a hundred years later, that would be totally inconceivable: even general histories now commonly devote entire chapters to economic and social matters.

Having emerged therefore in the second half of the nineteenth century, the new discipline underwent such extraordinary development during the period from 1930 to 1970 (despite the intervening Second World War) that some of its branches began to go their own way. There are now specialized journals (see table 1) and even university courses given over specifically to the history of population, the history of commerce, the history of agriculture, the history of industry, the history of money and banking, the history of transport, business history, and social history. The history of economic history over the last three centuries thus provides a fascinating example of the birth, growth and evolution of a new discipline.

Economic history and to an even greater extent those disciplines that have grown up around it are, however, the result of an artificial partitioning of human activity. Like *homo faber* or *homo philosophicus*, *homo oeconomicus* is a pure abstraction. Reality consists of people in all their biological, psychological and social complexity. Similarly, society does not function in watertight compartments: it operates rather as a vastly complex whole, articulated at different but inextricably interdependent levels. In real life, there is no such thing as economic history, just as there is no such thing as political history, social history, cultural history, or history of technology. Instead there is just *history* – that is to say, life in its infinite and complex variety, a magma in continual flux, powerful yet fragile. For the sake of descriptive and analytic clarity one is obliged to make use of the categories mentioned above. But one must never lose sight of the fact that such categories are the product of heroic efforts at simplification, at times verging on absurdity.

This means that, in order to gain a fully rounded picture of the phenomena that they wish to study and describe, even when these phenomena are of a purely economic nature, economic historians must take into account the findings of other disciplines, such as the history of technology and science, the history of medicine, archaeology, anthropology, numismatics, the history of law, the history of philosophy, diplomatic and military history, the history of religions, the history of art, and the history of architecture. All these disciplines (not listed here in order of importance) are able to make substantial contributions to our

Table 1   Journals of social and economic history: date of first issue and country of publication

Hansische Geschichtsblätter	1871 Germany
Vierteljahrschrift für Sozial und Wirtschaftsgeschichte	1903 Germany
Revue d'histoire économique et sociale	1908 France
Business History Review	1926 USA
Economic History Review	1927 UK
Journal of Economic and Business History	1928 USA
Annales d'histoire économique et sociale	1929 France
Rivista di storia economica	1936 Italy
Journal of Economic History	1941 USA
Past and Present	1952 UK
Scandinavian Economic History Review	1953 Sweden
Agricultural History Review	1953 USA
Journal of Transport History	1953 UK
Kwartalnik Historii Kultury Materialnej	1953 Poland
Economia e storia	1954 Italy
Australian Economic History Review	1956 Australia
Afdeling Agrarische Geschiedenis Bijdragen	1956 Netherlands
Journal of the Economic and Social History of the Orient	1957 Netherlands
Histoire des entreprises	1958 France
Technology and Culture	1959 USA
Comparative Studies in Society and History	1959 USA
Jahrbuch für Wirtschaftsgeschichte	1960 Germany
Rivista di storia dell'agricoltura	1961 Italy
Indian Economic and Social History Review	1963 India
Annales de démographie historique	1964 France
Explorations in Economic History	1964 USA
Journal of Social History	1967 USA
Histoire sociale	1968 Canada
Anuario de historia económica y social	1968 Spain
Journal of European Economic History	1972 Italy
Revista de historia económica e social	1978 Portugal
Società e storia	1978 Italy
Revista de historia económica	1983 Spain
Boletín de la Asociación de demografía histórica	1983 Spain
Annali di storia dell'impresa	1985 Italy

understanding of economic history, and might therefore be considered subsidiary to economic history. Yet this would involve a distortion in perspective. For economic history might equally well be considered just one of the subsidiary disciplines of any of those listed above. It depends on one's vantage point.

In the term 'economic history', the word 'history' is liable to give rise to misunderstandings regarding the object of the discipline. After all, 'history' tends in everyday usage to refer to antiquarian matters. It is therefore all too easy to draw the inference that economic history is about, or ought to be about, economic events of the distant past. This notion, however, is quite mistaken. It is true that history is concerned with the past. But all events, inasmuch as they are indeed events, have already occurred and therefore belong to the past. The difference between the past and the future is that, whereas the former consists of events that can be neither blotted out nor modified, the future offers a range of alternatives. What we call the present is no more than that fleeting instant which as soon as it is perceived as factual reality already belongs to the past. History, inasmuch as it is concerned with events and not with predictions, is about the past; but this past may be extremely distant or on the other hand very recent, dating back to palaeolithic times or no further than the day before yesterday. Accordingly, I find nothing to quarrel with in the definition of economic history given in the *Dictionary of Modern Economics*, by Horton, Ripley and Schnapper (1948, p. 106): 'Economic history is the study of past and *present* economic events in one or more countries' (my emphasis).

It does of course make a considerable difference whether one studies events that occurred hundreds or thousands of years ago, or events that happened only a few years or months ago. The disparity in time is bound to be reflected in the type, quality and quantity of information available. Furthermore, the historian who studies the distant past has greater opportunities for placing events within a historical framework that takes account of their long-term consequences. On the other hand, the greater the period of time separating the historian from the events studied, the more difficult it becomes to gain an understanding of the mentality and culture of the people concerned.

There are therefore marked differences in the methods and training of economic historians, according to whether they study periods that are remote or recent. Economic history, however, is concerned with the whole of the past. As W. Kula has written, 'the notion that economic history is a science of the past and economics a science of the present just won't bear scrutiny' (1972, p. 78).

Like economic history, economics is a relatively young discipline: it was not until the second half of the eighteenth century that it underwent substantial development. In the course of its development, it too has split into numerous sub-branches, each giving rise to a specialized literature, specialist journals and specialized university courses. As a result, one now speaks and writes of macro-economics, micro-economics, political economy, econometrics, industrial economics, labour economics, the economics of transport, the theory of money and banking, agricultural economics and health economics. In Italy there are university courses on the economics of tourism. There is an evident parallelism between the sub-branches of economics and those of economic history. The counterpart of macro-economics is general economic history. The counterpart of econometrics is cliometrics. The counterpart of micro-economics is business history. And so on.

To clarify the relationship between economics and general economic history, it is useful to consider,

(a) the issues addressed by the two disciplines and the conceptual instruments they deploy in their analysis;
(b) the aims of the two disciplines.

Let us first look at the kind of issues that the two disciplines tackle and the conceptual instruments that they deploy. Clearly, a study that sets out to establish the date of birth of a particular tradesman cannot be deemed a work of economic history simply because the key character under investigation happens to have been engaged in trade. Similarly, a paper detailing the marital mishaps of a banker cannot reasonably be viewed as a work of economic history unless the said mishaps were the principal cause of the man's subsequent bankruptcy. In order to qualify as economic history, a given piece of research must tackle issues of an economic nature – that is, to put it crudely, issues that relate in some way to the three basic questions in economics:

(1) What to produce?
(2) How to produce it?
(3) How to distribute the product?

In practice, these three questions branch out into a series of more specific questions relating to the determination of prices; the allocation of scarce resources; short-term and long-term variations in production, employment, and demand, and their structure; variations in the distribution of wealth and income; and so on.[1]

To qualify as economic history a piece of research must employ the conceptual instruments, the analytical categories and the type of logic forged by economic theory. This point was made back in the late nineteenth century by Luigi Cossa, when he wrote that economic theory 'must supply economic history with the theoretical criteria indispensable for the selection, co-ordination and evaluation of the facts, circumstances, and institutions which represent the substance of economic history' (1892, pp. 26–8).

One may be tempted to object that the conceptual instruments and the paradigms developed by contemporary economics are ill suited to the interpretation of a very remote and hence different reality. The objection is fundamentally incorrect, or at least is in need of substantial qualification – we shall return to this point in chapter 5. The fact remains that, if a particular analysis, taking events of economic history as its subject, fails to employ concepts, categories and paradigms borrowed from economic theory, not only will it not qualify as economic history, but its findings are also liable to be highly questionable. On the other hand, it must be conceded that the most sophisticated techniques of economic

[1] But see the points made below in chapter 2.

theory can safely be ignored by economic historians. As T. W. Hutchinson has pointed out, ' [sophisticated] abstract analysis has no real-world use. . . . Evidence fed back from real-world users seems to . . . suggest that the analysis which is actually useful . . . is of a basic and fairly unsophisticated "sophomore" level, and that more sophisticated models are just as likely to be misleading as helpful in real-world advising' (1977, p. 93).

There is of course nothing to prevent the economist from delving into and taking examples from the past, and, equally, nothing to prohibit the economic historian from studying contemporary economic phenomena. Moreover, within certain limits, to be examined below, economic history and economics should not only address the same issues, but also use the same conceptual instruments and analytic categories. It is thus not surprising that an economist of the calibre of A. K. Cairncross should have written, 'I find it difficult to think of economists and economic historians as separate animals. Their interests are fundamentally the same. The job of the economist is to explain how the economy works; the job of the economic historian is to explain how it worked in the past. But the one runs into the other.' Yet economic history and economics are and remain two quite distinct disciplines.

As a rule, economists are future-oriented. John Maynard Keynes argued that 'the economist must study the present in the light of the past for the purpose of the future'. And John Hicks reiterated that 'much of the work of economists is concerned with the future, with forecasts and with planning' (1979, p. 62). Having identified certain economic variables as relevant, economists look for regularities in the relations between those variables. To put it crudely, they are interested in uncovering 'laws' on the basis of which they can produce reliable forecasts and plans. Economists arrive at their 'laws' and paradigms either by way of concrete factual analyses (hence, by way of an analysis of a more or less recent past) or by means of formal deductive logic. Even when using abstract deductive logic, they rely on notions and relations which, however intuitive they may be, are substantially derived from experience. Hicks, then, after making the remark quoted above, quite rightly feels obliged to add, 'But forecasts are trivial and planning useless unless they are based on facts; and the facts that are at our disposal are facts of the past. It may be recent past, but it is past all the same.' Yet economists remain future-oriented and, to a lesser or greater degree, depending on whether their forecasting techniques are merely extrapolative, or adaptive, or reflect so-called rational expectations, implicitly assume that the future will somehow reproduce the past.

Historians, by contrast, are resolutely past-oriented and thus neither worry about the future nor claim any ability to influence it. At times they may feel tempted to emphasize certain apparent analogies and even to rough out a few 'laws'. But these are perilous deviations. Whereas economists use past experience to predict or to attempt to influence the future, historians content themselves with observing the past in order to understand it on its own terms. As Hempel remarked, 'history – in contrast with the so-called physical sciences – is concerned with the description of particular events of the past, rather than with the search for general laws which might govern those events'.

This difference in the orientations of economists and historians entails two different methodological approaches. Anxious to identify working paradigms, economists tend to consider only those variables that seem to display certain regularities in their reciprocal relations, and that reflect predictable and rational forms of behaviour. Numerous other variables, summarily condemned as 'exogenous', are jettisoned or ignored. As R. C. O. Matthews and C. H. Feinstein aptly observed, 'what economists usually do is try to set up a limited model of the system's laws of motion, embracing some aspects only and relegating the rest to the category of exogenous. . . . Exogeneity [however] is an attribute of the chosen framework of the thought, not an attribute of the events themselves' (1982, p. 13). The number of endogenous variables accounted for by economists in their models may be taken as k.

Economic historians cannot proceed in the same way. To explain the functioning and performance of a particular economy, economic historians must endeavour to take into consideration as many variables and as much evidence – both economic and non-economic – as possible.[2] They have to take account of legal institutions, social structures, cultural factors and political institutions, both as regards the impact of such institutions and structures on the performance of the economy in question, and, equally, as regards the impact of the economic situation on the said institutions and structures. Historians must consider geographical and environmental circumstances, climatic variations, the biological conditions of the human population, as well as the populations of animals, microbes and viruses coexisting with or afflicting the human communities.

Nor can economic historians afford to neglect any of the other minute variables and accidents – be they rational or irrational, predictable or unpredictable – that play a part in the development of a given historical situation. To the economic historian, the stomach-ache that prevents a businessman from clinching a particular deal, the unforeseen and unforeseeable outbreak of an epidemic, the declaration of a war, and the erratic action of a fanatical Middle Eastern leader in sabotaging oil supplies are all relevant endogenous events. In other words, economic historians have to take into account as many as possible of the n variables of a given historical situation.[3] What economists dismiss as 'noise', 'disturbance' or

[2] This is true as a first approximation. The issue is investigated in greater detail in chapter 4.
[3] The difference between the economist's and the historian's points of view of accidental events was already clear to Karl Bücher at the end of the nineteenth century when he wrote, 'The historian of a particular epoch must not forget anything of importance that occurred, whereas the economist can limit himself to indicating that which is normal while calmly leaving to one side whatever is fortuitous' (1893, ch. 3).

as 'exogenous' features may, in the eyes of economic historians, be the very essence of a unique set of historical circumstances.[4]

The set of k variables that interests theoretical economists is considerably smaller and more homogeneous than the set of n variables that historians take into account. It is the limited nature of k as compared to n and the rigidity of the correlations assumed within the set k that give the theorizing of economists its unreal and artificial complexion. And it is the vast range of n, its extreme heterogeneity and its chaotic character that prevent historians from formulating laws and that compel them to recognize the uniqueness of each historical situation.

Keynes held that the very act of substituting numbers for letters to measure the variables or the relations among the variables of a theoretical model was sufficient to render the model unusable as the conceptual instrument of the theory. 'It is of the essence of a model', Keynes wrote, 'that one does *not* fill in real values for the variable functions. To do so would make it useless as a model. For as soon as this is done, the model loses its generality and its value as a mode of thought' (1973 edn, XIV, ii, p. 296). In other words, economists are limited by the generality of their paradigms just as historians are limited by the unavoidable specificity of their narratives.

This point becomes clearer when applied to the distinction that economists make between the 'short run' and the 'long run'. The definition of the 'short run' supplied by standard economic texts is relatively simple and apparently precise: it is that period during which the fixed capital of a firm may be assumed to remain unaltered. Similarly, at the macro-economic level, economists work on the hypothesis that any short-run variations in capital stock will not have any significant impact on the potential or the real gross product. Taking a closer look, however, it is apparent that economists working with macro-economic models assume that in the short run a range of other historical variables remain fixed, including population size and age structure, the level of education and skills of the working population, the technology of the society in question, its legal institutions, political and social structures, its value scales, organization systems, tastes and fashions. This does not constitute a serious problem since the factors mentioned tend to undergo significant change only during periods of upheaval (social and political strife, scientific and technological revolutions, and wars) and then to settle down to relatively slow rates of change. Except during such periods of upheaval, the economist's rough 'short-run' model is therefore a fairly accurate depiction of reality.

---

[4] As Lord Bullock observed, any historical reconstruction would be incomplete and misleading were it to exclude 'the impact and chronological order of events frequently unpredictable in their combination and effects, the interplay of personalities, the conflicts of particular interests, the mixture of rational and irrational behaviour, the element of chance' (1977, p. 18).

It is when the focus is switched from the short run to the long run that problems suddenly emerge. In the long run everything is subject to change and it is possible neither to postulate invariable factors or quantities nor to get rid of awkward variables by labelling them 'exogenous'. In the long run everything changes and everything is endogenous. For economists the problem becomes intractable. During the 1930s Keynes shrugged it off with a quip: the long run is of no interest to economists because 'in the long run we are all dead'. After the Second World War, this dismissive stance could no longer be maintained. The problem of long-term economic development forced itself on the attention of everyone – politicians, economists, the general public. A branch of economics known as 'development theory' became fashionable, though it was and remains a total failure. The point is not that 'in the long run we are all dead', but that in the long run every problem is historical. This point is relevant not only in terms of description but also in practical terms. It means that economists and engineers cannot single-handedly orchestrate the development of a country's economy. Back in the 1940s, as China prepared to industrialize, M. Chiang had already grasped this when he wrote,

since we were knocked out by cannon balls, naturally we became interested in them, thinking that by learning to make them we could strike back. But history seems to move in very curious ways. From studying cannon balls we came to mechanical inventions, which in turn led us to political reforms; from political reforms we began to see political theories, which led us again to the philosophies of the West. On the other hand, through mechanical inventions we saw science, from which we came to understand scientific method and the scientific mind. Step by step we were led farther and farther away from the cannon ball – yet we came nearer and nearer to it. (1947, p. 4)

The twists and turns of history point to another problem with economic theory: its assumption that people will tend to act in a rational way. In order to formulate a logical and generally applicable theory, economists have to assume strong associations of a repetitive character between certain basic variables. But this assumption is unrealistic: people rarely behave as expected. 'Man', wrote Cairncross, 'is a wayward and inconsistent creature and his behaviour, as Keynes put it, is not homogeneous through time.' However hard they endeavour to introduce elements of probability, economists work with models that are inspired by what Pascal termed *l'esprit géométrique*.

Historians are concerned not only with a very much greater number of variables, but also with unmeasurable, irrational and unpredictable elements, and with continually changing associations among variables. No convenient assumptions can be made. It is important to stress that the difference between n and $(n-k)$ is not merely quantitative. If it were, one might naïvely believe that in this computer age it would be possible to set up systems equations with a number of variables approaching n and then to effect a massive 'co-optation of the exogenous'. This is nonsense. Whereas *k* represents an artificial homogenous set of more or less rational and predictably associated variables, $(n - k)$ is a chaotic set of heterogeneous elements, many of which are utterly unpredictable, irremediably irrational and/or unquantifiable. As if this were not enough, history deploys great imagination in a game involving the perpetual modification in unforeseeable ways of the links by which the variables in this set are related. *L'esprit géométrique* cannot cope with this intractably complicated and variable set. What is required is the finer and more malleable – but arguably less scientific and harder to define – *esprit de finesse*.

But what is this subtle *esprit de finesse*? Even Pascal, who intuitively sensed its existence, was hard-pressed to provide a definition: he stumbles, repeats himself, and falls back on vague and confused phraseology.[5] Paraphrasing Pascal, I would suggest that the ingredients of the *esprit de finesse* are a gift for sensing the existence and importance of an infinite number of variables many of which cannot be known, measured or defined; an acute awareness of the high frequency of non-linear and (in physicists' terminology) chaotic associations; a deep suspicion of strict relations of causality; and, lastly, a sense of the continuous presence of conditions under which chance and chaos play an important role. *Esprit de finesse* is, as it were, a sixth sense that evolves in gifted historians as a result of their familiarity with their sources, enabling them to be flexible in their conclusions, cautious in their explanations, always aware of the inherent and unmeasurable imprecision of their reconstruction.

History often appears to repeat itself in various ways. Yet, however striking the resemblances to what happened on other occasions, every historical situation is unique and can never be repeated. To resort to a crude analogy, the historical situation is like a person – bound to resemble other individuals but none the less unique for all time. The fundamental fact that history *does not* repeat itself gives the traditional saying *historia magistra vitae* a special significance. Indeed the notion that history repeats itself and the maxim 'history is life's teacher' are incompatible. For, if a particular situation really did recur, those who had emerged as losers on the first occasion would, with the benefit of experience, behave in a

---

[5] 'In the [*esprit géométrique*] the basic principles are palpable, but remote from ordinary usage. . . . in the [*esprit de finesse*] the basic principles are those in common usage and in full view of everybody . . . it is only a question of good sight; but it must be good, for the principles are so subtle and so numerous that it is almost impossible that some will not escape notice. . . .

'But the reason why geometers are not subtle-minded is that they do not see what is before them, and that, accustomed to the exact and plain principles of geometry, and not reasoning till they have well inspected and arranged their principles, they are lost in matters of subtlety. . . . [The principles of subtlety] are scarcely seen; they are felt rather than seen; there is the greatest difficulty in making them felt by those who do not of themselves perceive them. These principles are so fine and so numerous that a very delicate and very clear sense is needed to perceive them, and to judge rightly and justly when they are perceived, without for the most part being able to demonstrate them in order as in geometry'. (1960 tr., pp. 264–5)

different manner the next time round. Owing to their change in behaviour, the new situation would differ from the previous one.

Henry Kissinger once wrote that history 'is not a cookbook offering pre-tested recipes' (1979, p. 54). This is the corollary of the previous claim that history does not repeat itself. I imagine that some people at this juncture might wonder what the point of studying history is. To my way of thinking, the pursuit of knowledge is its own justification. In the specific case of history, I find it hard to conceive of a civilized society that would be uninterested in the study of its own origins. History tells us who we are, where we come from, and why we are what we are. To me, all this is elementary. Yet I am certain that some might consider this viewpoint elitist and socially unjustifiable. To such people, infected with Benthamite utilitarianism or current notions of narrow relevancy, it should be pointed out that the study of history has an eminently educational significance. As Huizinga wrote, history is not only a branch of knowledge; it is also 'an intellectual form for understanding the world'. Moreover, the study of history makes it possible to see the current problems that we have to face in their true dimension and, as Richard Lodge wrote in 1894, 'it furnishes the only means by which a man can fairly understand the present'.

The study of history is a practical exercise in understanding human beings and their society. We all tend to be parochial, intolerant and ethnocentric, and hence all need continuously to strive to be informed and sensitive about lifestyles, values and behaviours that differ from our own. After all, this is the basis of all civilized coexistence, both within and between societies. In this respect, it is essential to study history, and to make that journey into the past that historical inquiry entails. Travel opens the eyes, enriches the traveller with knowledge, and broadens the mind. The longer the journey and the remoter the destination, the greater is the challenge to our vision of the world. This is why I believe that those historians who study the more remote periods possess – other things being equal – a subtler and more sophisticated sense of history than those who specialize in periods closer to our own. I do not, however, believe or wish to suggest that the study of history (or, indeed, travel) is all that is required to turn someone into a sage. Were that so, professors of history would all be sages – which is far from being the case. Travel and a knowledge of history are necessary but insufficient conditions for an understanding of human events.

2   Identifying the Issues

Any piece of research must, if it is to be of some worth, attempt to supply an answer, no matter how partial and provisional (there are no definitive answers in scientific matters) to a problem or set of problems. The first thing to do, therefore, when embarking upon an investigation or sitting down to draft a paper, is to formulate the problem (or set of problems) to which an answer is sought. The quality of the answer depends to a considerable degree on how clearly the problem has been formulated. A problem set out in confused, imprecise or inappropriate terms can only give rise to confused and imprecise answers.

In chapter 1 it was argued that economic history has to address problems of an essentially economic nature. This is valid as far as it goes, but needs some qualifying. It does not mean, for example, that economic historians should pounce unquestioningly on issues addressed by the sacred texts of economic theory and then proceed to rerun, within a historical framework, debates already held by economists. This may happen, of course, but in practice a variety of factors come into play that provide for a broad margin of flexibility. Hence, although the problems addressed by economic historians are of an economic nature, they may none the less differ in significant ways from those addressed by economists. There are several different reasons for this.

First, as has already been pointed out, economists aim to identify particular associations among variables, interactions or even 'laws' which hold valid in different historical situations, whereas economic historians aim to describe and reconstruct particular economic circumstances in their historical uniqueness and specificity.

Secondly, with the emergence of economic history as a discipline in its own right, a set of issues has taken shape which, while remaining of an essentially economic nature, pertain to economic history.

Thirdly, the emphasis placed by economists and economic historians on particular phenomena differs according to the type of economy studied. An economic historian studying the slave economy of classical antiquity or the manorial economy of the early Middle Ages is unlikely to worry

14

about fluctuations in employment levels in the same way as an economist interested in modern industrial societies is.

Lastly, while it is not impossible for economists to refer to economies, economic structures and economic events of the more distant past, their prevailing interest in making forecasts and drafting plans for the near future means that they normally investigate the contemporary economic scene. The issues that arouse their curiosity reflect the current interests of the culture and society in which they live. As consumers of information, economists are therefore more or less attuned to the producers of economic information, since the latter are part of the same culture and the same society as the economists, and therefore share their curiosity and concerns. This match – albeit imperfect – between the demand and the supply of information means that economists normally unearth without great difficulty the kind of information that they need.[1]

Economic historians usually work under very different conditions. It has been argued in chapter 1 that there is nothing to prevent an economic historian from studying contemporary economic developments. Indeed, both in Europe and America economic historians have recently shown an increasing interest in the economic events of the twentieth century. Where this is their field of study, they often find, like economists, that documentary evidence of the kind that they require is available. But more often, economic historians concentrate on societies and economies from a distant past. Inevitably the concerns of researchers are not matched by the information at their disposal. The reason for this lies in the fact that the questions raised by historians (like those raised by economists) reflect and arise from the culture and the society to which they belong, whereas the documentary material with which historians must grapple responds to the questions, concerns and curiosity of a different culture, a different society, a different world. As I have written elsewhere, 'we would like to know the size of the population, the patterns of consumption, the level of production of, let us say, the province of Rheims in France at the beginning of this millennium. The documents of the time give us instead detailed information of the miracles performed by St Gibrian in the area' (Cipolla, 1976, p. XIV).

---

[1] Even among producers and consumers of economic information who live in the same period and country, this match is not always perfect. The consumers are not always sufficiently aware of the conditions and methods by which information is produced. Those who produce information within the public sphere are bureaucrats who, either owing to the nature of their training or for budgetary reasons, are not always able to produce information of the quality desired by the consumers, many of whom belong to the academic world. As regards information originating in the private sector, it is not always in the interest of companies to reveal the details that economists require to complete their investigations. Lastly, governments may find it to be to their advantage to conceal or blur data to which certain groups of scholars would like to gain access. For example, in the United States the budget of the CIA is hidden in the budgets of numerous other government departments. In the Soviet Union, military expenditure has until recently been kept completely secret. In Germany, the Nazi government published information that deliberately underestimated the country's gold reserves.

An essential part of the historian's job is therefore to mediate between the subjective nature of the demand for information and the subjective nature of its supply. This is what Paul Veyne must have had in mind when he wrote that historians are constantly involved in 'a struggle against the viewpoint imposed on them by their sources'.

Economists, sociologists and anthropologists are forced to wage the same battle when they turn their attention to contemporary societies that are economically and socially backward. Towards the middle of the nineteenth century, an English scholar turned to a Turkish Cadi for information about the region he administered – its population, trade and industry, and its archaeological remains. Eventually he received the following reply:

> My Illustrious Friend, and Joy of my Liver [an Islamic expression of friendship]!
> The thing you ask of me is both difficult and useless. Although I have passed all my days in this place, I have neither counted the houses nor have I inquired into the number of the inhabitants; and as to what one person loads on his mules and the other stows away in the bottom of his ship, that is no business of mine. But, above all, as to the previous history of this city, God only knows the amount of dirt and confusion that the infidels may have eaten before the coming of the sword of Islam. It were unprofitable for us to inquire into it.
> Oh my soul! oh my lamb! seek not after the things that concern thee not. Thou camest unto us, and we welcomed thee. Go in peace. (Layard, 1853, p. 663)

The greater the cultural gulf between the society to which historians belong and that which they investigate, the greater the mismatch between their interests and the available information. There is some sense in applying a set of questions derived from current monetary theory to the study of the monetary history of the British Empire during the nineteenth century. But there can be no sense whatever in an attempt to repeat the exercise with the Roman Empire of the second century AD: not a single question could be answered.

For such reasons, historians have to adapt their questions to their sources: in other words, they have to frame their questions with regard to the period and culture that they are studying and the surviving evidence. In this process, historians inevitably distance their concerns so far from those of economists that in extreme cases the latter no longer find the historians' research of any interest whatsoever.

When an economist and an economic historian put their heads together to investigate the economic history of a much earlier society, the inevitable clash occurs right at the beginning of the project, when drawing up a list of issues to be addressed. The economist is likely to suggest topics and problems that strike the historian as anachronistic and ahistorical, since available evidence will not be able to support such an inquiry. On the other hand, the questions raised by the historian – representing an attempt at mediation between what one would like to know and what the sources disclose – may seem to the economist to be devoid of any economic significance. Indeed, the economist may mistakenly conclude that the economic historian is ignorant of economics.

Recently, especially in the United States, there has emerged a school of economic historians who, having been trained primarily as economists and being concerned above all with contemporary economic history, fail to appreciate the problems posed by the available sources. Concerned first and foremost with the theoretical 'model' that they have fabricated, and failing to unearth adequate sources to substantiate and verify the same 'model', they readily turn to so-called 'proxy evidence', assuming equivalences which instead should often be demonstrated.

It is of the utmost importance for the success of a given piece of research that it should clearly identify at the outset the problem that it seeks to address. This does not mean that the initial formulation of the problem must govern the whole of the subsequent research, for as the investigation progresses unexpected evidence may – and usually does – emerge, bringing to light imperfections, weaknesses or even downright mistakes in the theoretical models and working hypotheses with which the researcher began. To respond to this by digging in one's heels and blindly pursuing a preconceived approach is proof of a closed mind. Historians have to be always on the look-out for indications that they need to modify or overhaul their initial model. In other words, there must be perpetual feedback between the formulation of problems and the process of gathering evidence. It is a sign neither of fickleness nor of inconsistency to modify or reformulate the issues and models with which one is working: rather it is evidence of mental flexibility and intellectual honesty. The aim of research is not to twist facts to prove a theory, but rather to adapt the theory to provide a better account of the facts.

3 The Sources

Economic historians (as well as general historians – or, for that matter, scholars in any other branch of history) differ from novelists in that they do not invent their stories, even if at times their intuition or imagination may tempt them to fill in certain gaps with more or less gratuitous hypotheses. Whatever field they specialize in, historians reconstruct the past on the basis of evidence which they must treat with circumspection, and in accordance with strict criteria, as outlined below. The ability of a historian may indeed be measured by the scrupulous rigour and intelligence that he brings to bear on the available evidence. When students and general readers pick up a history book, they tend to concentrate on the thread of narrative and to place an implicit trust in the historian: they rarely stop to question the quality of the documentary research that underpins the work. The bad habit that publishers have of relegating notes to the end of the chapter or even to the end of the book (instead of putting them where they belong, i.e. at the foot of the page) reinforces this trend towards acritical credulity. Yet it is precisely the quality of the documentary research that validates (or invalidates) the historical narrative.

Langlois and Siegnobos wrote in 1898 that 'without documents there is no history', and in 1961 Samaran echoed this message word for word. In his book *The Practice of History* G. R. Elton stated that 'knowledge of all the sources and competent criticism of them . . . are the basic requirements of a reliable historiography' (1967, p. 86). Lucien Febvre wrote that he considered history 'an inquiry conducted scientifically, not a science' – that is, an inquiry based on documentation diligently gathered and critically evaluated. Historians must always base their work on documentary evidence. Even when relating events that have occurred in their own lifetime, they need to utilize sources that complement, flesh out and corroborate their own direct observations. A sentence that Conan Doyle put into the mouth of Sherlock Holmes in 'The Adventure of the Copper Beeches' applies well to the historian: 'Data! Data! Data! I can't make bricks without clay.'

The documentary work undertaken by historians may be divided into three stages:

(1) the collection of documentary sources;
(2) the critical examination of these sources;
(3) their interpretation and use.

COLLECTING SOURCES

The gathering of documentary sources and the collation of the information that they contain demand particular effort and are liable to run into considerable difficulties. The documentation available is often patchy. There are essentially three reasons for this: the documentation sought may never have been produced; if produced, it may have been deliberately destroyed; or it may have been accidentally destroyed or lost. Each of these possibilities deserves a brief comment.

The documentation that the historian seeks may never have been produced simply because the society concerned felt no need to answer the questions that interest him. This situation has been discussed in chapter 2. Some kinds of evidence, however, may never have been produced for more banal reasons. Many agreements are sealed with a simple handshake. Especially in periods and societies where illiteracy prevailed, oral agreements would have been the norm. Even nowadays, in advanced societies, many messages, decisions and instructions are relayed by telephone and leave no trace behind. Other events fail to generate any evidence because contemporaries judge them to be obvious or trivial.

Even when documentation is produced, it may be destroyed at a later date. It may for example be in someone's interest to see that particular documents disappear, thereby ensuring that no trace is left of the events to which the documents referred. But the deliberate destruction of documents is not always a criminal act. Documentary materials are often destroyed simply because people do not think they are worth keeping. In 1692, and more drastically in 1720, the government of the Republic of Venice, even though it was extremely careful to preserve all its own administrative documents, instructed the archivist in charge of the records of the city's public health services to 'separate the useful from the useless' and to get rid of everything deemed 'useless', to make room for all the new documents that were piling up (Carbone, 1962, pp. 19–20). It is far from certain that the material that the archivist judged 'useless' and sent to be destroyed would be considered 'useless' by today's historians.

Lastly, evidence may be destroyed by accident. The classic instances of this are fires, floods and earthquakes, all of which have been known to obliterate entire archives. In 1574 and 1577, two disastrous fires laid waste to the Doge's Palace in Venice, destroying a great many of the administrative documents kept there. In 1755 Lisbon was devastated by an earthquake which destroyed many of the records relating to Portuguese explorations and trade in Africa and Asia in the sixteenth and seventeenth centuries. Acts of war must also be numbered among the accidental causes of destruction, however barbarously wilful the act responsible. The account of the destruction of the great library in Alexandria during the Bellum Alexandrinum may be essentially a legend. The 'library' that caught fire in 47 BC may in fact have been no more than a warehouse for books awaiting export (Rice Holmes, 1983, III, pp. 487–9). But there is no counting the acts of vandalism perpetrated by men during the course of wars and conflicts, nor are they confined to some dim and distant age of barbarism. On 30 September 1943, in the village of San Paolo Belsito, a detachment of retreating German troops, for reasons that have never been fully clarified (some say on account of a pig that the villagers had failed to declare), set fire to a villa containing a vast wealth of documentary material from the Naples State Archives. This material had been moved out of Naples in the hope of preserving it from the bombardments that the city was suffering at the time. Approximately 55,000 parchment manuscripts and 35,000 books went up in smoke, including documents of the Duchy of Naples, parchment registers containing the deeds of the Angevin monarchs from 1265 to 1434, registers of the deeds of the Aragonese monarchs, registers of some of the main judicial organs of the state and of several Bourbon ministries, and part of the archives of the houses of Bourbon and Farnese. Looking back on the episode, the Director of the Naples Archives wrote, 'It appeared on that dismal morning that all the sources of the history of the Kingdom of Naples, spanning eight centuries, had vanished forever, leaving such a void in the science of our past as could never be filled' (Filangeri, 1954, p. 99; see also Filangeri, 1946, pp. 76–81).

The continual dispersal and destruction of documents owing to carelessness, neglect and aging may also be classified as accidental. It is not known how, when or why the registers of the forty or more notaries of the fairs of Champagne, originally kept in special archives at the fairs themselves, came to be mislaid or destroyed, but with them was lost an extremely precious fund of documentary evidence on the main centre of commercial and financial exchange of the thirteenth century. In April 1682, in London, the directors of the East India Company observed that 'old books and papers . . . are in a confused manner layd in the upper garret of India House'. In January 1717 it was noted that one of the registers relating to Surat had been cut out of its covers and stolen and that 'great quantities of the Company's packets and other papers were thrown in heaps in the Back Warehouse'. A committee was appointed to find a place to store the old papers and to appoint 'a proper officer' to look after them. However, as late as March 1720, the directors observed that 'great numbers of papers, packets, and old books, [have been] removed out of the Secretary's, Accountant's and other offices of the House, and carried into the warehouse on the other side of the garden, where they lye in utmost confusion, and it is feared many of them are destroyed' (Foster, 1966, pp. i–ii).

Losses of this order are not confined to the distant past. In 1938, M. Moresco and G. P. Bognetti warned of the alarming deterioration of one of the most important documentary sources for the economic history of twelfth- and thirteenth-century Europe: the Genoese notarial cartularies of that period. 'It is a threatened treasure', they wrote.

> Owing to the precarious condition to which exceptional events have reduced these documents, now over seven centuries old, and owing to the wear occasioned by the repeated albeit necessary reference made to them, the paper of almost all the oldest of the cartularies is gradually flaking and crumbling away, not only along the outer margins but in many cases in the body itself of the text. To save them, it is essential that they be published. (1938, p. 1)

In this particular case, effective measures were taken: the cartularies were microfilmed, much of their contents was published, and special steps were taken to preserve and restore the originals (see below, Part II, chapter 6). But, for every document that has been saved, a hundred have been left to decay. As regards carelessness, it has to be added that in previous centuries in the West the dispersal of public documents was abetted by the deplorable habit, among those in positions of authority, of taking public documents home with them to study at their leisure. They then frequently forgot – or couldn't be bothered – to return the documents to the office where they belonged and where they ought to have been kept.

In many instances, documents have been preserved more by chance than through deliberate policy. As we shall see, important documents belonging to Jewish merchants trading during the tenth and eleventh centuries in North Africa, the Near East and around the Indian Ocean were preserved by chance in a storehouse (*geniza*) annexe of the Cairo synagogue, merely because Jewish tradition opposes the destruction of writings. The case of the Tebtunis Papyry is even more curious. In Ptolemaic Egypt, the crocodile god Sobk was venerated in a variety of forms and under different names in different villages. In 1900 an American archaeological team was excavating the vast Ptolemaic necropolis at Umm el Baragat. Day after day, all they found were embalmed crocodiles used in the cult of the god Sobk. On 16 January one of the diggers employed by the team became so frustrated by the continual discovery of mummified crocodiles instead of the hoped-for sarcophagi that he thrust his pick into one of the beasts. To everybody's surprise, beneath the mummy's outer cloth bands the crocodile's body was wrapped around with broad leaves of papyrus, which had originally been used for registering contracts, payments and similar transactions. Inspection of the mummies of the other crocodiles led to the recovery of papyrus documents with valuable information on the economic and administrative history of the era (Grenfell et al., 1902, I, pp. v–vii).

Two points may be made at this juncture. First, the bulk of documentary evidence surviving from a particular society is the product of logical but subjective choices (the culture of the society in question, and subsequent decisions about which documents to preserve) and of what Emilio Gabba calls 'capricious fortuity' (earthquakes, floods, fires, acts of vandalism, gradual deterioration, religious convictions, the embalming of crocodiles, and so on). Historians have to take into account the varied reasons for gaps in the documentary evidence, since the lack of a particular kind of evidence may be just as significant as its existence. Secondly, whether owing to conscious choices or to 'capricious fortuity', the remoter the periods studied, the patchier the documentary evidence available. From the point of view of evidence, economic historians of contemporary industrial societies and economic historians of the early Middle Ages or of classical antiquity work at opposite extremes. The former, faced with boundless quantities of evidence, are spoilt for choice.[1] The latter, by contrast, have to work with a small number of paltry and niggardly documents. The evidence available to economic historians specializing in the late Middle Ages or in the early Modern Age falls between these two extremes.

The relative abundance of documentation in the Western world on the modern and contemporary periods is related among other things to the creation of archives – that is, to offices set aside for the arrangement, preservation and consultation of public and private documents. In Part II, chapter 2, mention will be made of the circumstances that in the second half of the eighteenth century led to the creation of the Archivo General de Indias, one of the most important archives in Europe. Here it is also worth mentioning the circumstances surrounding the creation of another famous archive: the Public Record Office in London.

In 1836 a Select Committee of the House of Commons was created to examine the possibility of establishing a public record office in London. At that time the realm's collections of documentary material were scattered in several different deposits, none of which was suitable for their preservation. The most important deposits were in the Tower of London, the Chapter House of Westminster Abbey, and Rolls House. Documents were continually being destroyed by the damp or by rats. Furthermore, the ill-considered and deliberate elimination of documents judged on dubious and selective criteria to be of little value was continually eroding this previous heritage of records. In 1858 documents thought to be of doubtful interest were systematically discarded, and between 1861 and 1865 approximately 400 tons of War Office and Admiralty documents were destroyed.

The situation improved with the setting-up of the Public Record Office, but as late as 1911 an American scholar, N. S. B. Gras of Harvard,

---

[1] This does not mean that future historians of today's industrial societies will be overwhelmed by an abundance of information. Future historians will raise problems that we at present do not consider or cannot imagine and for which therefore we produce no documentation or information. Furthermore, a considerable amount of the documentation that we produce is written or printed with inks and on paper that have a very short life expectancy. It is too soon to tell quite how the situation will be affected by the spread of computers.

informed the directors of the Office that he had discovered the important series of Port Books stacked carelessly in one of the building's attics.

The patchier the documentary material available to historians, the more they have to sharpen their wits and apply their powers of detection, scrutinizing their sources as if under a microscope, sentence by sentence, word by word. It took all the keen ingenuity of Claude Nicolet to draw from a few vague passages in Livy, Cicero, Caesar, Dio Cassius and Tacitus his brilliant inferences regarding the financial system operating in Rome during the first century BC and the first century AD (Nicolet, 1963; 1971). Scholars working on the early Middle Ages had to exercise saint-like patience to extract from tedious stories of saints and miracles a reference to some worthy who, before becoming a monk, had been a merchant, and thence to arrive at conclusions about the existence of mercantile groups and trade movements during the periods and in the areas under consideration (Dopsch, 1922; Ganshof, 1933; Pirenne, 1937; Sabbe, 1934).

But the written sources surviving from certain periods – from classical antiquity, for example – are so few and far between and so insubstantial that even the most powerful magnifying glass is of no avail. In these circumstances historians have to look around for other evidence. A detective who lacks documentary proof of the murderer's identity utilizes the clues afforded by fingerprints, cigarette butts, stains, and so forth. Similarly, historians hunt for clues in linguistics, archaeology, numismatics and epigraphy. Any piece of information may in the end turn out to be useful. Findings of coins and especially of Greek vases in the various countries of the Mediterranean basin can be used (with caution) to plot and date trade movements in the period when Greek commerce was expanding and a growing population was founding colonies abroad.[2] Discoveries of Roman coins in India may afford clues to the history of trade between Rome and the Indian subcontinent.[3] Chemical analyses demonstrating the appearance of platinum in the gold used in Roman coins towards the middle of the fourth century AD may be evidence that new mines were being worked (Callu and Barandon, 1986, p. 572, graph 3). In their description of the sources for ancient history, Crawford and his colleages (1983) devoted seventy-four pages to written sources, fifty-five to epigraphy, forty-six to archaeology and fifty-one to numismatics.

However, it is not only historians of ancient times who turn for clues to archaeology, epigraphy, numismatics and linguistics. Historians of the Middle Ages also make regular use of these disciplines in order to make

---

[2] See for example Cook, 1959, pp. 114–23. On the critical caution essential when using archaeological material in the investigation of Greek economic history, see Will, 1973.

[3] In the southernmost tip of the Indian peninsula, Roman imperial coins were discovered in an excellent state of preservation, dating back to the times of Augustus (63 BC–AD 14) and Tiberius (42 BC–AD 34): more specifically, from the last issue under Augustus to the last under Tiberius. Only a few Roman denarii dating from an earlier period and a few denarii and aurei from a later period have been discovered in India. See Warmington, 1974, p. 272ff; and Crawford, 1980, pp. 207–17.

Plate 1 Aerial photograph of an English lost village

up for gaps in documentary evidence or to corroborate information gained in other ways. The fact that in English domesticated animals such as the ox, calf, pig and sheep are called by names of Anglo-Saxon origin while the words for their meat (beef, veal, pork, mutton) derive from the French terms for the same animals tells us more than any number of written documents about the different standards of living of the Norman invaders (who spoke French) and the Anglo-Saxon populations whom they subjugated after the Battle of Hastings in 1066. Similarly, the distinction in Italian between *onorario* and *salario* and in English between *fee* and *wage* says a great deal about the different status accorded to professional work and manual work in the Middle Ages. The history of mediaeval currency simply cannot be told without the aid of evidence that numismatics alone can supply. The history of the 'lost villages' in England and Germany, abandoned following the demographic decline of the fourteenth and fifteenth centuries, has benefited enormously from aerial photo reconnaissance (see plate 1), while historians of the Industrial Revolution have been assisted by the development and findings of industrial archaeology.

Whatever period they study, historians have to adopt the detective's practice of leaving no stone unturned in the search for proof. As a result, terms such as 'document', 'documentation' and 'documentary sources' eventually take on a very broad meaning indeed. In its narrowest acceptation, the word 'document' refers to 'written evidence of a fact of a legal nature, compiled in compliance with certain well-defined procedures, which are intended to accord it authority and the force of proof' (Paoli, 1942, p. 18). But to the historian, such as Croce (1938, p. 19), every item of evidence, whether written, oral, archaeological, numismatic or epigraphical, constitutes a 'document'. To borrow an elegant phrase from the jurist Paolo (*Pandette* XXII.iv.1), one might say that to the historian under the name of 'documents', 'sources', 'evidence' 'ea omnia accipienda sunt, quibus causa instrui potest' ('all things must be included which may serve to the setting up of a trial'). As Lucien Febvre wrote, 'history is doubtless pieced together from written documents, when there are any, but also from the observation of countrysides, from the study of bricks and the shapes of fields, from the account of eclipses of the moon and draught-horse collars, from chemists' analyses of metal spears, and from geologists' research into rocks'.[4] The field is wide open. And, as G. R. Elton argued, 'ideally, the student should never consider less than the total of the historical material which may conceivably be relevant to his enquiry' (1967, p. 66).

---

[4] The reference to the draught-horse collar alludes to the work of R. Lefebvre de Noëttes, who, on the basis of iconographic research, showed how, as a result of the development in the early Middle Ages of a new technique for harnessing horses, the use of horses became considerably more widespread. See also White, 1962, p. 57ff. The reference to spears alludes to recent investigations into chemical and metallographic analyses of the remains of spears used by invading Germanic peoples; these suggest that the invaders practised advanced techniques of metal working.

Writing a brief history of the Roman Empire, Colin M. Wells noted that

> the relationship between literacy and archaeological evidence is not that of mistress and 'handmaid' as used to be said. The archaeological data are as much a primary source as the text by Tacitus or an inscription. The historian must recognize that they may complement the literary evidence; contradict it (Caesar claims the Rhine as a major ethnographic and cultural boundary between Gauls and 'Germans', but archaeology refutes this); or provide us with information about matters on which the literary record is wholly silent. (1984, p. 49)

Whether one studies ancient, mediaeval or modern history, the validity of numismatic, epigraphic and archaeological evidence remains unaltered. But the relative importance of the information that can be derived from these disciplines, in comparison with written documentation, diminishes very rapidly with the dissolution of the ancient world.

In practice it is impossible to produce a complete inventory of sources relevant to economic history. Years ago, when Armando Sapori published his *Saggio sulle fonti della storia economica medievale* (Essay on the sources of medieval economic history), he listed and illustrated only those types of document that refer to mediaeval trade. Then, at the end of his essay, realizing, as it were, that the contents of the bottle didn't measure up to the claims made on the label, he felt obliged to add that he had accounted for 'the main sources' only and that 'every collection of archives, belonging to every institution, may contain material of interest to historians of the economy' (1955, I, p. 23). The delineation of a descriptive inventory of the sources of economic history is daunting not only because of the colossal size of the enterprise, but above all because references to facts and economic factors can be discovered in the most disparate and diverse documents, ranging from the list of purchases made by a serving woman at market to the daily financial newspaper, from the memoirs of a politician to a peace treaty. In spite of all this, I have made a brave (or reckless?) attempt to provide examples of the most important documents or sets of documents available to economic historians of the period between AD 1400 and the present day. As I stated in the Preface, the fruit of this laborious and risky effort is confined to Part II. There the reader will find a description of some of the documents that no student of European economic history can possibly afford to ignore, set within the framework of the socio-economic and cultural development of which the documents themselves are the expression.

PRIMARY AND SECONDARY SOURCES

A detective seeking to discover exactly how a road accident occurred is unlikely to waste time listening to an account of the incident from someone not actually there at the time. He will want to question those persons, and those alone, who were at the scene of the accident at the moment when it happened. Assuming that there are five witnesses, the detective will in all probability hear five slightly different versions, since we all see things from our own particular physical and psychological viewpoint. The detective will take care to correlate, contrast and evaluate each of these five eyewitness accounts, and will overlook any interpretations suggested by people who were not present and are therefore relying on mere hearsay. In this way, the detective will apply the common-sense rule making a clear-cut distinction between primary and secondary sources.

Since, in the past also, many historians were intelligent and sensible people, it may be presumed that they were aware of this rule. But, when the historians of ancient times and the chroniclers of the Middle Ages could find no primary sources on which to base their attempts at historical reconstruction, rather than worry about it they turned to legends, oral traditions and secondary sources, casting everything into the pot pell-mell. As M. I. Finley commented, 'the ability of the ancients to invent and their capacity to believe are persistently underestimated' (1986, p. 9). It was in late-seventeenth-century Europe that scholars began systematically to distinguish between primary and secondary sources and to draw up precise rules of conduct for historians to observe in their use of different sources. The masterwork that hailed the dawn of a new era in historiography was Mabillon's *De re diplomatica*, published in 1681. As Marc Bloch has observed, 'in that year, 1681, document criticism was at last founded'. Nowadays, as Arnaldo Momigliano has written, 'historical methodology is based on the distinctions between primary and secondary sources'. Even the least expert historian now knows that whenever possible he must refer back to primary sources, and that, if there are none available, it is only with great caution that he may proceed to make use of secondary sources. However, as will become clearer further on, primary sources too are a minefield. Langlois and Seignobos have written, 'we don't know of a single contemporary witness who assures us that he saw Pisistratus; yet millions of "eyewitnesses" swear they saw the devil' (1898).

The distinction between primary and secondary sources is crystal clear to all historians and ought to be self-evident to any educated person. The hypothetical example of the road accident, distinguishing between those who were present at the scene of the accident and those who merely heard an account of it from others, should clarify the two concepts. However, what in one context may be defined as a secondary source can in another become a primary source. Henry Pirenne's book *Mahomet et Charlemagne* (1937), is a decidedly secondary source in terms of an investigation of the economy of the early Middle Ages. But, for any biography of Henry Pirenne, the said book is a primary source. Furthermore, it is also possible for a given source to be a primary and secondary source at one and the same time. Giovanni Villani's *Cronaca* is a primary source in terms of events in the Florence of his day, but a secondary source in any other context.

The sources described in Part II are almost all primary sources. Secondary sources appear in the bibliography at the end of the book. Of the primary written sources available to economic historians, one has to distinguish between (1) narrative sources and chronicles and (2) documentary sources.

Whenever possible, professional historians base their work on primary sources. Historians who rely exclusively on secondary sources might be compared to surgeons who have read textbooks on surgery, but have never been near an operating table or handled a scalpel. But we are living in strange times. A few years ago Momigliano wrote that 'a bibliography can act as a drug, encouraging vice – the vice, when studying the past i.e. history, of reading modern accounts instead of original documents' (1974, repr. 1987, p. 15). The publishing explosion of the late twentieth century has promoted or imposed the reading of a growing number of modern works, thereby encroaching on the time available for reading the sources. Especially in the United States, the increasing preoccupation with the formulation of theoretical models and with statistical methodology has been totally to the detriment of the study of the primary sources of economic history. The invasion of economic history by sociologists and anthropologists has also encouraged bibliographical study at the expense of recourse to primary sources. This has had pernicious consequences. It is not merely that by relying on second-hand sources historians risk repeating the same errors of reading or interpretation committed by the author of the secondary source. It is more serious than that. As we shall see in chapter 5, every historical reconstruction is to a differing degree vitiated by simplification, generalization and subjectivism. Anyone who relies on secondary sources when writing history inevitably piles his own simplifications, generalizations and subjectivism onto the simplifications, generalizations and subjectivism of the secondary sources he has used. This normally results in the kind of work that experts can recognize at a glance – work that is laden with shallow abstract generalizations, and with rigid and at the same time simplistic patterns of thought: work that lacks any awareness of that infinite range of single variously-graded exceptions and variations that characterize the real world.

To return to our hypothetical case: any detective attempting to reconstruct the dynamics of a road accident is bound to harbour suspicions and to feel sceptical about declarations from people who were not themselves present at the scene of the accident. Likewise, historians have to use particular caution when obliged by the lack of primary sources to fall back on secondary sources. However, it should not be imagined that the use of primary sources in some way relieves historians of their constant duty to stand guard over the evidence. For even primary sources can lie: and this is true not only of narrative sources, but also of documentary material.

4 Source Criticism

The sciences owe their spectacular achievements to a methodology founded essentially on rigorous attention to three processes:

(1) the formulation of a logically structured theory;
(2) the collection of data the reliability of which is measured by the statistical estimate of their margin of error;
(3) the verification of the theory by means of data the reliability of which has been ascertained.

In the historical disciplines and in economics, this three-cornered approach has never been fully adopted. Historians and economists have been left stumbling, but curiously enough they stumble in different places.

Since the very beginning of historical inquiry, historians have been obsessed by the possibility that they might be misled by false information or that they themselves might be accused of giving an untrue account of events. When Thucydides wrote his *History of the Peloponnesian War*, he made a point of stating that 'my narrative is based on what I myself have seen and on accounts from others, after careful research aiming for the greatest accuracy' (1919 tr.). Cicero insisted that historians have the duty 'firstly, never to say anything that is not true; secondly, not to suppress anything that is true; and, thirdly, to prevent any suspicion of partiality or deception in their own writings' (1913 tr.). In the second half of the fourteenth century, the Arab historian Ibn Khaldun wrote,

False information creeps into histories . . . one of the reasons is the partisan spirit that seeks to spread particular opinions and ideas. A second cause of false accounts is blind faith in those who recount them, whereas those who pass on accounts ought to undergo the same kind of investigation as witnesses undergo at the hands of judges. A third cause of error is the failure to understand ends: many narrators don't know what the actions that they have seen or heard about were leading to; by relating matters according to their impressions and conjectures, they fall into error. Fourthly, mistakes can arise due to excessive self-assurance, or an exaggerated faith in one's own sources.

29

For centuries these and other high-minded concerns had no noticeable effect on the practice of history. What was lacking was method. It was not until the end of the seventeenth century that the foundations were laid for the formulation of a systematic methodology, which was brought to completion during the nineteenth century. This methodology, based on the distinction between primary and secondary sources, on the philological reconstruction of the archetypal text by means of an investigation of manuscript genealogies, and on tests of concord or compatibility between different sources, came to be known as 'source criticism'. As a rigorous methodology it has justified history's current claims to scientific status.

The methodological corner in which historians have been left stumbling is that of theory. As we shall see later in this chapter, historians have seldom taken the trouble to formulate explicitly – even for their own benefit – the theory that underpins their collection and reassembly of data, or to check its logical consistency. They have tended to place all their trust in 'common sense'.

Economists have been left stumbling in the opposite methodological corner. From Ricardo onwards (with the exception of the nineteenth-century historical school in Germany) economists have shown increasing concern with the logical coherence, the simplicity and the formal elegance of their models, while behaving carelessly in their collection and use of data. They often accept data that agree with the proposed theory without bothering to establish how the data were generated, without rigorously checking their reliability, and without ensuring that all the available data of proven reliability are consistent with the proposed theory. Indeed, as far as the last point is concerned, economists frequently disregard facts that fail to fit in with their theories, while welcoming data that are more amenable (even without sufficient proof that they are well-founded). In this way, they force reality into the strait-jacket of their theory instead of adapting their theory to fit the facts. As J. K. Galbraith has written, the attitude of most theoretical economists in the end 'undermines efforts to gather information and . . . encourages a disregard for inconvenient facts'.

Economic historians who share their methodology with historians and economists are prone to suffer from one or other of the concomitant defects. Economic historians from a prevalently historical background usually turn out to be strong on source criticism but weak on theory. Economic historians from a prevalently economics background usually turn out to be strong on constructing models but weak on source criticism. The basic aim of good economic history should be to combine the positive aspects of both approaches, starting with source criticism.

Source criticism basically involves four processes:

(1) deciphering texts;
(2) interpreting their substance or content;

(3) confirming their authenticity; and

(4) ascertaining how reliable they are.

These processes are inextricably interdependent.

Deciphering a contemporary document does not normally pose problems, unless it is in code. But, when one turns to ancient, mediaeval or early modern documents, things are not so straightforward. The Knossos tablets could not be read until 1952, when Michael Ventris managed to decipher the script that archaeologists call Linear B (see Part II, chapter 1). The tablets written in Linear A, which are still awaiting their Michael Ventris, retain their secrets.

In sources dating from the Middle Ages and the early centuries of the Modern Age, economic historians often have difficulties with the symbols used to indicate units of currency or weight. In sixteenth-century Florence, every scribe had his own way of writing the symbols for the monetary units soldi, florins, scudi and ducats. As a result, even the most expert of palaeographers sometimes trips up. The same problem occurs with the symbols indicating units of weight – the mark, pound, ounce, pennyweight, grain, and so on. When preparing an edition of the sixteenth-century *Cronaca*, written by the Florentine merchant and man of letters G. de' Ricci, Giuliana Sapori, herself a first-rate palaeographer, took the sign for pound to mean ounce, thus rendering aspects of the Florentine monetary system totally incomprehensible.[1] And, when E. G. Parodi was preparing a critical edition of a manuscript dating from 1235–6, he read the symbol for soldi as that for florins, setting the price of a pair of shoes at the improbably high level of six gold florins (1887, p. 195).

'TRUE' AND 'FALSE' SOURCES

In a healthy democracy, individuals are presumed innocent until proved guilty. This makes the proper attitude for historians to take to their sources appear distinctly undemocratic. Perhaps Jacques Le Goff pushes his point too far when he argues that 'every document is a lie', but the fact remains that historians must never presume their source to be innocent, must always be suspicious of it, and always ready, at the slightest hint of inconsistency, 'to take the document to court', as Foucault put it.

As we saw in chapter 3, historians should treat secondary sources with particular suspicion and refer, whenever possible, to primary sources. The use of primary sources keeps out certain kinds of distorted information, but the historian's duty of unending and suspicious vigilance does not stop there. A primary source may, to put it crudely, be any of the following:

---

[1] Cipolla, 1987, p. 131. Since I have not had the opportunity to consult the original manuscript, I cannot say whether the error really is attributable to Sapori or whether it was made by whoever produced the manuscript.

(1) a false source containing false information;
(2) a false source containing true information;
(3) a genuine source containing false information; or
(4) a genuine source containing true information.

An example of a false source containing false information is provided by the so-called Donation of Constantine, by which Emperor Constantine the Great in AD 313 supposedly donated the city of Rome to Pope Sylvester, thus legitimizing the temporal power of the Bishop of Rome and his supremacy over all the other bishops of the Catholic Church. The falsity of this document was demonstrated in the mid fifteenth century by Lorenzo Valla (1406–57), relying on incontrovertible philological arguments.[2]

Another false document containing false information is a deeds certificate dated 13 October 874, attributed to Emperor Louis II and made out in favour of the Benedictine monastery of San Clemente di Cesauria in the Abruzzi (Italy). This fake cannot be compared for notoriety with the Donation of Constantine but is worth recalling on account of its implications for the history of technology. The fake probably dates from the thirteenth century and was produced by Benedictine monks who, like others of the same period, wanted to make their monastery's ownership of its possessions appear more ancient (and consequently more noble and more legitimate) than it really was. In the document in question, the Emperor reconfirms the monastery's ownership of courts, castles and serfs along with 'molendinis, acquarum decursibus, piscationibus, *valcatoriis*, silvis, rupibus, domibus' (my emphasis). The *valcaturae* were fulling mills (i.e. mills that had been specially equipped for cloth-fulling) – an important technological innovation of the Middle Ages. Were the document authentic, it would provide evidence that fulling mills existed in the ninth century. The proof that the document is a fake allows economic historians and historians of technology to stick to the view that fulling mills were first developed in the tenth century (Malanima, 1988, pp. 49–50).

The notion of a false document containing true information may seem rather far-fetched. But imagine an authentic document certifying the purchase of a particular property by an abbey. Now imagine an accident causing the loss or destruction of this document. In such a case, mediaeval monks might well produce a new document replicating the substance of the original. The new document would be false in so far as it purported to be the original, but its contents would be true. The reader who is interested in the fascinating tale of documentary forgeries will find plenty of good examples in the six volumes of Fälschungen im Mittelalter (Forgeries in the Middle Ages), published in Hanover in 1988.

There is no counting the number of genuine documents containing false information. During the Middle Ages, Church condemnation of usury

---

[2] For the text of the Donation, see Mirbt, 1924. For Valla's refutation see Valla, 1928; and Giannantonio, 1972.

(interest-bearing loans) led to a massive increase in fakes of this type. For example, in Siena on 19 May 1223 a notarial act was produced in which Ugolino and Ranieri, cutlers, acknowledged a loan from Bonaventura di Piero of 8 Sienese lire. The two craftsmen undertook to repay this sum by the beginning of November. The document makes no mention of any interest, but the historian, alerted by innumerable similar cases, is bound to suspect that the amount actually loaned was somewhat less than the 8 lire specified, and that the amount to be repaid represented the capital plus interest (Lopez and Raymond, 1955, p. 160). Another practice that was quite common in the Middle Ages, and also during the Renaissance, was to disguise loans at interest as contracts of exchange. These contracts are therefore suspect. In Genoa on 12 February 1190, Riccuomo and Egidio de Uxel acknowledged receipt from Rufo and Bernardo of a sum of money for which they promised to pay the said bankers 69 lire in Pavia denari the following Lent. Formally the document is authentic, but it is hard to say whether it was really a contract of exchange or a disguised loan at a rate of interest concealed by the exchange rate (Lopez and Raymond, 1955, p. 164).

There is one quite sizable category of authentic documents that contain false information: declarations of income or wealth submitted to tax authorities by private individuals and companies. Indeed, many company balance sheets contain figures that conceal rather than disclose the true state of affairs. Nor is the private sector alone in producing financial statements that contain fraudulent information. For example, in official statistics published between the two world wars, the Nazi government deliberately understated the size of the nation's gold reserves held by the German central bank (Morgenstern, 1965, p. 20).

The crudity of our quadripartite categorization of primary sources according to the genuineness/falsity of the document and the truth/falsity of its contents emerges most clearly in relation to our last category: genuine sources containing true information. Identifying a genuine source may be straightforward enough: analysis of the writing materials, the style of handwriting, the language used and the seals used may lead straight to a favourable verdict. According to the rule laid down by H. Bresslau, a document is formally false 'when it seeks to appear that which it is not' (1889–1931, I, p. 7). If the document is not false, *ipso facto* it is genuine.

When it comes to evaluating the contents of the document, however, things are very much more complex. In this connection, two preliminary points have to be made. First, a clear-cut distinction must be made between sources that contain deliberately falsified information and sources that contain unintentionally incorrect information. Secondly, the dividing line between truth and falsehood is rarely as clear in practice as in theory. 'Truth', wrote Oscar Wilde in *The Importance of Being Earnest,* 'is never pure and rarely simple.' Between the utterly truthful and the utterly false there is an extraordinarily broad range of half-truths, half-lies, distorted truths, mystifying silences, gaps in information, and glaring errors.

Some documents are truthful and yet represent reality in such a way as to be misleading. Others intend to be truthful but, for 'technical' reasons, supply incorrect information, or the statistics given are unintentionally vitiated by wide margins of error. There is, in other words, a huge and extremely varied range of different cases. The following are but a few characteristic examples.

Many documents dating from the eighth, ninth or tenth century register debts (in respect of purchases, loans, and so on) to be settled by payment of a given sum of money. Taking these documents at face value, an economic historian might fall into the trap of inferring the existence of an economy based on monetary exchange. But these documents are deceptive. Debts are reckoned in monetary units but, precisely because the market economy was barely functioning and the monetary system was primitive, it was commonly understood that payment might take the form of any kind of goods acceptable to the creditor – *merce placibile*, as it was termed in one contemporary document. Marc Bloch, for instance, cites a French document dating from 1107 in which a debt of 20 sous is stipulated. But from a subsequent document it emerges that the debt was settled with a horse. If the second document had been lost, the historian might have been led to view the transaction in question not as a case of barter (as in effect it was) but rather as a monetary transaction (Bloch, 1954, p. 31; other examples in Cipolla, 1956, pp. 4–6). The first of the two documents does not contain anything that is false but, by failing to mention a condition which at that time was taken for granted, it could be completely misleading to an insufficiently wary historian.

Whereas some documents say too little, others say just enough to incriminate themselves. In Part II, chapter 1, mention is made of that extraordinary early-eleventh-century document known to historians as the *Instituta Regalia et Ministeria Camere Regis Lomgbardorum*, which contains a brief but precious description of the administration based in the royal *palatium* in Pavia (Italy). After enumerating and describing, with obvious relish for his subject, the dues and tributes paid by merchants and guilds to the royal chamber, the writer launches into an invective:

Gisulfus was in charge of the royal chamber and was a noble and rich man at the time of King Hugo and his son Lotarius, at the time of King Bengarius II and at the time of Emperor Otto I, and he held his office with much honour. After the death of Emperor Otto the office of Master of the Chamber was still held by the same Gisulfus and following him by his son Aijraldus, who held the office honourably, as his father had done, under both Emperor Otto II and under Emperor Otto III. After the death of Aijraldus, Master of the Chamber, the office ought to have passed to his son Agisulfus. But it was then that arrived that devil personified called Johannes the Greek, a true apostate, Bishop of Piacenza and a heretic, who was adviser to the Greek Empress and to her son Otto III, who was still a boy.

> The King yielded all his powers to that Greek, who gathered all power into his own
> hands and brought with him two servants of the Greek Empress, one called Siccus
> and the other Nanus, to whom he yielded every power. (Cited in Brühl and Violante,
> 1983, p. 25)

This writer is arguing a particular case: that the royal–imperial administration remained properly centralized as long as it was guided by the expert hands of Gisulfus and his son Aijraldus, but that, following the arrival of that 'devil personified', the apostate and heretic Johannes the Greek, and of his two sycophants Siccus and Nanus, the alienation and erosion of royal rights, progressively usurped by local potentates, commenced. This is the familiar process of the crumbling of central power, undermined on the one hand by the growing centrifugal forces of feudalism and on the other by the early demands for autonomy made by the cities. The writer – probably the very same Agisulfus ousted by Johannes the Greek, or a close relative of his – paints a picture of stark contrasts: he has nothing but praise for the old, efficient centralized system, and nothing but contempt for the changes brought about by the diabolical Greek. The partisan nature of the text is all too obvious and the historian has no difficulty in showing, with the help of other sources, that the crumbling of the central administration had begun prior to the arrival of Johannes the Greek (Solmi, 1932). The document none the less bears precious witness to the workings of the royal administration in northern Italy before the erosion of central power.

Other documents that incriminate themselves include those containing evident elements of propaganda. The law used by Henry VIII of England to dissolve the monasteries and confiscate their property carries the following preamble:

> Forasmoche as manifest synne, vicious carnall and abhomynable lyvyng, is dayly
> usyd & comytted amonges the lytell and smale Abbeys Pryoryes and other Relygyous
> Houses of Monk Chanons & Nonnes, where the congregacon of such Relygyous
> psons is under the nomber of xii psons, wherby the Gouvnours of suche Relygyous
> Houses and thir Covent spoyle dystroye consume & utterly wast, aswell ther Churches
> Monasteryes Pryoryes principall Houses Fermes Granges Londes Tenementes &
> Heredytaments, as the ornamentes of ther Churches & ther goodes & cattalls, to
> the high dyspleasour of Almyghty God, slaunder of good Relygyon & to the greate
> Infamy of the Kynges Highnes & the Realme if redres should not be hadde
> therof . . . . (Statutes of the Realm 27 Henry VIII, c. 28)

It is likely that there was some truth in these accusations. However, historians, aware of the financial straits in which Henry VIII found himself at the time, are bound to view the complaints as highly exaggerated, especially when they recall that between 1536 and 1545 in the county of Yorkshire alone the dissolution of the monasteries netted the King a profit of almost £30,000.

This case underlines the warning issued by Cantor and Schneider that not only secondary but also primary sources 'contain opinions or value judgements and the historian who seeks to use the primary source as evidence must be aware of the opinionated nature of all primary evidence and must evaluate it' (1967, p. 33). To this piece of advice should be added the rule, stated by Finley, that, when dealing with 'any document at all, the first question one must ask is for what reason or purpose the document was written' (1982, p. 701).

ERRORS OF TRANSCRIPTION

Prior to the invention of movable-type printing (in the mid fifteenth century), texts were reproduced manually by copyists. Few original documents have survived to our day: in most cases, copies alone have reached us. Philologists have developed very sophisticated and fairly reliable techniques to establish the 'family trees' of manuscripts and to reconstruct a text as close as possible to that of the original. When a text is reconstructed in this way it is commonly called a 'critical edition'. The relatively straightforward genealogy of the manuscripts of the *Instituta Regalia et Ministeria Camere Regis Lomgbardorum*, mentioned above, has been reconstructed in the following way (Brühl and Violante, 1983, p. 85):

A   Eleventh-century original, lost

X   Fourteenth-century copy, lost

H   Fourteenth-century manuscript, entitled *Honorantie Civitatis Papie*, including the text of the *Instituta Regalia*

C   Manuscript of the sixteenth–seventeenth centuries, the work of different hands, containing copies of various texts, including the *Honorantie Civitatis Papie*

Often the only surviving exemplum of a document is a transcription produced for the official registers. In such cases, the genealogy consists simply of the lost parent document and a first-generation copy.

With texts copied by hand, each new copy is liable to contain fresh errors of transcription. Old errors are likely to be repeated and compounded where the document that a copyist has to transcribe is not the original but itself a copy. It is therefore important to know how close to or remote from the original a copy is. The longer the genealogical line between the original and the copy, the higher the probability that the copyist's text is riddled with errors.

While I was researching the history of the Milanese currency in the fifteenth century, I happened upon orders, issued on 16 January 1456, to mint 4-soldi grossoni, 2-soldi grossi and sesini (6-denari coins). The document I had before me was a contemporary copy of the ordinance, made after the original document left the ducal chamber. It is entered on sheet 100 of the official register of ducal letters for the years 1456–61, now kept in Milan City Archives.

In the passage dealing with the fineness of the 4-soldi grossoni, the copyist wrote 'qui grossoni sint in liga a denariis X granis XVIIII hoc est tenentes onzias VII denarios IIII granos XXI argenti pro marcha' ('the grossoni should have a fineness of X pennyweights XVIIII grains, i.e. they must contain VII ounces IIII pennyweights XXI grains of pure silver for each mark-weight [of alloy]'). There is a glaring contradiction in this passage. A fineness of 10 pennyweights, 19 grains is equivalent in present-day terms to 899.31 thousandths of pure silver, whereas a fineness of 7 ounces, 4 pennyweights, 21 grains of pure silver per mark-weight (8 ounces) works out at 900.39 thousandths.[3] Were the 4-soldi grossoni to be coined at a fineness of 899.31 thousands or at one of 900.39? Obviously one of these two specifications is wrong. The right one must be that contained in the first part of the specification (10 pennyweights, 19 grains = 899.31 thousandths) because, according to the system of weights then in use, such a fineness was equivalent to 7 ounces, 4 pennyweights, and 16 grains of pure silver per mark-weight of alloy: in all likelihood, on copying the original minting order into the register the copyist, using Roman numerals, wrote 'granos XXI' instead of 'granos XVI', mistaking a V for an X.

In the subsequent passage, referring to the alloy used in the 2-soldi grossi, the copyist made a similar mistake by writing 'sint dicti grossi a denariis XI hoc est tenentes onzias IIII argenti fini pro marcha' ('be the said grossi at a fineness of XI pennyweights, i.e. they must contain IIII ounces of pure silver for each mark-weight [of alloy]'). If a mark-weight of alloy was to contain 4 ounces of pure silver the alloy must have been 'a denariis VI' and not 'a denariis XI'. Obviously in this case too the fifteenth-century copyist mistook a V for an X.

This document was published in 1893 by Emilio Motta in a collection entitled 'Documenti visconteo-sforzeschi per la storia della zecca di Milano' (Documents of the Visconti and Sforza for the history of the Mint of Milan).[4] Motta was a talented palaeographer and the director of the Milan Archives, but he was not an 'expert' in metrological and monetary matters. Consequently, he failed to notice the mistakes made by the fifteenth-century copyist and reproduced them. Worse, he unwittingly

[3] For more information on the complicated system of measurement used at the time in Milan to calculate the alloy percentages of coins see Cipolla, 1988, p. 17.
[4] Published in *Rivista italiana di numismatica*, VI (1893), VII (1894), VIII (1895).

added two new errors of his own. In the passage concerning the fineness of the 4-soldi grossi, the fifteenth-century text, as has already been mentioned, reads, 'hoc est tenentes onzias VII denarios IIII granos XXI argenti pro marcha', whereas Motta's printed version reads 'onzias VIII [instead of VII] denarios IIII granos XXI'. Obviously this was just a typesetting error, overlooked when the proofs were read, but it does make matters even more complicated. Moreover, as regards the weight of the 2-soldi grossi. Motta's text refers to a minting of 'CIIII' coins per mark-weight, whereas the fifteenth-century text reads 'CIIII'$_3$ – that is to say 104½ and not 104.

In 1961 Caterina Santoro, shortly after her appointment as director of the Milan City Archives, published an official edition of *I registri delle lettere ducali del periodo sforzesco* (The registers of the Ducal letters of the Sforza period). In the case of the monetary ordinance of 16 January 1456, Dr Santoro must have neglected to check the original text, preferring to place her trust in Motta's publication. Thus, not only did she fail to notice the errors made by the fifteenth-century copyist, but she also reproduced those committed by Motta. Ten years later, in the appendix to a long article on the production of the Mint of Milan during the period of the Sforzas, E. Bernareggi re-published the same ordinance. Unfortunately he too failed to go back to the original source, relying on the document printed by Motta, thereby reproducing all Motta's mistakes. In addition, he added a mistake of his own (obviously a misprint): in the passage referring to the fineness of the 4-soldi grossi, Bernareggi (1971–2) has 'fineness of XVIIII pennyweights' instead of 'fineness of X pennyweights XVIIII grains'.

I have reported this case in some detail because in my view there are a number of lessons to be learnt from it. First, it highlights the point that copyists often made errors when transcribing documents. Secondly, it reveals that even modern critical editions may be less than accurate, owing to errors in typesetting, misreading of the document, and so on. Lastly, it demonstrates one of the fundamental rules of historical criticism: that even when two or more different sources agree about a particular reading this is no proof of their accuracy. It is perfectly possible for one source to reproduce the errors of another, as Santoro did in following Motta.

DOUBTFUL STATISTICS

General historians mainly work with narrative texts and use their critical expertise to lay bare distortions of information occasioned by partisan views, personal value judgements, vested interests, political convictions or ideology. In order to assess the reliability of a source, they check on its internal consistency (or inconsistency) and its compatibility (or incompatibility) with other, independent sources.

Most people believe that economic history and quantitative history are the same thing, but this is a mistake. There are forms of quantitative history that have nothing to do with economic history, and vice versa. However, it has to be acknowledged that most sources used by economic historians contain numbers referring to quantitative variables. As a result, economic historians have to deal almost routinely with quantitative information, and the problem that faces them is how to estimate the degree of error in the measurements that the sources supply.

In the exact sciences the term 'error' has a precise statistical meaning. There is 'bias' (systematic error) and there is chance error. Bias cannot usually be detected merely by examining the measurements: they have to be compared to an external standard. The probable size of a chance error, on the other hand, can be estimated fairly accurately. In a series of repeated measurements the standard deviation of the series gives an estimate of the likely size of the chance error of a single measurement. The calculation of the standard error provides an estimate of the likely chance error in the average of the series. For example, in order to ensure the accuracy of the various kinds of scales available on the market, the National Bureau of Standards in Washington DC regularly measures the 10-gram sample weight kept at the Bureau. In 1962 and 1963, Almer and Jones carried out a hundred weighings of the sample weight, taking care to use the same room each time, the same set of precision scales and, as far as possible, to maintain atmospheric pressure, temperature and ambient humidity constant. Despite all these precautions, a different weight was recorded every time. These were the first ten measurements (weights in grams):

1	9.999591
2	9.999600
3	9.999594
4	9.999601
5	9.999598
6	9.999594
7	9.999599
8	9.999597
9	9.999599
10	9.999597

The mean of the 100 measurements turned out to be 9.999595 grams. If, instead of 100, 1,000 measurements had been made, the mean result might have been different. In any case, the greater the number of measurements the closer the mean will come to the exact value of the weight, which in 1962–3 it was not possible to determine to seven decimal points. The standard deviation of the series is roughly 6 micrograms and supplies the probable chance error of a single measurement. The standard error of the average measurement (being the square root of the number of measurements multiplied by the standard deviation) is roughly 0.6 micrograms. The standard deviation tells us that a single measurement is accurate to approximately 6 micrograms. The standard error tells us that the average of the 100 measurements is accurate to approximately 0.6 micrograms.

Historians cannot carry out experiments of this type. In their analysis of series, they therefore normally use the term 'error' rather loosely, to give a broad indication of the lack of precision in their data.

Sometimes it is the sources themselves that alert the historian to the presence of errors in the data. On sending to Vienna population data for Lombardy in 1787–8 (when the province was part of the Austrian Empire), the Milanese civil servants warned Minister Kaunitz of 'the fallaciousness of the results in the tables . . . the total fallaciousness of the calculations and data on the population . . . the misunderstandings that can occur in the muddled compilations in a register pieced together from over 2,000 notes by many different administrative hands' (quoted in Cipolla, 1943, p. 50n). As late as 1978 in the United States, a country where statistics are treated with particular care, the House of Representatives Select Committee on Population reported that, despite the statistics produced by official government publications, 'we do not know how many legal immigrants enter the US labor market in various occupations; the length of stay of either legal or illegal migrants, that is how many return to their native land and how many remain here permanently; the age–sex structure of the illegal population; how many persons emigrate from the US.' Another report guessed that illegal immigration to the United States amounted to well over 500,000 people a year, who obviously do not figure in the official statistics on emigration and immigration (US Government Printing Office, 1978).

Historians' doubts about the reliability of available statistics are often prompted by their feeling for the period and the society that they are studying. The culture of the fundamentally agricultural societies of the past favoured approximation. Generally, numbers were used not with precision, but to give a general notion of abundance or scarcity. This explains the frequent use of quantifications that had no foundation in fact. People didn't even know their exact age and, if asked, frequently gave a round number (see figure 1). Werner Sombart was not exaggerating when he wrote,

> To be exact, to make calculations balance is something modern. In all previous ages numerical statements are always only approximate. Anyone who is at all acquainted with calculations in the Middle Ages knows that if you check the columns the general thing is to find the totals quite incorrect. Mistakes in arithmetic were common occurrences. . . . All these errors are clearly seen in the so-called book-keeping of the Middle Ages. If you look through the books of a Tölner, a Viko von Geldersen, a Wittenborg, or an Ott Ruhland, you will find it exceedingly difficult to believe that the writers were all great merchants in their generation. (1915, p. 18)

As the head accountant of the Fugger company himself admitted (see Part II, chapter 6), book-keeping was a much more advanced art in Italy than in

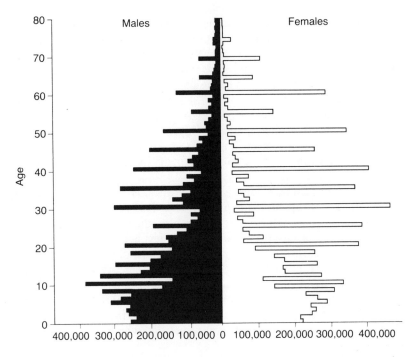

Figure 1 The population of Turkey in 1945 by gender and age. The anomalous structure of the pyramid, with its exaggerated peaks at ages 5, 10, 15, 20, 25, and so on, clearly indicates that people did not know their own exact age and gave the census officers an approximate round number.
Source: United Nations, 1955, p. 34.

Germany. In the fourteenth and fifteenth centuries, mints all over Europe called on Tuscans to serve as mint directors because Tuscans knew how to balance accounts. And yet there is a good deal of truth in what Sombart wrote. Until the beginning of the nineteenth century, approximation certainly prevailed throughout the whole of Europe. In both public and private administrative accounts, errors in calculation were commonplace. For every fourteenth-century Villani, fifteenth-century Sanudo, or sixteenth-century Guicciardini, who reported quantitative economic data that have by and large been confirmed by historical scholarship, there are scores of cases in which the figures given are demonstrably exaggerated in one direction or another. (On Villani see Sapori, 1929, repr. 1955; on Sanudo see Luzzatto, 1929b.)

In Europe, the precise use of numbers began to spread beyond the circle of Italian merchants, of mint masters and watchmakers at the end of the eighteenth century. But the habit of producing and citing grossly inaccurate and fanciful figures died out only very slowly. Authoritarian pressures also sometimes fostered the production of bogus statistics. Commenting on the mass of statistics produced in Brandenburg in the eighteenth century, David Landes expressed his conviction that 'one has the sense with a ruler like Frederick II ("the Great") . . . that even with the best of will, his servants could not keep up with his demands and may on occasion have manufactured numbers rather than plead ignorance' (1972, p. 78). Gilles, Festy and Landes harboured similar suspicions with regard to Napoleonic statistics (see Woolf, 1984, p. 160; Landes, 1972, p. 62). Personally, I have the same feelings about many of the figures published nowadays by international agencies, figures widely used by economists in the construction of scatter diagrams, charting per capita incomes or capital–output ratios or rates of investment in many of the so-called developing countries.

Suspicion is one thing, evidence quite another. Historians have the duty to be perpetually suspicious of their sources. But, if they make the leap from suspicion to accusation, they are also duty-bound to prove the grounds of their accusation. Sometimes they are able to do this by highlighting the absurdity of a report or the contradictions present in the source. The report, attributed to Aristotle, that there were 470,000 slaves on the Greek island of Aegina may be written off as nonsense in view of the fact that the island has a surface area of only 80 square kilometres. The Milanese monetary ordinance discussed in the previous section provides an example of internal contradictions which put the historian on his guard.

On other occasions, the reliability or otherwise of a source can be ascertained by comparing it with other sources, or by combining this with an assessment of the document's internal consistency, taking into account the tendency to round figures off. The thesis that in the days of Augustus and Tiberius the Roman Empire had a balance-of-payments deficit with the East is confirmed by Chinese sources (see Warmington, 1974, p. 274) and by numerous discoveries of Roman coins in India (ibid., p. 278ff; Crawford, 1980, pp. 204–17). Pliny the Elder (AD 23–79), in his *Naturalis Historia* (VI.23, 101; XII.18, 84), maintains that this deficit amounted to 50 million sesterces per annum for trade with India and to 100 million sesterces per annum for trade with India, China and Arabia taken together. The gross roundness of these figures makes one think that they do not derive from official surveys but are imaginative 'guesstimates'. E. H. Warmington (1972, p. 276) doubted the accuracy of Pliny's figures, since they appear rather small given the value of the estates of certain wealthy people of the time: Seneca and Pallas were each said to be worth 300 million sesterces, and Narcissus 400 million sesterces. This line of argument does not, however, appear very logical and, besides, the figures purporting to represent the estates of the three plutocrats themselves seem dubious. Judgement on Pliny's figures must therefore be suspended.

Diocletian's edict fixing the prices of more than a thousand goods and services might be considered the ideal source for systematic investigation of the structure of prices in the Roman Empire after the devastating pressure of more than a century of inflation. Unfortunately we do not know how the prices and wages imposed by the edict were arrived at. Were they averages of data gathered in the market-place or were they simply dreamt up by bureaucrats? The fixing of nine salaries at 25 denarii and of sixteen at 50 would appear to have more to do with bureaucratic planning than with market reality. The fact that identical prices and wages are set for all parts of the Empire also gives rise to serious doubts about how realistic the edict was (Duncan Jones, 1982, p. 367). All price-fixing ordinances are suspect and Diocletian's edict is no exception to the rule. In this particular case, the extreme scarcity of other data that might provide a basis for comparison makes it all the more difficult to assess the source.

Lactantius in *De mortibus persecutorum*, chapter 7, wrote that following the edict 'much blood was spilled owing to the scarcity of goods and the poor quality of products, and fear caused the merchandise to vanish from the market. Hence the cost of living rose yet further until, after the death of many, the edict had of necessity to be revoked.' Lactantius hated Diocletian and was prone to describe him as a wild beast in human form. The assertion that many traders were violently eliminated for not complying with the edict should not be accepted at face value. But it is not hard to believe that in the last analysis the edict was a failure.

Historians are justifiably suspicious of data drawn from fiscal documents. Estimates of taxable income, income declarations, and customs registers are all particularly suspect. Examining Spanish sources on trade between Seville and the Americas during the sixteenth and seventeenth centuries (see Part II, chapter 2), Huguette and Pierre Chaunu have drawn attention to the various ways in which merchants could and indeed did defraud the tax collector. The data entered in the ship loading and unloading registers were distorted, and as a result the figures for the value and volume of both incoming and outgoing trade are understimates. Tax fraud is by its very nature, hard to assess and any attempt to correct the data is complicated by the fact that 'fraud was not constant over time: it grew considerably from the sixteenth century onwards and fluctuated from year to year for a variety of reasons, depending also on the state of the economy' (Chaunu and Chaunu, 1955, I, pp. 88–124). At the start of the seventeenth century, smuggling reached very high levels. Contemporary reports on smuggling are eloquent. J. H. Elliott (1986, p. 156) cites a confidential report sent to the Spanish Council of State in 1617, which asserts that, when fleets returned from the Americas to Sanlucar, large quantities of silver, which those responsible had been careful not to register at the time of loading, were smuggled off the galleons under cover of night, and secretly reloaded onto North European ships lying at anchor close to the harbour. In a letter of July 1633, the Count-Duke of Olivares wrote that the fleet that had docked in Spain on the 13th of that month officially carried 7 million pesos (pieces of eight) in silver, but that it was suspected that there were a further 2 million pesos in contraband on board (Elliott, 1986, p. 465). In 1624 a book-keeper for the royal administration, Cristóbal de Balbas, produced documentary evidence that at least 85 per cent of goods transported by the fleet that had sailed from Seville that year bound for Portobelo in Panama had not been declared, and that no export duty had been paid on them. In the last analysis, the Consulado of Seville, a powerful association of merchants exercising a trade monopoly with the Americas, was responsible for this vast fraud. The royal administration threatened to set up a rigorous inquiry, but the Consulado paid a fine of 206,000 ducats and the affair was hushed up (Vila Vilar, 1982).

The registers of ships passing through the Sound, the principal strait linking the North Sea to the Baltic (see Part II, chapter 2), belong in this same category of suspect documents. Both Axel Christensen (1934; 1941) and S. van Brakel (1915) have expressed serious reservations about the information that they contain. Recently, Pierre Jeannin has re-examined this whole time-worn issue, and among other things has compared the information in the Sound registers with that contained in the *Pfundzollbücher* kept at the port of Königsberg. In Jeannin's view, the registers were virtually complete. But for many centuries, given the considerable variation in tonnage of seafaring vessels, it was unclear exactly what qualified as a 'ship'. Many nations had merchant ships, and this adds to the difficulty of arriving at an average tonnage for the ships in any given period. The interpretation of information on the size of ships' cargoes is even more complicated. Alex Christensen, on the basis of analyses of the amounts of duty paid, estimated that in the period 1574–97 fraud amounted on average to 40–50 per cent of the value of a cargo. Jeannin, however, brought to light evidence that suggests less simplistic conclusions. Most important, it would appear – and this seems logical enough – that fraud varied in relation to the value of the goods transported. Furthermore, it seems that there were sharp fluctuations in the level of fraud from one period to another. From 1562 (when duty was first imposed on the cargo as well as on the ship) until the late 1570s, fraud seems to have remained at a very modest level – especially between 1562 and 1567, when the duty payable was very slight and evasion simply was not worth the risk. But in the first half of the 1580s fraud reached very high levels indeed. Dutch captains of the time apparently declared to the customs less than half of each cargo. This triggered a clamp-down, and between 1586 and 1588 Danish customs officers intensified their checks. Fraud again became rife between 1590 and 1598, however, and in 1618 the Danish authorities introduced regular checks on ships and their cargoes. From then until 1650, comparison with information on shipping traffic in the Baltic ports confirms the information contained in the Sound registers. For the period 1650–1710, the granting of exemptions to Swedish ships (it was in this period that the east side of the Sound became Swedish territory) creates fresh problems, but the under-registration resulting from the Swedes' privilege appears to have amounted to no more than 5 per cent of the cargoes that passed through the strait (Jeannin, 1964, esp. pp. 68, 97–102; see also Nilsson, 1962).

A similarly complicated question is that of the reliability of English sources on foreign trade. As explained in Part II, chapter 2, there are three main sets of documents on English foreign trade (or at least, for particular periods, on one sector of that trade): the Exchequer Enrolled Customs Accounts from 1275 until the mid sixteenth century, the Port Books from 1565 until 1799, and the Ledgers of the Inspector General of Imports and Exports from 1697 until 1780. These sources are exceptionally rich in information, but, like all sources rich in information, they also pose numerous problems.

In the case of the Exchequer Enrolled Customs Accounts, it should not be forgotten that these documents were of fiscal origin. Eleonora Carus Wilson thought that in the fourteenth century the margin of error of the data in the Customs Accounts 'probably never exceeds some 8% and is seldom likely to be so much' (1941, p. 178), but just how this distinguished scholar arrived at such a precise estimate is hard to comprehend.

As luck would have it, the port of Hull's Particular Accounts for 1453–90 have been preserved. These were used to compile the briefer and more succinct Exchequer Enrolled Customs Accounts. In 1986, on editing the Particular Accounts of Hull, W. R. Childs concluded that 'a final judgement on the completeness of the accounts involves a balancing of probabilities rather than certainties' (1986, p. xvi).

As for the Port Books and Ledgers, goods were initially valued at market levels. As time went by, however, their value became arbitrarily fixed, with the result that figures for the 'value' of goods imported and exported in fact represent not the actual value of the trade, but rather an index of its volume. But the common problem of smuggling was much more serious.

With regard to the sixteenth century, N. J. Williams has uncovered the case of Francis Shaxton, a merchant active in the latter half of the century in the small port of (King's) Lynn. The authorities became suspicious of him in 1572, and an inquiry was set up. This brought to light not only Shaxton's large tax evasions, but also those of almost all the other local merchants (N. J. Williams, 1911, pp. 387–95). As for the seventeenth and eighteenth centuries, D. Woodward has written that

during the early Stuart period large-scale smuggling probably remained restricted to a narrow range of commodities. The level of duty on most commodities remained low and widespread evasion of duties in the ports probably varied according to the honesty and diligence of the custom officials. But between the outbreak of the Civil War and the early years of the eighteenth century the situation changed considerably. The introduction of the excise in 1643 increased the incentive to smuggle certain commodities, but the greatest inducement to the smuggler came with the substantial increase in the level of duties during the 1690s. Following this, smuggling almost became a national sport in the eighteenth century. (1973, pp. 158–9)

Editing Boston's Port Books for 1601–40, R. W. K. Hinton commented that 'Port Books are seducers. They have an air of plausibility which they may not merit. It is necessary to resist the temptation to take at face value the commercial information that can be extracted from them (1956, pp. xxxii–xxxiii). B. Dietz, when he came to edit the London Port Books for 1567–8, advanced the hypothesis that, owing to smuggling, 'the port books . . . under-record imports [of high-cost goods] like spices and silk but . . . give an accurate account of the trade in "mass" wares like timber, canvas, and fish'. Dietz concluded sagely that 'the most realistic attitude . . . is one which avoids . . . the extremes either of uncritical acceptance or of complete distrust', but he acknowledged that 'the debate on smuggling and its share of the nation's trade is likely to be endless' (1972, pp. xii, xiv).

Concentrating his attention on a single year (1685) and on a single commodity (iron), W. E. Aström compared the information in the London, Hull and Newcastle Port Books with that contained in the Sound registers and in other Baltic port sources. His verdict was that the various sources were in rough agreement as to the number of ships, that problems arose when it came to information on cargoes, but that on the whole the Port Books were 'fairly reliable' (Aström, 1963/5; 1968). It is worth pointing out, however, that smugglers were less interested in the bulky and relatively low-cost goods (such as iron) that were shipped out of the Sound than in high-cost, low-volume goods such as tea, on which until 1784 a heavy import duty was exacted. The work of W. A. Cole (1958) is relevant here (see also Nash, 1982).

As explained in Part II, from 1697 onwards there are two parallel sets of data on English imports and exports: the Port Books, and the Ledgers of Imports and Exports. Several scholars have attempted to compare these two sources and as a result grave doubts have been cast on the Ledgers.[5] C. M. Foust (1986) has compared information in the Ledgers on English imports of Russian rhubarb with information in a Russian source on rhubarb exports from the port of St Petersburg. These two sources tallied, rhubarb thereby demonstrating its strongly invigorating properties on those historians whose faith was reeling under the blows dealt by W. A. Cole, R. G. Wilson and D. Woodward. Be that as it may, the seductive statistics available on English foreign trade from the Middle Ages until the end of the eighteenth century should be used with great caution, because, as Foust himself conceded, 'for certain specific commodities at certain times they can arouse suspicions that the national series is flawed by under-reportage', owing above all to smuggling (1986, p. 552).

In the case of Mediterranean ports, historians have another reason for remaining on their guard: the ban on exports of 'strategic' goods to Muslim

[5] Wilson (1971), comparing the information contained in the Port Books of Hull with that contained in the Ledgers, observed that the exports of two types of woollen fabric from Hull (according to the Port Books) exceeded in volume the total exports of these fabrics from all English ports (according to the Ledgers) in six out of the seven years for which the check was made. Similar discoveries were made by Woodward (1973, pp. 160–1) in comparisons between the Ledgers and the Port Books of Bristol.

countries. Popes Alexander III (1159–81), Nicholas IV (1288–92) and Boniface VIII (1294–1303) issued a series of bulls threatening to bar from trading and to excommunicate any merchant who dared to sell 'strategic' goods to 'the enemies of Christendom'. As late as 1620 at the port of Leghorn, which for those times enjoyed an exceptionally liberal regime, the Grand Duke of Tuscany, in compliance with papal precepts, decreed

> that in the commerce and trade of Barbary with the wharf of the port of Leghorn the observance of the good and holy commands be more strictly supervised . . . enjoining all merchants that they venture not to send, either directly or indirectly, with or without intermediary, neither in response to any petition nor under any pretext, to those parts, prohibited merchandise and goods – that is to say, weapons, iron, wire, tin, steel and any type of metal, powder and munitions, timber, hemp, rope or material for making rope, as well as any other thing prohibited in the papal bulls.

The consequences of this and similar bans are easy to imagine. For example, on 24 August 1652, according to official port documents, the English ship *Dolphin*, moored at the quayside, was laden with two bales and three bundles of Florentine cloth, twenty-five casks of alum, two sacks and one bag of pepper bound for Tripoli on behalf of Salomone Ressin; 100 pigs of lead bound for Messina on behalf of a certain Felice Pigott, an English merchant resident in Leghorn; fifty cases of Greek pitch and fifty cases of black pitch bound for Malta; and new hawsers bound for the Venetian fleet in Crete, also on behalf of Felice Piggot. On the evening of 24 August, the authorities received a tip-off that the black pitch and the hawsers, both goods deemed to be 'strategic', were bound not for Malta and Crete, but for Tripoli, and that 'Felice Pigott' was just a front: the person really responsible for sending the banned merchandise to the Barbary pirates stationed in Tripoli was an English merchant named George Norlens.

It is not only in relation to periods when statistical records were crude or unknown that historians need to be wary of quantitative data. From registers of population kept by the various Belgian provinces, J. Stengers counted a total of 24,717 Belgian emigrants to North America (Canada and the United States) in the period 1906–13. But, on examining American and Canadian immigration registers, he counted 53,279 (Stengers, 1970, p. 438).[6] R. P. Swierenga, studying the Dutch migrations in the period 1820–60, reached the conclusion that 'the number of Dutch emigrants to the United States was 48 per cent more than the Dutch emigration records showed and 90 per cent more than US official immigration records showed' (1981, pp. 453–4).

---

[6] See also Stengers' comments (1970, p. 444) on the statistics published by the International Labour Office in its official *Annuaire statistique du travail* on female employment in the Belgian Congo in the 1950s.

Oskar Morgenstern uncovered a similar but even more sensational case, involving statistics on the international gold trade. Comparing French statistics on exports of gold to Britain with British statistics on imports of gold from France in the years 1876–84, Morgenstern (1965, p. 140) noted the following extraordinary discrepancies (figures in millions of gold francs):

	French data on exports	British data on imports
1876–80	41.5	94.4
1881–4	52.9	112.2

Gold is involved here, not potatoes. And gold is a well-defined commodity: there is no difficulty in identifying or classifying it. In Jean Stengers' view, 'the problem posed by bogus statistics is very widespread. . . . Statisticians themselves are happy to challenge mistaken methods in the use made of statistics and readily denounce the casual manner in which some scholars feel they may compile statistics without getting to know the rules of the game' (1970, p. 47) but they don't take enough trouble to denounce the unreliability of many official statistics. It should also be appreciated that so-called 'official statistics', even when they have not been brutally distorted for political ends, always bear the hallmarks of the prevailing political and cultural climate. Widely differing criteria and judgements are in fact implicit in the choice of what is measured, of how it is measured, of how frequently measurements are taken, and of how the resulting data should be presented and interpreted. The notion that it is possible to produce statistics on purely a technical and scientific basis and in accordance with purely technical and scientific criteria is a pious illusion.[7]

Sometimes historians are forced utterly to reject the data at their disposal and to forgo any type of quantitative analysis. On other occasions, they can demonstrate that they are justified in accepting the available information only in part or as a rough guide. The trouble is that historians do not always engage in source criticism with the necessary thoroughness and objectivity. Worse still, on occasion economic historians themselves contribute to the production of bogus statistics. This danger will be examined in chapter 5.

INTERPRETING CONTENT

As we saw earlier, deciphering texts, interpreting their content, confirming their authenticity and ascertaining how reliable they are are inextricably interdependent processes. It is in practice impossible to undertake one of these tasks without somehow getting involved in the others. Here, however,

---

[7] On the inevitable 'politicization' of 'official statistics', see Alonso and Starr, 1987, pp. 3–4.

I shall concentrate on 'interpreting content', in order to illustrate what this means. I shall also give examples of the traps that always lie in wait for historians.

In Part II, chapter 1, mention is made of the Augustan censuses carried out in 28 BC, 8 BC and AD 14. These gave the total number of *civium Romanorum capita* (literally 'heads of Roman citizens') as 4,063,000, 4,233,000 and 4,937,000, respectively. There is no doubt about what the text says; the problem is the meaning of *civium Romanorum capita*. What demographic groups did this expression cover? All Roman citizens including women and children? Or only men fit for military service, as was usual in Roman censuses of the Republican era? Augustus did not cite these figures in a technical document but in the context of what might be called his political testament. He therefore did not explain an expression that he expected his contemporaries to understand. But for historians the doubt remains. K. J. Beloch in 1886 believed that the Augustan totals included women and children. Tenney Frank in 1924 favoured the hypothesis that Augustus was using the expression *civium Romanorum capita* in its traditional Republican sense of men fit to bear arms. Brunt (1971) returned to Beloch's thesis but suggested that Augustus's figures should be increased a little to allow for soldiers under arms and for a hypothetical under-registration (without, however, explaining how he worked out the number of serving soldiers and the extent of under-registration). The diversity of assumptions and interpretations leads to drastically contrasting results. Whereas Beloch and Brunt interpreted the Augustan figures to mean that the population of Italy in this period was around 5–6 million, Tenney Frank put it at approximately 12 million.

In the first few years of his reign (AD 270–5) Aurelian tried to reform the Roman currency, which had been progressively deteriorating since the times of Commodus (AD 177–92). The sign XX.I (see plate 2) appears on various issues of the antoninianus minted during his reign, including those bearing the image of his wife Severina. Diocletian (AD 284–305) made a more energetic attempt to reform the monetary system. The sign XX.I appears on coins of his reign too, but not on those that replaced the antoninianus; instead it appears on the follis, a coin of smaller value. The sign can be seen quite clearly, but what did it mean? Some numismatists argue that on Aurelian's coins it meant '20 antoniniani = 1 aureus'. But the fact that the same sign on the follis of Diocletian's time lends support to the hypothesis, advanced by other numismatists, that it indicated the composition of the alloy used in the coin: i.e. it meant '20 parts copper to 1 part silver'. But which interpretation of the sign XX.I is the right one remains uncertain.

In the previous section mention was made of the English Port Books, which provide information and data on the import and export trade passing through English ports in the sixteenth to eighteenth centuries. J. H. Andrews has pointed out that the term 'port' in the title of these books does not necessarily refer to a single place, but is to be understood rather in its

Plate 2 Antoninianus bearing image of Severina, wife of Aurelian. Above: obverse and reverse, actual size. Below: enlargement of reverse, clearly showing the sign XX.I

legal and administrative sense. In other words, minor ports were not treated separately, but were subsumed under the major port of the region. Thus, for example, details of trade passing through the ports of Folkestone, Hythe and New Romney are included in the figures for the larger ports of Sandwich and Faversham. Unless care is taken, this can create a false picture of the overall situation (Andrews, 1956, p. 121)

Statistics can easily mislead unless scrupulous attention is paid to their historical context. A young economic historian once worked out, for a north Italian city in the fifteenth century, what percentage of the population had died a violent death, and compared that with the corresponding percentage for the same city in recent times. The fifteenth-century percentage was much higher, so he concluded that life was much more violent in the fifteenth century than it is today. This is probably true, but the statistics cited do not constitute proof. If someone got a hard knock on the head in the fifteenth century, the chances were that that would be the end of him. But, if someone gets a very similar hard knock on the head nowadays, the chances are that the doctors will save him. Figures on violent deaths are not comparable, because they reflect not only the relative frequency of acts of violence, but also changes in the effectiveness of medical assistance.

Similarly, the rates of mortality among hospital inmates in previous centuries can easily trip up any historian who fails to pay sufficient attention to the conditions under which those hospitals operated. As explained in Part II, chapter 5, hospitals in the Middle Ages and at the beginning of the Modern Age customarily admitted destitute persons who were not really ill but who had nowhere to sleep and no bread to stave off hunger. After a night's sleep and a square meal, these basically healthy people were much better. However, when hospitals became better organized and admitted only or principally people who were really ill, mortality rates increased. In 1803 the famous doctor Giuseppe Frank reported, in his account of the hospitals of Europe, that he had had a long conversation with a certain Dr Borsieri, who held that 'the best-organized hospital is the one in which the mortality rate is the highest. The reason is easy to understand. The better a hospital is directed, the more care will be taken to ensure that only those who are really in need of medical assistance are admitted.' Indeed, it has been ascertained that in present-day New York those hospitals with a more efficient ambulance service, allowing for the immediate hospitalization of people suffering heart attacks, have a higher mortality rate than hospitals with an inadequate ambulance service: the reason is that in the latter case the sick have plenty of time to die at home, whereas in the former they die in hospital.

The examples cited in this chapter demonstrate that interpretation of a source cannot really be separated from evaluation of its authenticity and reliability, though for the sake of clarity of exposition and argument it has been necessary to distinguish different processes of investigation and their attendant problems. In real life scholars do not go through these processes one by one, like stepping from one room into the next. The collection, evaluation and interpretation of sources, and indeed the eventual reconstruction of the historical event – the purpose of all the other operations – take place, as it were, simultaneously, along a single broad front. Like detectives, historians, while gathering, examining, studying and interpreting their sources, are all the while developing in their imagination, as they tie one snippet of information in with another, a hypothesis about what actually happened at the time and in the society investigated. Then they may happen upon new sources, and read new documents, in the light of which they may review their previous judgements, revise their previous interpretation of the sources or modify the historical reconstruction they had previously hypothesized. And so the process goes on, a heady succession of approximations and revisions, with constant feedback between problems, hypotheses, assumptions, sources, interpretations and imagination. The final reconstruction of the historical event therefore emerges gradually in the mind of the scholar, rather like an image brought bit by bit into focus: at first blurred, distorted or even upside-down, it grows progressively more precise and better defined.

5 Reconstructing the Past

'The historian works on the assumption that he is capable of reconstructing and understanding the events of the past. If an epistemologist manages to convince him that this is not so, the historian should change profession' (Momigliano, 1974, repr. 1987, p. 14). At a time when the least-talented social scientist waxes eloquent about historial relativism, the subjective nature of historical reconstruction, and historicism, this typically concise, no-nonsense statement from an eminent scholar is a reminder that historians, when they write about history, are utterly convinced that their reconstruction truly reflects 'the way things really happened'. Otherwise, they are not historians but master forgers. Sometimes historians turn to forgery for fear of the powers-that-be, or for short-term gain, or even for the perverse thrill of fooling their peers. If historians are convinced that, despite their most strenuous efforts, their reconstruction is at best a crude and unwitting distortion of historial reality, they ought to cease writing and, as Momigliano suggested, 'change profession'. Of course, some historians may be ignorant or stupid, in which case their conviction that things happened in just the way they describe may be taken for granted without further ado. The fact remains, however, that talented historians too, even those prepared to give the epistemologist's relativist views a careful hearing, are convinced that their reconstructions are faithful descriptions of historical reality.

To reconstruct history, historians must rely on and confine themselves to attested facts, which they can then piece and link together. Some historians may have lived through the events they relate, in which case they act as sources and as historians at one and the same time. But historians usually draw their data from surviving documents, which, as we saw in chapter 4, they must examine and assess with a critical eye. Without documents there is no history. In their work of reconstruction, historians are heavily conditioned by the state of available documentation, and that, as we saw in chapter 3, depends on a variety of circumstances. These include the culture (and hence the 'curiosity') of the society in which the documents were produced, people's rational or irrational determination to preserve or to destroy evidence, and the vagaries of chance. Historians cannot, therefore, expect to find documentation on every aspect of the past. Besides, if each event, feeling, thought, sorrow, joy, smell, taste had left behind a documentary trace, the entire globe, both land and sea, would be chock-full of historical documents. The prime gift of the talented historian is an awareness of the significance of the abundance, scarcity or indeed the lack of documentary evidence, and the ability intelligently to pursue his or her own concerns within the bounds set by the state and type of the sources available.

While conveying a message from the past, these sources – whether they are narrative, documentary or archaeological – are at the same time a screen between the historian and the past. The distorting effect of this screen varies, and the historian's first task is to check its existence and assess its strength. Confronted with the facts, opinions and judgements that the sources transmit, the historian has to face a number of choices. Not only is it not feasible to gather up and pitch into one's book all the data transmitted by the sources; it is not part of the historian's job to do so – just as it is not the archaeologist's job to collect all the stones he can find at a particular site just because they can all claim antiquity. 'It is obviously impossible', Veyne wrote, 'to recount the totality of past events and one has therefore to make choices' (1971, p. 50). D. Lowenthal has remarked, 'No historical account can recover the totality of any past events, because their content is virtually infinite. The most detailed historical narrative incorporates only a minute fraction of even the relevant past. . . . Most information about the past was never recorded at all and most of the rest was evanescent' (1985, p. 214).

The choice is up to the historian. 'There is no such thing', Veyne wrote, 'as a special category of facts that may be said to represent History, and which accordingly demand to be selected' (1971, p. 50). The historical relevance of a fact or piece of evidence is not determined by any intrinsic quality. Mandelbaum argued that any fact can be of interest to the historian provided it possesses 'social significance' (1938, pp. 9, 14). In my view, this statement is misleading. The historical relevance of a fact or piece of evidence does not depend on its intrinsic qualities but on the nature of the historian's interests. Weather records tell us for example that Tuscany enjoyed an exceedingly hot autumn in 1630. To an economic historian interested in the monetary policy of Grand Duke Ferdinand II, this information is irrelevant. But, to a historian studying the fluctuations in wine production or the rise and fall of agricultural prices in Tuscany at the time of Ferdinand II, the same item of information is of historical interest. It all depends on the viewpoint and interests of the researcher.

In chapter 2 it was pointed out that historians normally start with a series of more or less intuitively conceived problems and that they may, during the course of research, as they delve into their sources and uncover new material, gradually modify their initial set of concerns, in response to promptings from the documentary evidence itself. If this happens, the historian's selection of data is influenced accordingly. All historians know how information that at first seemed irrelevant can turn out to be relevant after the original problems have been reformulated. There then follows the agonizing process of retracing one's steps in pursuit of the previously neglected evidence. Conversely, facts and evidence that seemed relevant may eventually be discarded in the light of changed priorities.

THE IMPORTANCE OF THEORY

'Facts', wrote Werner Sombart, 'are like beads: they require a string to hold them together, to connect them. But if there is no string, if there is no unifying idea, then even the most distinguished authorities cannot help producing unsatisfactory work' (1929, p. 5). The 'unifying idea' is the theory or, as they say nowadays, the 'model'. This applies not only to history and economic history, but to every other discipline. In his book *Scientific Man*, E. Cantore rightly observed that 'facts remain sterile until they are evaluated in the light of a theory' (1972, p. 33). It is only when they have been marshalled and arranged in accordance with a theoretical paradigm that facts – however carefully gathered and observed – acquire significance. Otherwise they are no more than drifting, solitary, meaningless atoms. The following curious example is instructive.

In the sixteenth and seventeenth centuries it was generally believed that plague was caused by lethal putrid vapours known as miasmas, the atoms of which would stick to clothing (especially to woollen garments and furs) and to skin, thus passing on the disease. During epidemics, at first in France and then in Italy, doctors working with plague sufferers took to wearing anti-plague clothing, in order to combat the pernicious effect of the 'sticky' atoms. This clothing consisted of ankle-length tunics made of waxed cloth and fitted with hoods. The idea was that the surface of the waxed tunics would be too slippery for the miasmic atoms to stick to. The anti-plague clothing in fact performed a most useful function, though not that intended by its inventors: it assured medical staff excellent protection against the fleas which were the true vector of the *Yersinia pestis* bacillus. At the time no one imagined that fleas had anything to do with the disease.

In 1657 Genoa was visited by an exceptionally virulent epidemic, which in a matter of months killed 55,000 of a total population of 75,000 inhabitants. In charge of the Genoese lazaretto was Father Antero Maria di San Bonaventura, who caught the plague and recovered but remained in that hellish environment for many more months. When it was all over, he related his extraordinary experiences in a volume of memoirs entitled *Li lazareti della città e riviere di Genova, del 1657* (Genoa, 1658) a work overflowing with humanity and good sense. As regards the anti-plague tunic, Father Antero wrote, 'the only good effect of the waxed tunic in a lazaretto is that fleas cannot easily find their way through it'. This was absolutely correct. Waxed tunics protected their wearers from flea-bites.

But who ever would have thought to link fleas with the plague? Because of the dominance of a mistaken theoretical paradigm (plague is caused by miasmas) and the consequent lack of a correct theory (plague is spread by living organisms), the importance of this isolated piece of information was missed. As a result, regardless of its accuracy and relevance, Father Antero's observation remained a mere anecdote. In other circumstances it might have provided the clue leading to the discovery of the aetiology of the plague – centuries earlier than in fact happened.

With the exception of the historical school of German economists in the nineteenth century, European economic historians – especially on the continent – have traditionally been extremely weak on theory. In the 1930s Eileen Power remarked, with reference to the work of economic historians of the Middle Ages, 'economic historians . . . have often approached their subject either with no theory at all, or with a theory that is inappropriate. . . . This has produced many valuable collections of facts and has deepened our knowledge of legal, institutional and political developments, but it has not given us economic history in any valid sense of the term.' 'Economic history', she added, '. . . has suffered from the fact that it has not always known what questions to ask itself' (Power, 1934, pp. 17, 15).

The inadequate use that most European economic historians (including such major figures as Pirenne, Sapori and Braudel) have made of the conceptual tools of economics may be largely owing to their training as historians or lawyers. To put it bluntly, if they have failed to deploy economic theory in any adequate way, it is because they were not familiar with it. But many historians also express a methodological objection which merits some consideration. It is asserted that to apply modern economic theory to the interpretation of a historical context radically different from our own period is an anachronistic and anti-historical procedure which entails a dangerous distortion of the historical context under examination.

The first response to this line of argument is that consciously or unconsciously every historian makes use of an interpretative theoretical paradigm – however crude or wrong-headed – for without one historians would not know which data to collect. Besides, without a theory historians would be unable to arrange their data in any logical order. As Werner Sombart wrote,

Most historians . . . have . . . some kind of theory at the back of their minds – even the most primitive historian would be unable to write history without some understanding of the way in which the events he describes are linked together. But the theory could hardly be described as scientific; it was little better than the loose notions of everyday life. There are historians who believe that, with a few vague and ambiguous notions of this kind – good enough for everyday life – they are fully equipped and qualified to write economic history. The result has been exactly what one should expect . . . almost valueless compilations. (1929, p. 4)

In cases where a theoretical paradigm is adopted unconsciously, on the promptings of common sense or the experience of ordinary everyday life, it generally turns out to be inadequate and often downright misleading. Moreover, the failure to make one's theoretical model explicit involves a dangerous concealment of its possible defects: its inadequacy, its internal contradictions or its utter absurdity. For example, Pirenne's classic work *Mahomet et Charlemagne* (1937) is based on the implicit theory that the economic, social and cultural structure of Western Europe in the early Middle Ages, along with its levels of consumption, investment and employment, was a function of trade (or lack of trade) with the Orient. Formulated explicitly, Pirenne's interpretative model reveals its simplistic absurdity and, as a result, his entire ingenious, erudite and brilliant construction collapses like a house of cards.

The notion that the explicit application of modern economic theory is a ridiculous anachronism is essentially founded on ignorance of economic theory, ignorance for which economists themselves are largely to blame. In chapter 1 we noted Henry Kissinger's comment that history 'is not a cookbook offering pre-tested recipes'. Likewise – despite the way it is taught in most universities – economic theory is not a cookbook offering thaw-and-cook theorems. Keynes rightly held that 'economics is a branch of logic, a way of thinking. The theory of economics does not furnish a body of settled conclusions immediately applicable to policy. It is a method rather than a doctrine, an apparatus of the mind, a technique of thinking' (1973 edn, XIV, ii, p. 296). Alfred Marshall remarked, 'Economics is not a body of concrete truth but an engine for the discovery of concrete truth' (1885, p. 25); and T. S. Ashton added that economics 'has ceased to be a set of conclusions and has become an apparatus of thought: no longer a doctrine, it has become a method' (1962, pp. 170, 176). Eli F. Heckscher observed, 'Economics is not concerned with any particular set of external facts but with a particular point of view about all human activities' (1953, p. 426).

Economic theorems, incorrectly referred to as 'theories', are contingent on specific historical situations: they are logical formulations which respond to the demands and aspirations of a given society at a given historical moment. It is no accident that the theorem of comparative advantage emerged in early-nineteenth-century England rather than in Portugal; that the theorem of tariff protection for fledgling industries emerged in Germany in the second half of the nineteenth century rather than in England; or that in the twentieth century the Keynesian theorem of deficit spending to sustain demand and employment emerged during the crisis-torn thirties rather than the 'roaring' twenties. These theorems are contingent, their validity restricted in both time and space, whereas economics as 'a branch of logic, a way of thinking' is universal. It is obviously wrong to apply to a past economy a theorem suited to a contemporary economy. But the mistake consists not in the use of a theoretical paradigm to organize one's data, but in choosing the wrong one. The economic historian's problem is how best to use that 'branch of logic' known as economics to elaborate a theoretical and interpretative model or paradigm suited to the specific historical situation under examination. This demands (1) mental elasticity and creativity, i.e. a willingness to discard fashionable models and the ability to create models suited to the period studied; (2) a profound knowledge of the historical context surrounding the events studied, i.e. an appreciation of the legal, political, social – as well as economic – structures and institutions of the society analysed. This wider socio-cultural context provides the framework for the economic system, and conditions its functioning and its responses to particular stimuli.

Although this may seem obvious or even trite, it is in fact both awkward and problematic. Scholars, in particular those with a background in economics, find it very hard to tear themselves away from the magical charm of this year's theorems. Their minds have been 'modelled' on them. The concrete evidence before their eyes each day relates to their own society and confirms the validity of current models. To undertake historical research they have to unlearn what it took them so much trouble to learn, and to imagine situations and circumstances that strike them as alien.

The following is a simple and clear-cut example. It has recently become fashionable for economists to question the once-popular hypothesis that during prolonged periods of inflation wages rise less rapidly than prices. One distinguished economist went so far as to assert that 'a more careful analysis shows that in most cases of inflation wages do not lag behind prices'. With special reference to the so-called 'price revolution' of the sixteenth century, another economist observed that, 'if in the short run wages may lag behind prices, it is hard to conceive of conditions under which individuals for entire decades might fail to react to a state of monetary turbulence whittling away at their real incomes'. The scepticism implicit in this comment arises from the fact that its author sees things through the eyes of the society in which he has grown up, a society in which labour is sufficiently well-organized to demand and obtain adjustments in wages.

But this has not always been the case. As L. P. Hartley wrote in the Prologue to *The Go-Between*, 'The past is a foreign country: they do things differently there.' In a document dated 1590 the employees of the Magistrature for Public Health of the city of Milan complained,

> These wages were fixed by the Duke of Milan when this Magistrature was first founded [May 1534], and there has never been the slightest increase made to them, about which each of the said ministers has often complained, for at the time when the said wages were established the cost of dwelling, dressing and living was not a quarter of what it is today, and they consider it a grave matter that with such a considerable increase in costs the smallness of the originally established wages should ever have remained unchanged. (Visconti, 1911, p. 426)

As can be seen, there existed in sixteenth-century Milan 'individuals' from a background anything but humble who 'for entire decades' were quite unable to obtain the slightest increase in their nominal wages or 'to react to a state of monetary turbulence' that was whittling away their real incomes. It is not difficult to give other examples of prices that remained unaffected by inflation over long periods. In ancient Rome, the Twelve Tables ordered that anyone proved to have struck another person should pay a fine of 25 asses (the as was a Roman copper coin). Several centuries later, the fine was still 25 asses but, owing to the effect of inflation, the amount had become derisory. To underline the absurdity of the situation, L. Veratius, a wealthy eccentric, went around hitting people left and right. Behind him ran his slave who, by way of compensation, paid his master's victims the 25 asses prescribed by the Twelve Tables (Gellius XX.i. 12–13).

TRAPS FOR THE UNWARY

The theoretical and economic deficiencies of traditional economic historiography have been more apparent in continental Europe than in Britain and the United States. In these countries, a broader-based understanding of economics, and a more precise usage of economic terms, many of which were first coined in English, have meant that even those economic historians who lack any special training as economists are often able to put together arguments that in terms of economic logic are proof against severe criticism. And it is in the United States that the reaction against the traditional approach to economic history has been most radical. From the 1960s onwards, a growing number of young American economics graduates, well-grounded in economics and statistics, have addressed issues of economic history in a new manner. They begin by setting out, usually in algebraic and geometrical form, the explanatory theoretical model that they have constructed or adopted, and then run regressions and check the validity of this model against historical material of a prevalently statistical nature. Unfortunately, this brand of economic history, which is widespread in the United States and has a handful of adherents in Europe, has very shallow philosophical and epistemological foundations. Worse, it is severely handicapped by four defects which always bedevil economic historians, whatever school they belong to – namely, oversimplification, *ex post* reasoning, special pleading in defence of a thesis, and subjectivism. These four traps constantly threaten to ensnare unwary economic historians, whether American or European, traditionalist or revolutionary. It is worth looking closer at each one of them in turn.

Oversimplification

In 1970 Kenneth E. Boulding wrote that

a state description is what the term implies: it is a description of the state of the system at a moment in time. Such a description has to be abstract in the sense that we would be quite incapable of producing in language of any kind a full description of the state of even quite simple systems. A great descriptive writer like James Joyce can spend a whole novel describing the events in the mind of a single person for a single night; to do this he has to strain the resources of the English language to the breaking point and even then he cannot encompass more than a fraction of the reality. The description of the enormous complexity of the sociosphere even at a single moment in time must involve abstractions to an extreme degree. (1970, p. 2)

In chapter 1 it was argued that one of the differences between the methodologies of historians and those of economists is that, whereas economists limit their attention to a small number of variables, historians must (or at least should) take into consideration a much greater number of variables, indeed as many as possible. The description provided by the economic historian should therefore be more complete and realistic than the normally paradigmatic description produced by the economist. Yet even the most detailed description of a historical situation given by the most pedantic and meticulous historian nevertheless remains an extreme simplification of historical reality. Surviving evidence furnishes the historian with limited and partial information, giving a more or less distorted view of reality. Moreover, historians have to select from the array of facts before them, in accordance with their particular concerns and their implicit or explicit theoretical model. The inevitable result of deficiencies in evidence and of the subsequent selections made is a drastic simplification of the historical situation studied. One only has to think of how much a verbal description gains when supplemented by a photograph to realize how much one misses when no photograph is available. And there is always something missing. We know that Caesar decided to lead his troops across the Rubicon. But we know nothing of the state of his digestive apparatus at the time he reached his decision, nor whether he was feeling tired or rested, nor whether he was surrounded by delicate perfumes or by foul smells, nor whether he was feeling hot or cold. One should also bear in mind that, owing to the generalizations forced on the historian by the need to provide an account of as many cases as possible, the space available for any particular case is strictly limited, and this entails a loss of direct contact with reality. The net result of all these circumstances is that all historical reconstructions are more or less drastic simplifications of reality, and this means that distortions, misrepresentations and downright falsifications result. For there are important differences between a simplifying and generalizing approximation and a hugely more complex reality made up of a vast gamut of exceptions, variations, anomalies, oddities, eccentricities, idiosyncracies and peculiarities scattered across what a statistician would call a broad deviation from the mean. The talented historian is the one who, though forced by the very nature of his task to deliver a simplified reconstruction of historical reality none the less manages to convey the sense that the actual events related were vastly more complex and complicated than his account of them. In essence, the sense of history is an awareness of the tremendous complexity of human affairs.

The foregoing considerations provide more substance to the statement made in chapter 3 that historians must base their work on primary sources. For it is only from first-hand material that one can derive a realistic notion of individual cases and of their wide 'scattering' around the average. Those scholars who rely on second-, third- or fourth-hand sources are bound to fall victim to the most atrocious generalizations and simplifications. In the end, the 'translator of Homer's translators' turns out simplifications of simplifications. Lacking any notion of the number and range of the exceptions and variations that are the very stuff of history, he erects constructions vitiated by pretentious, unrealistic and misleading oversimplification.

The comments apply to economic as well as to general history. In the case of economic history, however, there is a further factor that strongly encourages oversimplification. In the economic literature there is no shortage of biographies of business people and managers. But business history has never achieved a systematic merger with economic history. Current economic history fundamentally ignores individuals, as if they didn't exist. Attention is focused instead on units of capital, patterns of consumption, natural resources, imports, exports and technology. When people are brought into the picture, it is only as anonymous atoms who happen to belong to populations whose collective behaviour is studied through rates of birth, death and marriage.

Many years ago, Joseph Schumpeter drew attention to a grave defect within economic theory: its 'inhumanity'. He sought to introduce a human dimension by highlighting the personality and role of the entrepreneur. But not even Schumpeter was able to graft the unfathomable, many-sided and shifting essence of entrepreneurial activity onto the framework of a general theoretical formulation.

Paradoxically, economic historians have not fared any better. Even the French 'Annales' school, despite all its rhetoric about *l'homme et la realité humaine*, in fact deals above all with the anonymous dynamics of structures.

Ex post *reasoning*

What we commonly refer to as 'the present' is a small slice of the future tacked onto a small slice of the past, the size of the slices being left up to whoever uses the term. To the historian 'the present' may mean a few years or decades; to the person in the street, a few days or weeks; to the stock-exchange dealer, a few minutes or hours. The present is really that fleeting instant in which the future becomes the past. We live in the present and yet, owing to its insubstantial and fleeting nature, our gaze is forever fixed on the immediate, near or distant future. As Søren Kierkegaard noted in his *Journals* in 1843, 'life must be understood backwards, but it must be lived forwards' (1938 tr.).

Essentially, life is an uninterrupted succession of problems. When you think you have solved one problem, the conditions for the emergence of a new one are automatically created. In practice people simply replace one problem with another. There is no let-up. Confronting problems as they arise, individuals and societies are faced with options. Sometimes or for some people the range of such options is narrow. At other times or for other people the range is very broad. And there are infinite shades and gradations between these two extremes. To be confronted with options obliges one to make choices. The choices made are not always rational. Whether rational or irrational, choices demand decisions. Both individuals and societies are forced constantly to take decisions. If an individual or society retreats into slothful inertia it is because of a decision not to decide. Some decision – even if it is the decision not to decide – is unavoidable.

The degree of uncertainty of the future varies from case to case and from one moment to the next. But uncertainty is part and parcel of the future. The fact that choices must be made and decisions taken in a climate of uncertainty entails risks. The various options open to the individual or to society and the various decisions that can be taken entail different degrees of risk. But, even for those individuals most averse to running risks, when they take a decision about the future there is no escaping a certain degree of risk, however cautious and prudent the decision may be.

There is a continual vital bond between past and future. The past never dies and is never exorcized. Decisions taken yesterday limit and constrain tomorrow's choices. But there is no symmetry between past and future. In that fleeting instant when the present turns the future into the past, one's options vanish, choices made can no longer be altered, what is done cannot be undone. Uncertainty and risk disappear, making way for the semblance of a process determined by an iron logic – even when events have been heavily influenced by chance or irrationality. *Ex post* everything can be justified, everything appears logical, rational and inevitable. As Aldo Schiavone has written, *ex post* even 'the subtle workings of chance appear to us in the unbending shape of historical necessity'. Centuries ago Diodoro da Megara asserted that it was a mistake to say that the future holds options. He argued that there was only one option: that which would in fact come about. But, if events succeed one another in accordance with a strict logic, as seems to be the case when one looks at the past, why then is prediction so tricky and more often than not impossible? As Hempel rightly observed, a line of argument that fails to demonstrate *ex ante* predictive powers cannot be deployed *ex post* for the purposes of explanation.

It is all too easy for historians to fall into the *ex post* trap – all the more so because, as H. Stuart Hughes put it, 'whatever may be the nature of history "as it actually happened" statements about history can only be logical – otherwise they would be incomprehensible. Whatever may be the ultimate reality, one can communicate one's finding about history only in rational terms, i.e. terms that are coherent and reproducible, although not necessarily rigorous' (1968, p. 8). The tendency to reconstruct human history as a logical and unavoidable concatenation of events is accentuated by the tendency to import into historical discussion the scientific concept of cause. It is part of human nature to try to pinpoint one or more causes for every occurrence of even minor importance. Mere description fails to satisfy. An 'explanation' is called for. 'Felix qui potuit rerum cognoscere causa' ('happy is he who can know the cause of things'). But, as far as historical reconstruction is concerned, the term 'cause' must be uttered as seldom as possible, and preferably *sotto voce*. For in historical reconstruction there is no way of checking empirically what would have happened in a given sequence of events if one particular variable had been different while all the others had remained as they in fact were, because in history everything constantly changes. As E. Kahler (1968) has written, 'Only seldom can the historian justifiably say *why* something happened. In the vast majority of cases he must limit himself to describing *how* things happened, that is to describing the conditions under which an event took place. Thus the concept of cause loses its sense in an intricate web of interacting conditions where everything is "caused" by everything.' The assertion of causal relations that cannot be demonstrated to be such is simply another way of arbitrarily imposing *ex post* a developmental logic on reality which *ex ante* is anything but apparent.

For their own good as well as for that of others, historians (but this is equally true of biologists and physicists) cannot denounce too vigorously (1) the fallacy of the *post hoc ergo propter hoc* (after this, therefore on account of this) argument and (2) the fallacy that a correlation between two or more variables implies a causal relation. Often what are passed off as 'causes' in historical reconstructions have earnt this ill-merited status on the strength of one or both of these fallacious arguments.

Ex post reconstructions hide instead of illustrating the decision-making and problem-solving processes at the heart of human history. We know that Caesar crossed the Rubicon. But for Caesar the question was whether or not to do so. Hindsight is liable to cloud one's outlook. In April 1974, the Interuniversity Centre for European Studies in Montreal, Canada, hosted a conference on 'Failed Transitions to Modern Industrial Society: Renaissance Italy and Seventeenth-Century Holland'. The title of the conference reflects our knowledge that after the Renaissance and the seventeenth century came the Industrial Revolution. This *ex post* knowledge prompted the question, 'Why did the Italians of the Renaissance and the Dutch of the seventeenth century fail to carry out an industrial revolution *ante litteram*?' Taking a closer look, however, the question is absurd. The Italians of the sixteenth century and the Dutch of the seventeenth century did not set their sights on industrial organization: they didn't even know what industry meant. To speak of *failure* suggests that those societies planned to equip themselves with an industrial base but somehow didn't pull it off. Likewise, simplistic judgements based on hindsight are to be avoided when describing cases of economic groups that introduced a particular technological innovation while others did not. When a technological innovation makes its appearance it is merely an option, the benefits of which are usually far from obvious. The first motor-cars were slower than horses. And, for every successful technological innovation, there have been scores of failures. *Ex ante*, tricky problems of assessment and evaluation are almost always involved. Historians who with hindsight put it all down to shrewdness or stupidity are wide of the mark.

On referring to the past it should never be forgotten that the people of that past had to grapple with options and choices, whereas we, with the benefit of historical perspective, are in a position to assess the results of those choices not only in the short but also in the long run. The people living in that past worked from an *ex ante* position. We judge them *ex post*.

Special pleading in defence of a thesis

Books that expound a thesis are much more interesting than books that merely describe events, and their content is much more likely to remain impressed on the mind of the reader. There is nothing wrong in an economic historian setting out a thesis – provided certain conditions are respected. As R. H. Tawney pointed out long ago, although historians are habitually rigorous in their criticism of sources, they do not always exercise the same critical severity over what they themselves write or expound. Where there is a thesis to be argued, scholars may get carried away and lose their criticial edge. Props can easily be found for the most extravagent of theses, especially through a rhetorical and uncritical use of quotations. For, however preposterous a thesis may be, its inventor is bound, on sifting through the vast bibliography at his disposal, to find a book or article with statements that fit his thesis. Quotations from second- and third-hand texts, with no credentials as evidence, are the trademarks of such attempts at camouflage.

In the specific field of economic history, two further practices are often relied upon to embellish misbegotten theses with a semblance of scientific objectivity. An error frequently committed by economic historians of antiquity and mediaeval times is to attribute significance over the long run to documentation referring to the short run. For example, to support the thesis that a particular century was a 'century of crisis', 'depression' or suchlike, a historian usually has no trouble in tracing documents that mention downturns in business, unemployment, increases in the number of the 'poor', 'shortages of money', and so on. Mostly, however, such evidence refers to specific periods lasting only a few years and their use to demonstrate long-term trends is wholly improper. It is probably no exaggeration to say that most generalizations about long-term trends in the classical and mediaeval periods are based on an improper use of documentation that is valid only for the short run.

An even more dangerous form of camouflage is provided by statistical apparatus. Work by economic historians usually abounds with statistical tables, and numbers bestow an often spurious scientific and objective cachet. A few years ago a book entitled *How to Lie with Statistics* was published. The book itself was superficial, but its title was inspired. Numbers are easy to manipulate and 'statistics' can be tailored to the most far-fetched of theses, thereby misleading unwary or ill-trained readers. Admittedly, in historical measurements it is often hard to achieve a high degree of accuracy. But it is one thing to admit a reasonable margin of error, quite another to produce or make use of fake statistics.

Even when no deliberate manipulation is involved, the intrinsic weakness of a thesis may be hidden from view behind a screen of specious precision. In his classic work *American Treasure and the Price Revolution in Spain*, Earl J. Hamilton calculated an index for nominal wages in Castile from 1501 to 1650, with the average salaries for the decade 1571–80 as base 100. For the year 1501 the index came out at 37.51. The two decimal places convey an impression of great accuracy and reliability. But taking a closer look one discovers that the index for this year for the entire kingdom of Castile is based on just three salaries, one of which was a sexton's, another that of a wet-nurse, and the third that of a weaver. In this particular case, the author showed his hand honestly in an appendix so that any fussy or meticulous reader could check what that figure 37.51 was actually based on. But clarity and transparency do not always prevail. (Hamilton, 1934, p. 271.)

Sometimes, even when a statistical source is acknowledged to be fundamentally unreliable, a historian may nevertheless decide to throw a veil of rhetoric over its defects if its figures are needed to support a particular thesis. The following account provides an example. French agricultural statistics for the year 1840 are one of the most impressive nineteenth-century collections of data. However, even at the time the figures were called into question. Subsequently Bertrand Gille (1964, p. 196ff) retraced a number of documents that justified these suspicions. Sebastian Charlety, who did not need to use the data in question, wrote in his *La Monarchie de Juillet* that 'one can make use of *La Statistique* with caution when sources are indicated and methods of collecting and processing evidence are specified, but it is better to make no use of it at all when such information is not supplied'. A. Armangaud, who needed to cite some of the data in his book *Les Populations de l'est Aquitaine*, acknowledged that *La Statistique* had certain 'imperfections' but added that, 'although it is open to criticism in detail, it may still be used to trace the main features of the agricultural system'. Michel Morineau, for whom the figures provided by *La Statistique* were just what were needed to prove his thesis on the question 'Y a-t-il eu une révolution agricole en France au XVIII siècle?', admitted that *La Statistique* 'is probably not unassailable by criticism' but then went ahead and used it unconditionally to support his thesis. (See Stengers, 1970, p. 455.)

Once a historian has produced fake statistics there is no limit to their subsequent use and misuse by other scholars who find them handy support for their pet theses. The naked poverty of the data is then bashfully disguised behind the rhetoric of quotation: by citing the work from which the statistics are derived without the slightest comment regarding its reliability. For example, in 1936 R. R. Kuczynski estimated that a total of 15 million Africans had been forcibly shipped as slaves to the Americas. Kuczynski took this figure from a study published in 1911 by Du Bois, who in his turn had lifted it from work by E. Dunbar, published in 1861, that lacked any claim to scientific status. The fact is that nobody knows how many Africans were shipped to slavery in the Americas. Similarly, quantitative estimates dreamt up by G. C. Parson in 1972, regarding silver stocks in ancient and mediaeval times, are being widely quoted by scholars despite their absolute unreliability.

The kinds of camouflage so far cited do not involve any malicious intent to mislead. I am thoroughly convinced that in most instances the historians in question acted in good faith. But, unless scholars practise continual and strenuous self-criticism, they are liable to become infatuated with their own theses and to delude first themselves and then others.

One kind of thesis-led work is the historical reconstruction that is heavily influenced by a particular ideology. As has already been argued, behind every historical reconstruction there stands a theory – however unconscious and formless. Likewise, behind every historical reconstruction there stands the religious, political, economic or social ideology of the historian. In other words, a given historical reconstruction cannot be divorced from the personality and the social and cultural convictions of its proponent. But there are historians and historians, and ideologies and ideologies. Some historians know how to exercise sufficient control over their own convictions, not allowing them to overwhelm their historical work. Other historians, by contrast, use their work as a battlefield on which to parade their political, religious or social convictions. While some ideologies are not too cumbersome, others play havoc with historical reconstruction. Over the last hundred years, the two most pervasive ideologies have been nationalism and Marxism.

Historicism and subjectivism

'Historicism', wrote Arnaldo Momigliano, 'is the recognition that each of us sees past events from a point of view determined or at least conditioned by our own individual changing situation in history . . . historicism is not a comfortable doctrine because it implies a danger of relativism. It tends to undermine the historian's confidence in himself' (1974, repr. 1987, pp. 24–5). Historians who study a distant past come into contact with cultures different from their own. But the questions that historians ask are conditioned by the culture to which they belong. The mental categories and conceptual instruments that they use in the reconstruction of the past are those of their own times. The language that they use to describe the past is contemporary language and not that spoken by the people studied. As Marc Bloch wrote, 'unavoidably the historian inevitably thinks in the categories of his own times. He expresses himself in the language of his own times and the very language is not a neutral instrument which leaves categories and concepts unaffected.' All of this entails grave risks of anachronism and subjectivism.

Nowadays, historians (or at least those who deserve the name) are more aware than ever before of these risks. At times they push caution too far. In the Preface to his excellent book *The Emperor in the Roman World*, Fergus Millar declared that

> in preparing the work I have rigidly avoided reading sociological works on kingship or related topics, or studies of monarchic institutions in societies other than those of Greece and Rome. . . . For to have come to the subject with an array of concepts derived from the study of other societies would merely have made even more unattainable the proper objective of the historian, to subordinate himself to the evidence and to the conceptual world of a society in the past. (1977, p. xii.)

This is obviously an extreme standpoint, and in the view of Keith Hopkins

> untenable. It is untenable on a literal level because Millar has written in English, not in Latin or Greek. . . . Besides, the historian interprets a lost world to modern readers through the medium of a living language; one of his objectives may well be to enter the thought world of his subjects, both actors and sources . . . but he must also relate the lost world to contemporary concerns, whether consciously or unconsciously. (1978, p. 180.)

The epistemological problem posed by historicism is particularly acute for economic historians. Economics as a discipline and as a system of conceptual instruments and logical categories emerged at the end of the eighteenth century. Until then there was no body of theory for the analysis of economic life. Those alive prior to the end of the eighteenth century had no inkling whatever of a branch of knowledge called economics, even though the Greeks from the end of the third century BC had used the term *oikonomia* with reference to public administration.[1] It is no accident that there are no works of economic history before the seventeenth century. Whenever we write economic history we inevitably project our present-day interests, curiosities, and conceptions onto the past. Even were an economic historian to share Fergus Millar's extreme historicist position, he would find it impossible to carry through the same contemptuous rejection of current theory, for that would simply preclude him from practising economic history. Referring to language (but language reflects

---

[1] The Greek term *oikonomia* originally meant the administration of the family group (*oikos*) but towards the end of the third century BC it had come to be used to denote public administration, as is testified by its appearance on a marble stele discovered at Olbia, a Milesian colony on the Black Sea. See Ampolo, 1979, pp. 119–30.

concepts), Paul Veyne wrote that 'the most serious danger is posed by words that evoke in our mind false images and that fill history with universals that do not in fact exist' (1971, pp. 164). He suggested that, instead of saying that Lucretius loathed religion and that Cicero praised liberty, historians should say that Lucretius loathed *religio* and that Cicero praised *libertas*. After all, what the Romans meant by *religio* and *libertas* was quite different from what we mean by 'religion' and 'liberty'.[2] Solutions of this nature are simply not available to economic historians. Modern terms such as 'demand', 'supply', 'elasticity', 'productivity', 'marginality', 'fixed capital', and 'floating capital' had no equivalent in the Greek, Roman, Mediaeval or Renaissance world, but economic historians have to make do with them or condemn themselves to total silence.

The solution to the economic historian's problem is to be found at the empirical level, in careful avoidance of the extremes of both historicism and 'presentism'. When Eduard Meyer and other eighteenth-century German historians use terms such as 'industry' and 'capitalist development' in their descriptions of the economy of ancient Greece, and when modern historians speak of the 'economic imperialism' of Athens, they are clearly guilty of anachronism. Yet there is nothing intolerably anachronistic about using current economic logic to devise an interpretative model with which to describe and reconstruct an economic event of the past, provided that the model takes into account the specific historical, institutional and cultural conditions and circumstances of the period analysed. As I have written elsewhere, scholars describing an epidemic of plague in the remote past are perfectly entitled to ignore what is now known about plague, and to concentrate on contemporary ideas on the nature and origins of epidemics. Alternatively, the historians might want to find out why and how the epidemic developed and spread, and in this case the beliefs of the time regarding divine wrath, the influence of the stars and the role of miasmas are of less relevance than is our own understanding of the role of microbes, rats and fleas. It is in no way anachronistic to account for the spread of the plague epidemic of 1348 on the basis of what is now known about the bacillus *Yersinia pestis*, and about rats and fleas. What would be anachronistic would be to criticize the people of the time for not organizing rat-hunts. Likewise, it is not anachronistic to seek to explain economic phenomena of the past using the conceptual instruments of modern economic logic. What would be anachronistic would be to force upon the past a model that presupposes a present-day social, political or cultural context.

Of course, the historian's evidence and data are to some extent the product of a subjective choice. The type and volume of the evidence depend

---

[2] This suggestion is valid only for scholarly discourse. In work intended for a broader public, an awareness of the difference between the Roman concept of *religio* and our present concept of religion, and between the Ciceronian concept of *libertas* and our current concept of liberty, cannot be taken for granted.

on the material resources available to the historian. The theoretical model used to marshal and interpret the evidence is necessarily subjective. All this seems to suggest that historical reconstruction is an intellectual enterprise completely devoid of objectivity. Yet the problem is not confined to historiography: it extends to all the sciences, including those commonly labelled 'exact'. In my view a degree of subjectivism is unavoidable in historical reconstruction as in any other kind of scientific analysis. But, as Geymonat has written, 'in the highly complicated process of science not everything is constructed by us, not everything is subjective'. There are facts; and honest researchers gradually modify their initial approach in response to the evidence that the sources (or, in the case of scientific work, experiments) reveal. Nor can their choice of evidence be totally arbitrary: if historians are honest with themselves and others, they cannot brush aside or distort relevant evidence provided by sources deemed reliable or accepted by other scholars. If such evidence clashes with the theoretical model adopted at the outset, it is the model that has to be changed rather than the inconvenient data. It is against such parameters that the worth of a historian must be assessed. As is equally the case in any other discipline, sound work in economic history is a product not only of intelligence, perspicacity and expertise but also of intellectual honesty.

MODEL-BASED ECONOMIC HISTORY

At the beginning of the last section mention was made of the contemporary American school of economists. In my view the focusing of attention on the model and its verification does nothing to help historians avoid the four traps just discussed. Indeed, the reverse is true.

As M. Salvati has written, 'the economic model redefines history with dangerously convenient assumptions, with the hypothesis of an unchanging external environment, while attributing to its agents stereotyped and excessively general purposes' (1978, p. 16). In a sense, Michael Stanford is right when he declares that 'any model is a falsification' (1986, p. 5). To turn the model into a kind of research fetish, transforming an investigation of what actually happened into an attempt to verify the model, is to reduce ends to means and to accord means the status of ends.

The champions of model-based economic history all too frequently allow their enthusiasm for economic theorems and statistics to soar dangerously at the expense of arduous and time-consuming research on the institutional, legal, social and political aspects of a historical context. Even the most talented historian can never know enough about the non-economic aspects of a historical context, and model-bound historians are generally far too ignorant in this area. This becomes strikingly apparent whenever they stray beyond the social, cultural and political confines of their own societies, into areas with which they possess no native familiarity. Ahistorical howlers then abound.

Last but not least, the 'vested interest' that scholars instinctively and unconsciously develop in their own models can easily lead them into what we have labelled 'special pleading', i.e. the desire to force historical reality to fit the model, instead of admitting the weakness of the model as an instrument for making sense of reality.

It has to be acknowledged that the rise of the model-based approach was a necessary reaction to the traditional continental European approach to economic history, which paid insufficient attention to theory and felt no need to make its own theoretical assumptions explicit. Regrettably, however, the pendulum has now swung from one extreme to the other. The model-based school may deplore the fact that traditional historical reconstruction fails to attain the 'degree of neatness and cogency that are the direct results of a model' (Salvati, 1978, p. 17), but the formal neatness and elegance of the model are misleading: they are not evidence of the validity of the model, but proof that the model is a caricature of reality. History is too complicated to be elegant. If the 'new economic historians' want to come to grips with historical reality in all its complexity they will have to abandon their *esprit géométrique* for the subtler if less elegant *esprit de finesse*. This may actually happen sooner than expected. There are clear signs in American historiography that an increasing number of 'modelists' are already abandoning their more radical positions and are paying more attention to institutions, intangibles, accidents and chaotic conditions. The pendulum may therefore revert before long to a more sensible mean.

'SOMETHING MORE'

In addition to the various *traps* outlined above, there is also a kind of 'black hole' into which every historian is liable to stumble. Despite all that has been written over the last few decades on economics, economic history, sociology and anthropology, when it comes to describing the dynamics of human societies we are still condemned to superficiality: the tips of the icebergs are visible, but no one can tell how far down they go. This results from a shortage of evidence, but even more from a lack of suitable analytical and conceptual tools. One observes creative booming societies and self-destructive declining ones. The outward features of such creativity or destructiveness can be noted and described, but what lies behind these appearances? What is the precise relative role of the innumerable economic, cultural, political, social and ideological factors?

In the mid twentieth century it was fashionable to view religion as that 'something' that determined the economic performance of a society. British, American and north German sociologists and historians, convinced of the economic superiority of their own societies over Catholic ones, put forward the thesis that the seeds of capitalist development lay in the characteristics and ramifications of the Protestant ethic. Nowadays a thesis of this kind seems almost laughable, with its arrogant and simplistic ingenuousness, its Eurocentric outlook, its confusion of correlation and causality, and its inability to recognize that religion is merely one aspect of social and cultural life. And yet our ability to analyse the deep processes of history has not progressed substantially.

Take economic development. Numerous studies conducted on nineteenth-century European and American economies appear to agree that increases in production had outstripped increases in capital and labour inputs. Economists have ascribed this phenomenon to (1) a clearer division of labour; (2) economies of scale; (3) more efficient allocation of production factors; (4) technological progress; (5) better education and training of the workforce. But these explanations are substantially gratuitous. The fact is that we just don't know.

Long before current investigations into this phenomenon, Joseph Schumpeter (1947), who suspected its existence, wrote that 'only in very rare cases' could economic development be explained 'by causal factors, such as an increase in population or the supply of capital'. An economy or a company manages to produce 'something more' and this 'something more' 'can always be understood *ex post*; but it can practically never be understood *ex ante*; that is to say, it cannot be predicted by applying the ordinary rules of inference from the pre-existing facts.' Schumpeter labelled this 'something more' 'the creative response of history'. This was tantamount to acknowledging the fundamentally mysterious and inexplicable nature of the phenomenon. Moreover, if history produces at times 'a creative response' (however one interprets this expression) it must also be capable of a 'destructive response', for there are societies that decline and companies that fail. Also, what is true for society as a whole and for companies must apply equally to individuals. If two people, A and B, receive violin lessons for six years from the same expert teacher, A may become a second Paganini while B remains a mediocrity. People will say 'A had what it takes'. But what in fact does it 'take'?

With all the relevant and up-to-date statistics, Japan provides an obvious and accessible example. Mountains of books and torrents of articles are published purporting to explain Japan's extraordinary success. Yet the explanations that are supplied hardly get any further than Schumpeter's 'creative response of history'.[3]

The fact is that as regards neither classical antiquity, nor the Middle Ages, nor the Renaissance, nor modern and contemporary times, are we able to get much further than the straightforward description of superficial results. Thanks to the statistics available on the contemporary period we now have evidence about the 'something more'; but this evidence does

---

[3] Some scholars will pull the wool over our eyes through the use of extravagant pseudo-scientific terms. To 'explain' the economic success of particular peoples or social groups as compared with others, one scholar coined the term '*n* achievement' and another the term '*x* efficiency'. Such terms in fact explain nothing whatsoever, and mean nothing more or less than 'We don't know!'

not provide us with explanations: it simply gives us a rough measure of our ignorance and of our inability to penetrate the movements of history.

COMMUNICATION

Lastly, there is the problem of communication between historian and reader. Thus far, attention has been focused on the historian's task of reconstructing a specific past reality. But historians do not set out to reconstruct the past for their own benefit alone. In the overwhelming majority of cases, they aim to communicate their findings to an audience by way of conferences, articles or books. This process poses a huge problem. Historians necessarily use the language of their time to communicate with their audience. In the minds of readers unversed in historical inquiry, contemporary terminology tends to evoke visions and images of a contemporary character. Veyne's warning against using the modern terms 'religion' and 'liberty' as straightforward equivalent for the *religio* and *libertas* of classical Roman times has already been noted. The problem is, that a historian who recognized this by employing the Latin instead of the modern terms would be understood by only a handful of specialists; most readers would be puzzled rather than enlightened. Besides, historical reconstruction is always a simplification. When one historian addresses another, the latter may be able to supplement the patchy information conveyed with his own specialist knowledge, and thus fill in some of the major 'gaps'. But, if the historian addresses a broader audience, the ability of this audience to fill in the gaps is severely limited. We have a deep understanding only of what we ourselves have experienced. It is much harder to explain the living conditions of a peasant in the Middle Ages to an American student than to a Sicilian student. The American will have no first-hand knowledge of a social context resembling the one described, whereas the Sicilian's familiarity with his own society will enable him, provided he makes a further imaginative effort, to understand something of what the historian is struggling to convey. Similarly, a description of the devastating effects of inflation will be much more readily grasped by someone who has experienced soaring inflation than by someone who has known only monetary stability. It is no easy undertaking to evoke in the mind of another person all the nuances of which the historian is aware in his effort at historical reconstruction. Anecdotes, images of contemporary artefacts, and pictures can all be helpful. It would be hard to exaggerate the evocative power of these and similar expedients. But they are not enough.

Words too can be treacherous. Beneath their apparently immutable surface, even ancient terms may conceal considerable shifts in meaning. The term *mercatores* crops up frequently in both tenth-century and fourteenth-century documents. In the tenth century the term meant *homines duri*, wandering adventurers, individuals whose roots in the feudal, manorial and agrarian world had been severed, and who now existed on its margins. In the fourteenth century, by contrast, the term denoted a group at the top of the social ladder, forerunners of the 'businessmen' of later centuries, i.e. people who not only were fully integrated but also, in certain parts of Europe, were actually involved in running their societies. To avoid being misunderstood by a non-specialist audience, a historian describing a distant society and economy would need to append an explanatory footnote to every significant term.

Obviously there are historians and historians. The best ones do not confine themselves to providing their audience with a well-documented description of what happened – within the inevitable constraints outlined above. They also communicate to the reader an appreciation of such constraints, a sense of historical perspective, and a feeling for the ineffable complexity of human life. They are able to convey a sense of something deeper that defies description, and to people the reader's mind with ghosts of a vanished world – a world that is indeed 'a foreign country' where 'they do things differently'. In other words, good historians know how to rouse their readers from passivity and to turn them into active participants in the great exploit of evoking the past. But to do this one needs more than science: one needs art.

6 Conclusion

In 1987 Oxford University Press published Donald C. Coleman's *History and the Economic Past: an account of the rise and decline of economic history in Britain*. The title and scope of this lively work could, however, be extended to cover the whole of the Western world. Economic history is in crisis more or less everywhere, and not only in Britain. The roots of this crisis are not hard to identify.

The boom of the 1950s and 1960s attracted a huge range of new students to the discipline, and the amount of work produced in economic history increased beyond measure. There is no end of new books and articles on economic history, but all too often they are lacklustre and uninspiring. In its turn, the rise of the American model-led school resulted in a crop of highly technical material accessible and comprehensible only to a limited group of specialists. And, when one takes the not inconsiderable trouble of reading such work, it turns out to be deadly boring, and its results prove startlingly unimpressive. Moreover, in the West in the mid-1970s the consumers of economic history, i.e. university students and the reading public, began to lose interest in purely economic phenomena. Historical work, too, attracted less attention, as interest shifted – especially among the young – to more obviously 'relevant' topics, such as ecological and social issues. Against this already unpropitious background, economic history plunged deeper into the identity crisis which had dogged it from its inception. Economic history, as its very name hints, has a schizoid status half-way between history and economics. In a sense, economic history came into being with the birth of economics, whereas history had already been around for some time. Adam Smith's classic work *An Inquiry into the Nature and Causes of the Wealth of Nations*, published in two volumes in 1776, contains many pages of first-rate economic history. This is no accident. Adam Smith thought and wrote within the tradition of scholars trained and accustomed to look to history for evidence to back their deductive assertions.

This close initial symbiotic relationship between history and economic history seemed certain to survive, and yet it did not. In Great Britain, the work of David Ricardo (1772–1823), James Mill (1773–1836) and J. R. McCullan (1789–1864) succeeded in ridding theoretical economics of its historical dimension, and shifting economic analysis onto the ground of logical and mathematical abstraction. In *The Theory of Political Economy*, William Stanley Jevons (1835–82) pronounced that 'if economics is to be a science it must be a mathematical science'. Attempts to reinstate the historical dimension of the discipline were made by the German historical school of economics (whose exponents included W. G. F. Roscher, G. von Schmoller, K. Bücher), by the less well-known English historical school of economics (including J. K. Ingram, J. E. Thorold Rogers, T. E. Cliffe Leslie and H. S. Foxwell) and by the school of American institutionalists (T. B. Veblen, W. E. Atkins, C. E. Ayres, and others). Karl Marx (1818–83) met with greater success by conceiving of economic analysis in dynamic terms, and thereby managing to maintain a close link between history and social and economic analysis. But mainstream economics, especially in its neoclassical version, was increasingly distinguished by its application of logical–mathematical methods to a static analysis devoid of any historical dimension. Economic history thus found itself in an absurd situation. As a historical and therefore fundamentally humanistic discipline, it could not easily pursue economics into ahistorical analysis. On the other hand, as a clearly 'economic' discipline, it could not divorce itself entirely from economic theory. Economic historians from continental Europe tried to solve the problem by loosening their ties with economics; those who took up the American model-led approach loosened their ties with history.

I am not alone in the view (see Hutchinson, 1977, p. 40) that Karl Popper had understood nothing when he wrote that 'the success of mathematical economics shows that one social science at least has gone through its Newtonian revolution' (1960, p. 60n).[1] The physical world displays a certain degree of complexity. The biological world displays a greater degree of complexity, the sum of the complexities of the physical and biological worlds. The socio-economic world displays even greater complexity, the sum of the complexities of the physical, biological and socio-economic worlds. The remarkable success of the Galilean–Newtonian revolution was achieved by applying logical–mathematical analysis to the investigation of the physical world. So far, so good; but, powerful and necessary as it is, this sort of analysis is not adequate to the task of explaining biological and socio-economic

[1] Just as economics was preceded by a protoeconomics – the so-called 'political arithmetics' of the seventeenth century (see Part II, chapter 3) – so too economic history was preceded by a protoeconomic history: the works by Isaac de Laffemas (1606), Defoe (1713) and Huet (1716) on the history of trade, and by Le Blanc (1692) and Vettori (1738) on numismatics.

phenomena.[2] To use it in this way is like using a pair of glasses when what you need is a telescope. The improperly termed 'social sciences' are still awaiting their 'revolution', which, if it ever materializes, will not be merely Galilean–Newtonian. Until this more complex 'revolution' is accomplished, economic history will continue uncomfortably to straddle two cultures.

[2] The epistemological problems facing the 'social sciences' have more in common with those facing the biological sciences than with those facing the physical and mathematical sciences. In the physical sciences (with the exception of meteorology and astronomy), one can always perform experiments. In the biological sciences, the biologist has to be content with observation and comparison, even when it is possible to perform an experiment. In physics, 'cause' is a functional concept; in biology, it is intelligible only in an evolutionary sense. Physical sciences may pronounce laws, but in biology laws have little point, given the overwhelming number of exceptions for which they would have to account. Deterministic prediction, admissible in the physical sciences, has no place in biology. The physical sciences investigate inert matter that is incapable of storing historical information. Biologists, on the other hand, deal with living matter endowed with historical memory. Information in the physical sciences is primarily quantitative, whereas in the biological sciences it is often purely qualitative.

Part II

The Sources of
European Economic History

1   In the Beginning

Any attempt to produce a reasonably complete survey of the sources of economic history is hampered not only by the mammoth scale of the task, but above all by the fact that material of interest to the economic historian is to be found scattered over a wide range of documents. The present survey, therefore, is not a complete catalogue, but an outline, with illustrations, of the main types of evidence available: fiscal and legislative documents, statistical sources, foreign intelligence reports, 'semi-public' and Church sources, private sources of various kinds, and data furnished by international organizations. In what follows, a chapter is devoted to each of these areas of documentation. However, for classical times and the Dark Ages the documents relating to economic matters are so scarce that it seemed advisable to assemble them in a single chapter.

Economic historians of Graeco-Roman classical antiquity are faced with problems of documentation that are in a certain sense insuperable. The Graeco-Roman world was neither structurally nor culturally disposed to the production of quantities of documents, let alone economic documents. As M. I. Finley has written, 'Modern historians have constantly to remind themselves that the *paperasserie* with which they are surrounded has not always been a "natural" product of human behaviour. In the long history of the Graeco-Roman world, massive documentation characterized only the peculiar society of Egypt' (1986, p. 15). In Rome, it was only during Caesar's first consulship that the decision was taken to put the orders of the Senate in writing. If relatively few documents were produced, the way they were kept was decidedly inadequate. Archives were few and rudimentary, and in the Roman world only a small number of privileged individuals had access to the *arcana imperii*.

Accidents, the passage of time, and above all the havoc wreaked by the barbarian invasions did the rest. Consequently, the little that has come down to us unfortunately provides a wholly insufficient documentary basis on which to undertake the work of economic and historical reconstruction.

Literary and narrative sources are unable to make good this lack. There are no genuinely primary sources for Greek history from the middle of the fourth century AD onwards, or indeed for lengthy periods of Roman republican and imperial history. For the long reign of Augustus, for instance, the only primary sources available are a few letters and speeches by Cicero, the Emperor's own account of his life's work, and the works of the poets of the age. The only history of the Augustan period that makes any effort to be systematic was written by Dio Cassius two centuries later. Furthermore, scrutiny of those texts that have survived, be they first- or second-hand, reveals that Greek and Roman historians were at least as inclined to indulge their literary imaginations by composing orations for their characters as they were reluctant to cite documents – especially documents relating to economic life. Any figures that they do give are presented in such a casual manner that they can only be treated with great caution. Numbers had not yet assumed statistical significance.

Sources for the economic history of the ancient world may be classified as

(1) either archaeological or manuscript sources (using these terms broadly);
(2) documentary sources, narratives (such as Thucydides' history) or treatises (for example, work by Aristotle, Cato, Varro and Columella); and
(3) of either public or private origin.

As already noted, sources of the narrative type yield very few precise economic facts and indeed very little reliable quantitative information of any kind. Private documentary sources are available above all for Ptolemaic and Roman Egypt, thanks both to Egyptian bureaucratic and administrative traditions, and to the dry climate, which has enabled many papyri to survive.

In the following discussion, I refer mainly to public documentary sources of an archaeological nature. In the discussion of company sources in chapter 6, however, a private documentary source recovered in the excavations of Pompeii is mentioned.

ANCIENT GREECE

After the excavations conducted by Heinrich Schliemann and subsequent archaeologists, it is clear that the economic history of ancient Greece should be divided into three distinct phases. The earliest is that of Minoan–Mycenaean civilization, whose initial centre of gravity and point of irradiation was the island of Crete but which later extended to the area around Mycenae in mainland Greece; its period of greatest splendour was 2000–1400 BC. Its economy remains rather mysterious, apparently organized around a number of grandiose labyrinthine palaces where, as in Kafka's Castle, everything was registered and accounted for in the minutest detail.

All the evidence about the Minoan–Mycenaean civilization is archaeological in nature. First, there are the remains of the imposing palaces of Knossos, Phaistos, Mallia, Mycenae, Tiryns and so on. Then there are the numerous tablets discovered among the ruins of the palaces. These tablets bear inscriptions in three different scripts: a hieroglyphic script, a script that archaeologists have named Linear A and another which they have named Linear B. These scripts remained undeciphered for decades until in 1952 Michael Ventris, a young English architect, managed to decipher Linear B, demonstrating that the language was an archaic form of Greek.

A considerable number of tablets bearing inscriptions in Linear B (see figure 2) have been discovered in mainland Greece, whereas on Crete they have been found only at Knossos. Unfortunately they are not dated. Their content consists of regular and monotonous calculations of rations, lists of herds of sheep, and inventories of goods belonging in the palaces. They

Figure 2 Mycenaean tablet showing Linear B script (MR II)

confirm the picture already suggested by the ruins of the palaces: that of strongly centralized and bureaucratic economies within societies that centred on the palaces themselves.

Between 1400 and 1200 BC, this mysterious world and its economy were destroyed, and its palaces razed to the ground. When exactly, and how, and why, and by whom? We don't know. All we can deduce from the archaeological sources is that a second phase began: a dark age during which the kind of centralized and bureaucratic economy that was centred on the palaces was obliterated for ever.

The third phase began in the seventh century BC, with the rise of the *polis* (city). The most ancient document containing a verbal formula denoting a collective decision (along the lines of 'it has been decided by the *polis* that . . . ') is a Cretan inscription from Dreros dating from the second half of the seventh century. The historical period then beginning was the one to which one generally refers when talking of classical Greece – the age of the Greek city states.

The sources available for the economic and social history of this third period are very much more varied and plentiful than for the two preceding ones. In addition to purely archaeological materials, we have the evidence of coins and written sources. Spoilt for choice, I shall cite just two examples.

From 490 BC onwards, the Greek cities were subjected to the deadly menace of a series of mighty Persian military expeditions over both land and sea. The Persians were beaten back at Marathon (490 BC), Salamis (480 BC) and Plataea (479 BC), but continued to pose a grave threat. Since Athens had been in the front line of resistance against the Persians, all the Greek cities intent on continuing the struggle against the Persian threat joined with Athens to form the so-called League of Delos (478 BC). The League members freely undertook to contribute towards the creation of a war treasury. Athens was acknowledged to have the right to administer this treasury and to determine the size of the contribution payable by each city in the League. Some cities were taxed in coin; others committed themselves to supplying a certain number of ships and armed men. Thucydides (I.96–7) recounts these beginnings in laconic but exact terms:

> [The Athenians] assessed the amount of their contributions, both for the states which were to furnish money for the war against the barbarians and for those which were to furnish ships. . . . The amount of the tribute first assessed was 460 talents, and the treasury of the allies was Delos, where the meetings were held in the temple. [Athens exercised] what was at first a leadership over allies who were autonomous and took part in the deliberation of common assemblies. (1919 tr.)

Every element of Thucydides' account has been confirmed by historical criticism; only the figure of 460 talents has been doubted (Meiggs, 1975, pp. 62–3).

Within a few years of the foundation of the League, Athens had managed to turn what had begun as a league of independent states into an 'imperial' system under its own rigid control and essentially at the service of Athenian power and economic prosperity. Language too underwent a change: the 'allies' became 'the cities which Athens controls' (Meiggs, 1975, p. 152). States that had committed themselves to contribute ships and soldiers to the League were now obliged to make their payments in ready cash. Cities that revealed a desire to quit the League were bullied into remaining. Other cities were forced or pressured into joining. In 454 BC the treasury was moved from Delos to Athens, and the Athenians, at the instigation of their leader (495–429 BC), began to dip into it to finance public works designed to embellish their city. The building of the Parthenon, for example, begun in 447/446 BC, was financed from the war treasury's funds (Meiggs, 1975, pp. 154–5). There commenced a period of extraordinary cultural, artistic and economic splendour, with which the names of Aeschylus, Sophocles, Euripides, Aristophanes, Herodotus, Thucydides, Socrates and Phidias are associated. Historians have often viewed the tribute paid by the cities of the League as a clear expression of Athenian 'imperialism'.

The most important sources relating to the tribute are the assessment decrees and the tribute quota lists. According to the quota lists, a sixtieth of the tribute each year was paid into the treasury of the goddess Athene. The donations to the temple began in 454/453 BC and ended presumably in 406/405 BC. The data were engraved on marble steles (slabs) kept on the Acropolis. The assessment decrees record the amounts of money that the allied cities were supposed to pay. This series is less complete than the quota lists.

The information provided by these two lists has been published in a critical edition by Meritt, Wade-Gery and McGregor (1939–53), who have supplied a detailed commentary taking into account other evidence. Provided due caution is observed, these data, even if in some cases they are distorted by particular political circumstances, may be studied as indexes of the relative economic power and the fluctuations in economic fortunes of the various cities of the League. Furthermore, they provide precise quantitative evidence of the considerable transfer of income and wealth from the 'allies' to Athens. As has already been mentioned, under Pericles the treasury was used to finance a grand programme of public works, thus boosting effective demand. This benefited Athens not only by enhancing its dignity and beauty but also by raising local levels of income and employment. This comment might appear crudely anachronistic – an absurd attempt to force an economic situation utterly different from our own into a Keynesian theoretical mould. The comment, however, is not mine but Plutarch's. According to Plutarch, there erupted in Athens at this time a violent dispute between a minority led by a certain Thucydides, son of Melesias, and the majority, led by Pericles. The argument turned on the question of whether or not it was just and moral to spend in Athens and for the exclusive benefit of Athens funds that in theory belonged to the League and that had been intended to provide for the League's defence against the Persians. Thucydides maintained that it was immoral and argued that the treasury should be left untouched. Pericles, however, championed the view that the money should be spent, and supported an impressive programme of public works. To justify the position taken by the Athenian statesman, Plutarch had him deliver an oration in which he asserted, among other things, that

> it is but meet that the city, when once she is sufficiently equipped with all that is necessary for prosecuting the war, should apply her abundance to such works as, by their completion, will bring her everlasting glory, and while in process of completion will bring that abundance into actual service, in that all sorts of activity and diversified demands arise, which rouse every art and stir every hand, and bring, as it were, the whole city under pay, so that she not only adorns, but supports herself as well from her own resources.

Afraid perhaps that he had not made Pericles' views sufficiently clear, Plutarch then provided the following gloss:

> it was true that his military expeditions supplied those who were in the full vigour of manhood with abundant resources from the common funds, and in his desire that the unwarlike throng of common labourers should neither have no share at all in the public receipts, nor yet get fees for laziness and idleness, he boldly suggested to the people projects for great constructions and designs for works which would call many arts into play and involve long periods of time, in order that the stay-at-homes, no whit less than the sailors and sentinels and soldiers, might have a pretext for getting a beneficial share of the public wealth. (Plutarch, *Pericles*, XII; 1916 tr.)

Plutarch lived from AD 46 to 120, i.e. roughly half a millennium after the events that he recounted. But he had at his disposal sources that we, almost two millennia later, no longer possess. Moreover, although he was essentially an amateur historian, he had the commendable habit of reading a great deal and of seeking out as much documentation as possible. Even if the concepts that Plutarch employed were not expressed at the time of Pericles in exactly the way that Plutarch presented them (though there is no obvious reason why this should be the case), there is no doubt that in practice the money spent would have created massive support for demand and employment.

Thanks to the unceasing research carried out by archaeologists, the text of another document relevant to this fascinating story of Athenian 'imperialism' has been reconstructed. Epigraphic fragments of this document – a decree – have been discovered in many places around the Aegean. The imperious tone of the decree indicated that it was addressed to communities that Athens considered subject. The substance of the document is of great interest: it was an attempt by Athens to bring the coinage, weights and measures of the localities to which the decree was dispatched into line with those used in Athens, and to oblige anyone who had silver to coin to bring it to the Athenian mint. The date of the document is uncertain, but there is some evidence to suggest a date between 440 and 415 BC.[1] As far as we know, the plan represented by the decree failed, but it was sensible, and in my view did not deserve the scorn that Aristophanes heaped on it in his play *The Birds*.

THE ROMAN EMPIRE

For the Roman imperial era I shall mention only two sources: the account written by Augustus of the censuses conducted during his administration, and Diocletian's edict fixing prices and wages, which André Piganiol, exaggerating somewhat, declared the finest economic document of the ancient world.

The *Monumentum Ancyranum* (see figure 3) and epigraphic fragments from Antioch and Apollonia have enabled historians to reconstruct Augustus's autobiographical text.[2] In this text, the authenticity of which is beyond doubt, the old Emperor records that during his administration three censuses were conducted, yielding the following results:

28 BC	4,063,000 *civium Romanorum capita*
− 8 BC	4,233,000 *civium Romanorum capita*
AD 14	4,937,000 *civium Romanorum capita*

During that period the vast majority of Roman citizens lived in the Italian peninsula, so the census figures refer *grosso modo* to the population of Italy. However, since he was writing a political rather than a technical document, Augustus did not bother to specify what he could safely suppose his contemporaries to know, i.e. the meaning of the phrase *civium Romanorum capita*. As we saw in Part I, chapter 4, historians have found this seemingly transparent and straightforward expression an intractable brain-teaser.

---

[1] The text of the decree has been published in Meiggs and Lewis, 1969, n. 45. On the significance and dating of the decree, see Meiggs, 1975, pp. 167–71; and Erxleben, 1969.
[2] Augustus's account of the censuses is part of a broader account of his political and administrative accomplishments – a sort of political testament. The text of the document was copied on the walls of the temples of Augustus throughout the Empire. Though marred in places by the scaling of the stone, the copy inscribed on the temple at Ancyra (Asia Minor) is the best preserved, and as a result the designation *Monumentum Ancyranum* has become synonymous with *Res Gestae Divi Augusti*. The Latin text is chiselled on both sides of the inner wall of the vestibule. The inscription is 2.7 m high and about 4 m long. One of the outer walls of the temple bears an inscription of a Greek translation of the Latin text.

The Dutch scholar Buysbech was the first to draw attention to the *Monumentum Ancyranum*, in 1555. The first faithful copy was made by Georges Perrot and Edmund Guillaume on commission from Napoleon III. They made a facsimile copy but no casts. In 1882 the Berlin Academy commissioned Carl Human to make a plaster cast, which Mommsen used in his great critical edition of 1883. Mommsen's edition became the basis for all subsequent work.

For the text, see Riccobono, 1945, p. 28.

Figure 3   The *Monumentum Ancyranum*: wall of the Temple of Ancyra, showing the Latin text of the *Acta Divi Augusti*

Fragments of the price-fixing edict issued by Diocletian (AD 284–313) were first discovered in the Caria region of Asia Minor in 1709 by William Sherard, British Consul in Smyrna. The edict was an integral part of a broader plan designed to halt the deterioration of the monetary system and to put an end to the inflation that for centuries had been undermining the economy of the Empire. To this end Diocletian introduced a monetary reform, about which we possess only patchy information. A few months later, between 20 November and 9 December 301, he issued a gigantic list of official prices. This set, by imperial edict, the prices of over a thousand goods and services, described in detail and classified in thirty-two sections. In the preamble to the edict, the Emperor lashed out at speculators – a typical example of the attitude of political leaders who, having created the economic conditions in which speculation can flourish, pour vitriol on the speculators and their greed as if they were the real source of all evil.

Diocletian wanted his price tariff engraved in stone in Latin in those areas where Latin was spoken and in Greek throughout the Greek peninsula (see plates 3 and 4). The first reconstruction of the text was completed by Theodore Mommsen in 1893, working from thirty-five epigraphic fragments. Since then, further reconstructions have been undertaken: by E. R. Graser in 1940, using sixty fragments; by S. Lauffer in 1970, using 126 fragments; and by Marta Giacchero in 1974, using 132 fragments. Further fragments have come to light since 1974. Fragments have been discovered over a very wide area, embracing Asia Minor, Egypt, Cyrenaica, Greece and Italy. This distribution bears witness to the huge effort made by the tetrarchs to disseminate and enforce the tariff. But, as we saw in Part I, chapter 4, the attempt did not succeed.

THE VALUES OF CLASSICAL ANTIQUITY

Before leaving the classical period behind, I should like to cite two texts – one by Herodotus and the other by Cicero. They both reveal scales of values totally alien to those that we think of as 'natural', simply because they form an integral part of our own culture. To understand how a given society functions and 'performs' economically, an understanding of its dominant values is no less important than a grasp of the economic parameters.

The text of Herodotus (c.480–c.424 BC) is taken from the *History* (II.166–7):

> [The Egyptian warrior class] are forbidden to follow any trade or craft [*techne*], and have an exclusively military training, son following father. I could not say for certain whether the Greeks got their ideas about trade, like so much else, from Egypt or not; the feeling is common enough, and I have observed that Thracians, Scythians, Persians, Lydians – indeed, almost all foreigners – reckon craftsmen and their descendants as lower in the social scale than people who have no connexion with manual work: only the latter, and especially those who are trained for war, do they count amongst the 'nobility'. All the Greeks have adopted this attitude, especially the Spartans; the feeling against handicraft is least strong in Corinth. (1972 tr.)

Cicero (106–43 BC) wrote in *De Officiis*, I.42,

> Unbecoming to a gentleman, too, and vulgar are the means of livelihood of all hired workmen whom we pay for mere manual labour, not for artistic skills; for

Plate 3 Fragment of Diocletian's price edict

Plate 4   Detail of fragment reproduced in plate 3

in their case the very wages they receive is a pledge of their slavery. . . .
Trade, if it is on a small scale, is to be considered vulgar, but if wholesale
and on a large scale . . . it is not to be greatly disparaged. Nay, it even seems
to deserve the highest respect, if those who are engaged in it, satiated, or rather,
I should say, satisfied with the fortunes they have made, make their way from
the port to a country estate, as they have often made it from the sea into
port. (1913 tr.)

The scales of values that emerge from these texts are typical of societies
dominated by warriors and by large landowners.

THE EARLY MIDDLE AGES

Written documents containing information of an economic nature are more plentiful for the early Middle Ages than for the ancient world, but they are still extremely few and far between. Both economically and socially, Europe was underdeveloped – not only by modern standards but also in comparison to other areas at that time, such as the Byzantine and Islamic empires. In Europe, the cities were in absolute ruin, mere seats of episcopal religious administration, stripped of any economic function. Trade and exchange had withered away. The market had virtually ceased to operate. The prevailing economic system was the so-called manorial system (*système domaniale* in French, *Hofsystem* in German, *sistema curtense* in Italian) based on villas or manors, i.e. on vast landed properties (whether secular or ecclesiastical) that functioned as largely self-sufficient 'economic microcosms'.[3] The documentary evidence that this impoverished, illiterate, primitive and essentially agrarian world left behind it obviously reflects these basic characteristics. The evidence mainly consists of

(1) a few royal or imperial ordinances or laws (usually in the form of a 'capitulary');
(2) documents relating to purchases and donations of land and buildings; and
(3) most important, *polyptyques*,[4] documents detailing the extent and external organization of the manors.

The manor was typically divided into a *pars dominica* (the lord's part or a demesne) and a *pars massaricia* (land held by tenants). *Polyptyques* give details of the extent of the estate and its holdings, the average yearly product of the *pars dominica*, the number of servants who worked there, the various dues, tributes, rents and labour due from the tenants, and the buildings and productive equipment (mills, boats, and so on). They served both as inventories of the property, and of the workers and animals attached to it, and as economic blueprints for the functioning of the manors themselves.

Of the various capitularies, the so-called *Capitulare de Villis*[5] deserves special mention. Dating from the first half of the ninth century, and issued either by Charlemagne or by his son Louis, this document contains detailed instructions on the administration and functioning of the imperial manors.

---

[3] This neat expression was coined by Volpe (1928, pp. 220–43).

[4] *Polyptycum* (French *polyptyque*) is a term employed from the fourth century AD onwards to signify either a sheet folded several times over or a notebook consisting of an indefinite number of sheets.

[5] This document was published by A. Boretius in *Monumenta Germaniae Historica. Leges. Capitularia Regum Francorum I* (1881), p. 83–9, and is the subject of a considerable bibliography. See Ganshof, 1958, p. 162.

The most famous surviving *polyptyque* relates to the possessions of the abbey of St-Germain-des-Prés near Paris.[6] It was composed between 810 and 826, on the initiative of Abbot Irminon. Since it was compiled by cross-examining the people involved (servants and tenants), its various chapters are in effect records of the proceedings. Regrettably, the document is incomplete: the first part, the size of which it is impossible to assess, is missing. What has survived amounts to a bound volume of 129 sheets, describing twenty-five fisci[7] and covering a total of 221,080 ha of land, thirty-five churches, eighty-four mills and 2,788 families (approximately 10,000 individuals). The distribution of the land described in the surviving sheets of the *polyptyque* is as follows (areas in hectares):

	Demesne	Tenancies	Total
Arable land	6,041	16,088	22,129
Vineyards	196	231	427
Meadows	176	327	503
Grazing land	6.5	86	92.5
Marsh	1.5	–	1.5
Woods	197,750	177	197,927
Total	204,171	16,909	221,080

As these figures show, the *pars dominica* was dominated by woodland, and the *pars massaricia* consisted mainly of arable land.

Comparable documents for Italy include the inventory of the manor of Limonta on Lake Como (835); the *adbreviationes* of the monastery of Bobbio (862 and 883 with later examples from the tenth and eleventh centuries); the inventory of the diocese of Lucca (890–900); the *breviaria* of the monastery of S. Giulia in Brescia (879–906); the *breve recordationis* of the diocese of Tivoli (945); and the *breviarium* of the monastery of S. Cristina di Olona (late tenth-century).[8]

Of the documentary evidence surviving from the early Middle Ages, most of which is of the type described above, three documents stand out as of quite exceptional importance. The earliest is the so-called Plan of St Gall (plate 5). This is in fact a copy made on parchment between 820 and 830 in the scriptorium of the abbey of Reichenau, from an original that has since been lost. In the twelfth century, after this copy had somehow found its way to the library of the abbey of St Gall, a monk chose to use the blank reverse side of the plan for an account of the life

---

[6] This *polyptyque* was published in 1844 by B. Guérard, who also provided a most erudite commentary.

[7] According to Guérard, 'the term *fisci* should be taken to mean a set of landed goods belonging to a single owner, under a single administration, and generally subject to a single system of rents or tributes' (1844, Introduction).

[8] These documents were studied by L. M. Hartmann, whose results were skilfully summarized, annotated and completed by Volpe (1928, pp. 220–43).

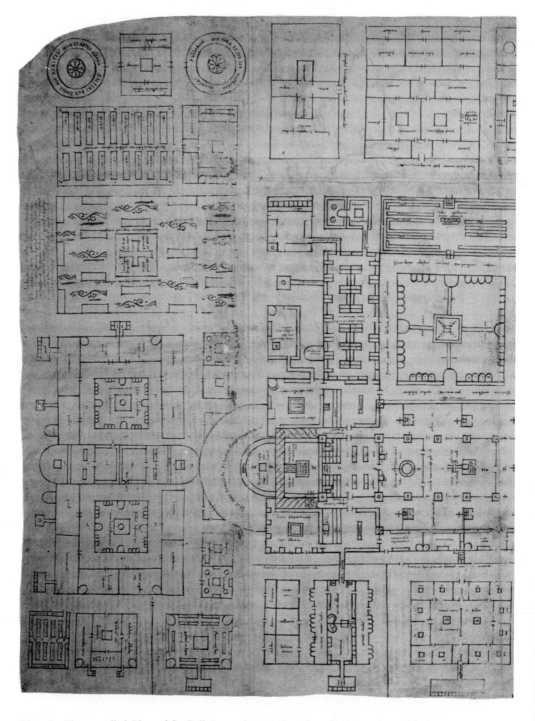

Plate 5 The so-called Plan of St Gall (a parchment sheet inscribed in red and black, about 112cm long)

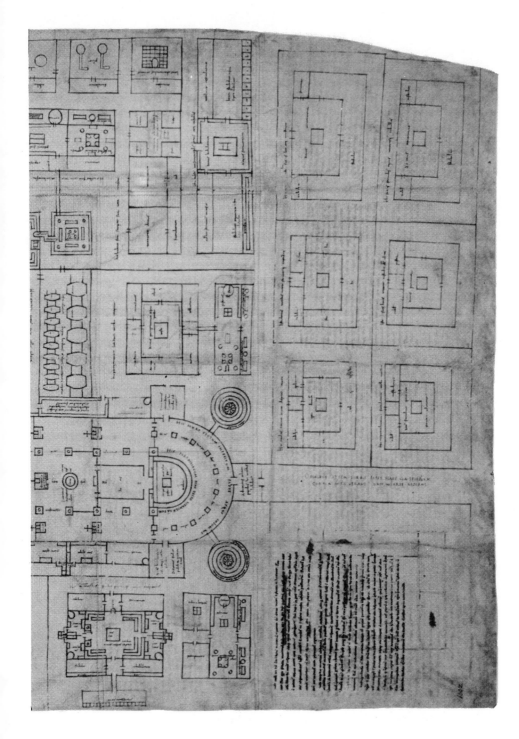

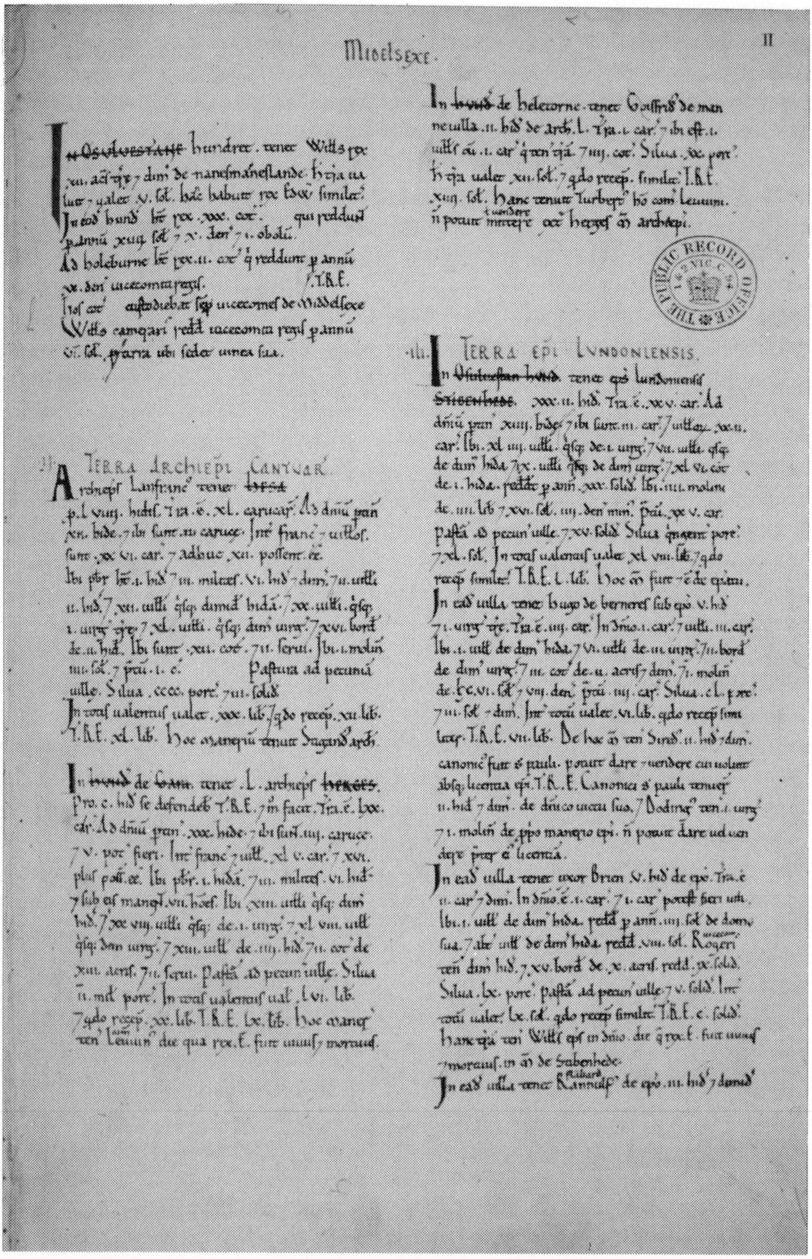

Plate 6 Page of the *Domesday Book* (Public Record Office, London)

of St Martin. This undoubtedly helped to secure the document's survival. The plan is an extraordinarily detailed and precisely drawn architectural plan of an imaginary model abbey encircled by thirty or so buildings and designed to house a community of roughly 270 people (including more than 110 monks), living and working within a manorial economy. (See Horn and Born, 1979.)

The second document is known as *Instituta Regalia et Ministeria Camere Regis Lomgbardorum et Honorantie Civitatis Papie* (text in Brühl and Violante, 1983, pp. 16–27). The original has been lost, but a copy reproduced on sheets 23–5 of a commonplace-book written in the seventeenth century has come down to us. It is a curious polemical text dating from the beginning of the eleventh century and commenting on the financial administration of the Italic kingdom and its revenues. Among other things the document lists the Alpine passes at which merchants and pilgrims were liable to customs duty; it also mentions traders from England, Venice, Salerno, Gaeta and Amalfi who on arrival at the fairs of Pavia had to pay tribute to the royal chamber. Where the author mentions the Venetians, he can't refrain from commenting, 'et illa gens non arat, non seminat, non vindemiat' ('and those people do not plough, do not sow, do not harvest grapes'), thereby expressing astonishment at a society that managed to live without agriculture. The document also mentions associations of workers such as soap-boilers, fishermen, leather-sellers, boat-makers, and people who prospected for gold in rivers. Lastly, it supplies information on the mints of Pavia and Milan.

The third document, however, is the most extraordinary of all. It was compiled in England between 1085 and 1086, just twenty years after the Norman Conquest (1066). Within a century of its completion, it became known as the *Domesday Book*,[9] because the information it contains was legally binding and irrevocable. The *Domesday Book* (see plate 6) presents an inventory (one is almost tempted to call it a *polyptyque*) of nearly the whole of England, with a list and description of all properties, workers, rents, animals and mills. It was compiled by order of William the Conqueror (d. 1087), who wanted a clearer picture of what he had conquered and of what it might yield him. The information was gathered with such diligence and punctiliousness that one overawed chronicler of

[9] The *Domesday Book* comprises two volumes. The *Great Domesday Book* contains 388 folios made with folded parchment sheets. It is written on both sides of each folio in double columns, and the folios measure approximately 15 by 11 inches. The *Little Domesday Book* covers three counties (Essex, Norfolk and Suffolk) left out of the Great Book. It contains 450 folios, 11 by 8 inches, written in a single column.

In 1744, the British Parliament ordered the printing of an exact transcript of the two volumes. An index was published in 1811. Facsimile copies were published a few years ago.

An enormous amount has been written concerning the *Domesday Book*. The bibliography compiled by Bates is comprehensive from 1886 and selective for the period before that date: it lists a total of 1,847 entries. Of recent contributions, those by V. H. Galbraith (1961) and Finn (1963) are particularly useful and informative.

the time was moved to write that 'no patch of land was left out of the count, no ox, no cow, no pig'.

The written documents surviving from the early Middle Ages have one feature in common with those of classical antiquity: since they are relatively few in number, they are mostly well known and have usually been published. The *Capitulare de Villis*, the *polyptyque* of Abbot Irminon, the Plan of St Gall, the *Instituta Regalia* and the *Domesday Book* have all been made readily available to scholars in editions with a full critical commentary.

2 Fiscal and Legislative Sources

THE LATER MIDDLE AGES

With the dawn of the new millennium, and in some areas a few decades earlier, there began in Western Europe a long process of development that was to peak during the thirteenth century. For reasons that remain far from clear, people had regained confidence in the exchange economy. The dynamic centres of the grand recovery were the towns, where a new social type emerged: the 'burgher'.[1] The term originally meant 'inhabitant of a town [*burg*]'; later its French version, *bourgeois*, came to be associated with the middle class and its values.

Population increased, and output in its dual components of consumption and investment grew faster than population. The economic system became increasingly monetary in nature (i.e. based on the exchange of goods and/or services for money, rather than on barter and robbery). At the end of the thirteenth century, Europe had been transformed from a backward continent continually threatened from outside into a highly dynamic area, able to boast a wealth of technological, financial and cultural innovations. The resulting expansionist thrust took a political and military form with the Crusades, the Germans' *Drang nach Osten* (push to the east) in the Slavic territories, and the reconquest of the Iberian peninsula by its Christian inhabitants.

As a result of these developments and of the changed economic system, from the end of the twelfth century documents on economic matters gradually became both more plentiful and more diverse. *Polyptyques* and other manorial sources petered out and an ever broader and more varied range of sources began to appear. To attempt to supply even a partial inventory of this documentation would be a colossal undertaking, so a

---

[1] In Flanders prior to the year 1000, this term is encountered in only three localities: St-Omer, Cambrai and Huy, all three of which were centres of some form of trading activity. During the twelfth century, the term gained currency throughout the whole of continental Europe. See Vercauteren, 1967, p. 20ff.

few examples will have to suffice. Some semblance of order can perhaps be obtained by distinguishing between public, 'semi-public' and private sources, as outlined at the beginning the last chapter. It must be remembered, however, that throughout the Middle Ages, and also to some extent during the first few centuries of the Modern Age, the boundary between the concepts of the public and the private remained blurred.

From the eleventh century onwards, public government became more forthright, continually extending its sphere of action. This was true both of the royal administrations (especially in France, England, Castile and Aragon) and of the Italian city states and the German free cities. For centuries, the principal functions of government remained those connected with the waging of war, the conduct of diplomacy, the organization of public celebrations and the minting of coins. From the beginning of the fourteenth century, military spending, which had always absorbed the bulk of public financial resources, became ever more costly, owing to the replacement of the civic militia (or feudal militia in France and England) by mercenaries, and the invention and spread of artillery. The history of government, from the earliest point at which it can be studied, is a relentless (and, one might add, tedious) history of a continually desperate search for funds. An English economist once wrote that 'where there are taxes there are statistics'. Indeed, until quite recent times a high proportion of public documents relating to economic matters were directly concerned with taxation. The main types of tax were

(1) a direct personal tax on people over a certain age (head tax or poll tax)[2] or on households (hearth tax);[3]
(2) a tax on wealth and/or income;
(3) a tax on production and consumption (usually in the form of excise duties and tolls).

In Italy, both head and hearth taxes were levied from the second half of the twelfth century, but, owing to the political and administrative fragmentation of the peninsula, both taxation and documentation relate to small administrative units. The same may be said for Germany. In France and England, on the other hand, the monarchies succeeded in asserting, albeit within certain limits, their centralizing power. As a result, the French king managed to collect a hearth tax in 1328, and the English king a poll tax in 1377. In each case, the tax was levied nationwide.

---

[2] In many areas the head tax gradually assumed the form of a tax on salt: the state obliged every family to purchase from it at an inflated price a certain quantity of salt, according to the number of members of the family, usually excluding children below the age of seven. This practice has left its mark on colloquial Italian, where *salato* (salty) is another way of saying excessively expensive.

It seems likely that the superstitious notion that the unintentional spilling of salt would be followed by dire consequences had its origin in the fact that for many families any wastage of salt spelled a tax increase.

[3] A 'hearth' was not, strictly speaking, the same as a family unit, though it would often have been so in practice.

In the words of Reinhard, Armangaud and Dupaquier, *L'Etat des paroisses et des feux* of 1328 is 'one of the classics of French demographic history: the earliest and perhaps the most famous' (Reinhard et al., 1968, p. 89; the first critical edition of the document was Lot, 1939). The survey listed 24,150 parishes and 2,411,149 hearths over an area roughly two thirds the size of 1789 France.

The English poll tax of 1377 was levied on most of the population, with the exception of children below the age of fourteen and the inhabitants of the counties palatine of Durham and Cheshire. The total number of people liable to the tax was assessed at 1,355,555 (Russell, 1948, p. 146).

Little more than two centuries later, in Spain, following the defeat of the Invincible Armada, the inhabitants of the kingdom of Castile were counted to prepare the way for the levying of a tax approved by the Cortes during its 1588–90 session. The objective was to raise a total of 8 million ducats. The census identified a little over a million *vecinos pecheros* (taxable inhabitants).[4]

Bearing in mind the times during which they were conducted, and their vast geographical scope, the three numerations cited were quite exceptional undertakings. Fortunately, the relevant documents and results have survived. The purpose of all the numerations was fiscal, though modern economic historians have seized on the results as evidence for the total populations of the countries in question. This provides yet one more example of the conflicting purposes of the producers and the modern consumers of sources (see Part I, chapter 2). The French survey counted 'hearths'; the English numeration covered persons over a certain age; and the Castilian census identified taxable inhabitants. Leaving aside the questionable accuracy of the three numerations, and temporarily assuming their totals to be exact, any effort to turn them into general population totals has to rely on some distinctly hazardous hypotheses. Taking their chances, economic historians and demographers have suggested that the population of France in 1328 amounted to some 15 million inhabitants, that of England in 1377 to some 2 million, and that of Castile in 1591–4 to about 6.5 million. But these figures are subject to large margins of error.

Around the beginning of the thirteenth century, and especially in the city states of central and northern Italy, the notion that citizens should contribute to the revenues of the state according to their financial resources began to gain ground. The authorities therefore set about producing assessments of the wealth and/or income of the various potential taxpayers. These assessments were called *libre* (in Tuscany) or *estimi*. A *libra* must have existed in Florence as early as 1242. The city of Siena ordered an *allibramento* in 1225–6, which was followed by further *allibramenti*

---

[4] Gonzales, 1829, p. 387, records a total 1,340,238 *vecinos pecheros* but Gonzales' work is not accurate. Moliné-Bertrand, 1985, p. 307, gives a figure of 1,084,072, but this excludes the population of the ancient kingdom of Granada. Ruiz Martín, 1967, pp. 189–202, puts the total of *vecinos pecheros* at 1,148,674.

in 1229–31, 1237, 1241 and 1248 (Fiumi, 1959, p. 442). In Pavia, an *estimo* was compiled in 1250–4. The wealth or income of the fiscal units was assessed on circumstantial evidence collected by special commissions. In Pavia in 1253, the commission entrusted with the compilation of the *estimo* for that part of the city known as Porta Palazzo consisted of 'nine money-changers [*campsores*], nine friars of the Humiliati Order, and twenty-seven notaries' (Cipolla, 1943, p. 9, n. 3).

The masterpiece among mediaeval assessments was conducted by Florence between 1427 and 1430 and took in the whole of the Florentine state at a time when, owing to the war with Milan, the Tuscan capital found itself in financial straits. Individuals were required to submit extremely detailed declarations of their possessions and incomes, and those returns were used to assess tax liability. The survey covered not only Florence but also the cities of Pisa, Pistoia and Arezzo and other communities then subject to Florence, as well as all the surrounding rural areas. Approximately 60,000 families, or more than 200,000 individuals, were affected – a sizable total in the small world of pre-industrial Europe, at a time when the population of the entire continent was under 80 million. Thanks to the detailed individual declarations, the age, occupation and place of residence of every member of every family are known. So are the size of each family's income and the extent and nature of its possessions: land and buildings; animals; public debt certificates; commercial, banking and manufacturing investments; debts and credits (always allowing for evasion, of course). This extraordinary documentation has been subjected to careful scrutiny by numerous economic historians and has formed the basis for several major works of economic and demographic history.[5] As has been authoritatively stated, 'thanks to the survey of 1427–30, Tuscany is probably the only European country in the fifteenth century that is so well described [economically and demographically].

From that time on, assessments and surveys were compiled with increasing frequency in different countries, and the resulting documentation represents an important source of information for economic historians. However – as is always the case when tax declarations are involved – the greatest caution must be observed in interpreting the evidence.

CUSTOMS REGISTERS

Until quite recently, taxes on production and consumption were mainly levied at town gates, at mountain passes, at fords, and at landing places. The lists of tariffs (many of which have survived) and the registers of tax revenue (unfortunately much rarer) supply indirect but precious information on the volume and composition of trade, on the type and volume of production in particular towns or regions, and also, of course, on one

[5] For example Conti, 1966; and Herlihy and Klapisch-Zuber, 1978. On the history of finances and taxation in Florence see Barbadoro, 1929; Conti, 1984; Palmieri, 1983.

of the principal sources of government revenue (see for example Daviso di Charvensod, 1961; and Noto, 1950). The English export registers, the Danish Sound registers, and the *libros de registros* of Seville together occupy a special place in the history of tax-based documentary sources.

Even at the end of the thirteenth century, England was, by comparison with most other parts of Europe, an underdeveloped country. Its exports mainly consisted of a single raw material – wool. This wool, however, was deemed of unparalleled quality. At the beginning of the 1270s Edward I found himself in grave financial difficulties, so in 1275 he imposed a customs duty – the 'ancient custom' – on all exports of wool and hides. This immediately boosted Crown revenues by an average of £10,000 a year. Having developed a taste for taxation, the King in 1303 brought in an additional duty, the 'new custom'. This tax only affected foreign merchants, who, however, were now liable to customs duty on all forms of merchandise, both on exports (including wool, on which they paid a surtax on top of the ancient custom) and on imports. At this time the manufacture of woollen articles was beginning to develop throughout the kingdom, leading to a rise in exports. In 1347 Edward III, who had recently repudiated his debts to the banks of the Bardi and the Peruzzi, introduced an additional *ad valorem* tax – the 'cloth custom' – on exports of woollen fabrics. This was payable by both English and foreign merchants.[6] Another duty, 'tunnage and poundage', was introduced the same year; at first levied intermittently, it later became permanent, and was payable on all goods exported or imported other than exported wool and hides and, later, English fabrics.

After 1347, then, all goods imported into or exported from England were affected by one or more of the following customs duties:

(1) the ancient or great custom of 1275, levied on exports of wool and hides;
(2) the new or petty custom of 1303, levied on all forms of merchandise imported or exported by foreign merchants;
(3) the cloth custom of 1347, levied on woollen fabrics and payable by all English and foreign merchants, with the exception of Hanseatic traders; and
(4) tunnage and poundage, which was first introduced in 1347, levied on all goods with the exception of those covered by the ancient custom and later also the cloth custom, and payable by all English and foreign merchants other than Hanseatic traders.

To collect these taxes, agents of the King, posted at every port of the realm, registered the name of every seafaring vessel that arrived or set sail, its port of origin, the name of its captain, its loading list, the names of the

[6] England had always exported woollen fabrics, though the volume of these had been tiny compared to the country's exports of raw wool. During the second half of the thirteenth century, a technique involving the use of the water mill for fulling woollen cloth was introduced into England and spread rapidly (see Carus Wilson, 1940). From that point on, the export of woollen cloth steadily increased, while that of raw wool steadily declined.

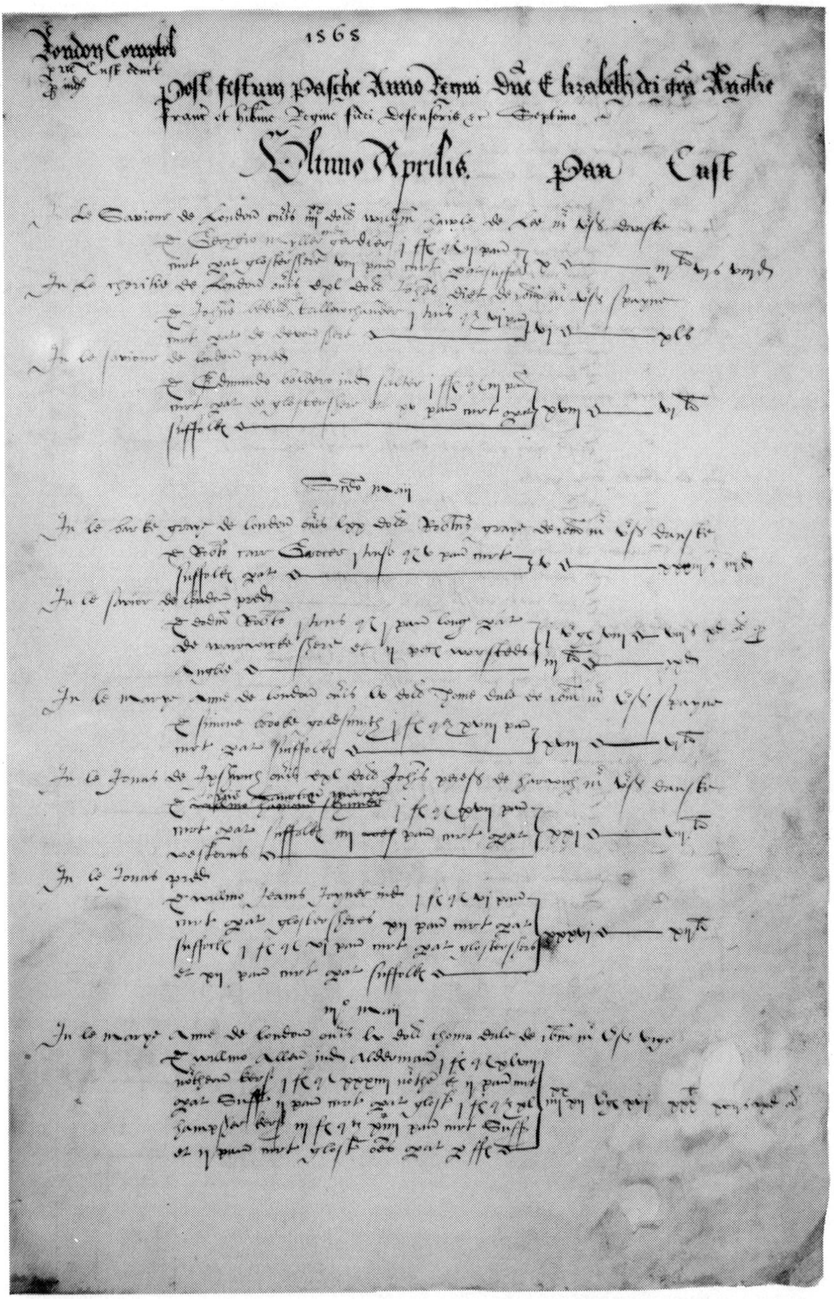

Plate 7 Page of a London Port Book, 1565 (Public Record Office, London)

merchants to whom its cargo belonged, and the amount of duty owed. Day in, day out, all this information was entered in registers or on parchment rolls. Vast quantities of these documents, known as 'Particular Accounts', must have been produced, though unfortunately very few have survived.[7] In each individual port, however, the King's agents also compiled summaries which they dispatched once a year to the Exchequer in London. The clerks of the Exchequer calculated the annual sums port by port and entered the results on long rolls of parchment approximately 16 inches broad. Known as 'Exchequer Enrolled Customs Accounts', these documents have survived to the present day in an almost unbroken series stretching from 1275 to 1547.[8] As late as the mid sixteenth century, exports of wool and woollen goods still accounted for approximately 85 per cent of England's total exports. Thanks to the Exchequer Enrolled Customs Accounts, it is possible to trace, year by year, fluctuations in the volume of these exports over a period of almost three centuries. No comparable information on the imports and exports of any other European state is available over the same period.

In the second half of the 1540s, the normal course of proceedings was disrupted, and in 1558 customs duties were sharply increased. Perhaps as a result of this, smuggling increased. In 1559 Elizabeth I reacted by ordering that ships should henceforth be loaded and unloaded only by day and only at specially designated places. At the end of the 1540s the Exchequer Enrolled Customs Accounts came to an abrupt halt, reappearing briefly in 1559–60. The series then gradually petered out during the second half of the sixteenth century (Clark, 1938, p. xi).[9]

But this situation did not remain without remedy. A new and remarkable series of registers came into being, known in contemporary officialese as the 'Exchequer King's [or Queen's] Remembrancer Port Books' (see plate 7). Begun in 1565, the Port Books were preceded by an ordinance issued by the Lord Treasurer in November 1564, in an effort to restore some order to the collection of customs duties. Under this ordinance, every Easter the Exchequer would dispatch to the sovereign's officials stationed in the various ports of the realm blank registers which the officials then had to fill with the relevant information on port traffic. There were two sorts of registers: those dedicated to trade with foreign countries, colonies, Scotland and Ireland; and those dedicated to coastal trade. For each port of the kingdom, the Port Books gathered information regarding the date of arrival and departure of vessels (or, alternatively, the date on which

---

[7] Many of the Particular Accounts relating to the port of Hull for the periods 1275–1325, 1378–1401 and 1453–90 have survived. Those covering the period 1453–90 have been published in Childs, 1986.

[8] The Exchequer Enrolled Customs Accounts are kept at the Public Record Office in London, entered under 'Exchequer LTR Customs Accounts'. The information they contain has been published in Carus Wilson and Coleman, 1963.

[9] For the patchily covered period 1545–61 see Gould, 1970, especially pp. 115, 119, 133–6, 170–82.

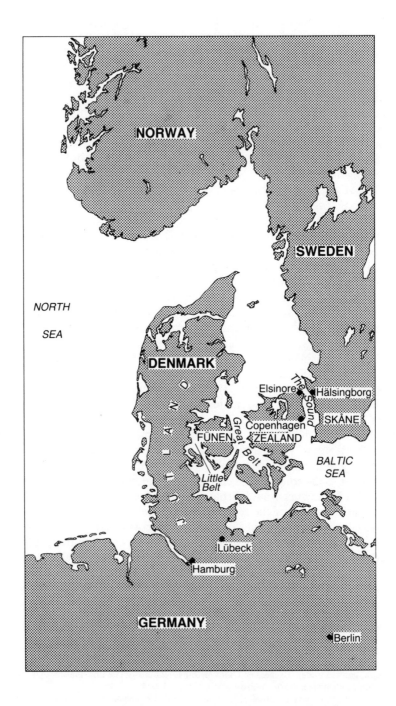

Figure 4 Sea routes between the North Sea and the Baltic

customs duty was paid), the name of the vessel, its port of origin and its tonnage, the name of its captain, its port of departure or destination, the name or names of the cargo-owners, information regarding the cargo itself, often its value, and always the amount of customs duty paid. As D. Woodward has observed, 'in essence the Port Books were customs records and not records of trade or shipping. This means that commodities which were duty free were sometimes omitted in the overseas books' (1973, p. 156).

Roughly 20,000 Port Books, a mere fraction of those originally produced, have survived to this day. It has been calculated that more than 4,000 registers must have been compiled for the port of London alone, but only 400 have come down to us. For the Elizabethan period (1559–1603), the only registers to have survived are those for 1567–8 and 1587–8. The London Port Books for 1697–1799 were destroyed in 1890 because, it was said, they had become illegible. For the port of Boston (Lincolnshire) between 1601 and 1640, registers have survived for seventeen years only, and no register survives from the period 1640–60. (See Woodward, 1973; Dietz, 1972; Hinton, 1956.) But even bearing in mind these serious gaps, the remaining Port Books represent a truly exceptional mine of information – even if the assertion that 'no other country can boast such comprehensive records for its commerce during these centuries' (N. Williams, 1955, p. 14, quoted in Woodward, 1973, p. 147) is a little overblown.

The English Port Books were compiled regularly until 1799, when the series was brought to an end. In the meantime, however, a third series of registers had come into existence: the 'Ledgers of the Inspector General of Imports and Exports', begun in 1696 (see below, chapter 3).

The second outstanding documentary source on maritime traffic is the series of Sound registers, which originated against a unique background of geographical, political, economic and technological circumstances. The geographical circumstances are as follows: Denmark, consisting of the peninsula of Jutland and the archipelago to the east (and formerly also of the southernmost provinces of what is now Sweden) divides the North Sea from the Baltic (see figure 4). The two seas are connected by three straits: the Little Belt, between Jutland and the island of Fünen (Fyn); the Great Belt, between Fünen and the island of Zealand (Sjælland); and the Sound (Øresund) between Zealand and the province of Skåne (from 1660 the southernmost province of Sweden). The Little Belt was used only for small-scale coastal trade. The Great Belt was used mainly by ships sailing between Norway and the ports of Lübeck, Danzig and Rostock. Between 1701 and 1748, the amount of traffic passing through the Great Belt was only 15 per cent or so of that passing through the Sound (Jeannin, 1964, pp. 68–9), which was the main route between the North Sea and the Baltic and by far the busiest of the three straits. The Sound is about 70 miles long and, at its narrowest, between Elsinore (Helsingør) on Zealand and Hälsingborg in Skåne, only 3 miles wide. The towns of Elsinore and Hälsingborg face one another across the strait, and whoever controls both or even one of them is in a position to control maritime traffic through the strait itself.

The German expansion into the Baltic area and into the Slavic countries (*Drang nach Osten*) and the foundation of towns in the newly conquered areas (Lübeck in 1143, Brandenburg in 1170, Riga in 1201, Mecklenburg in 1218, Wismar in 1228, Berlin in 1230, Stralsund in 1234, Danzig in 1238 and scores of others) quickened the expansion of trade between the North Sea and the Baltic. During the thirteenth and fourteenth centuries, the merchants of the Hanseatic League, and in particular those of Hamburg and Lübeck, virtually monopolized this trade. Hamburg is located on the estuary of the Elbe, which flows into the North Sea. Lübeck is located near the mouth of the Trave, which flows into the Baltic. Traditionally, trade between the North Sea and the Baltic was pursued without circumnavigating Jutland. Goods arriving by ship (from the west) in Hamburg or (from the east) in Lübeck were unloaded, transported overland (along the valley of the Eider or, from 1398, on the Stecknitz canal) from Hamburg to Lübeck or vice versa, then reloaded onto ships that bore them off to their destinations. This arrangement obviously brought considerable profits to Hamburg and Lübeck, the obligatory ports of transit and transhipment. Everything worked smoothly as long as the goods transported from the west (North Sea) to the east (Baltic Sea) were spices, wine and quality fabrics and the goods destined for the west from the east were furs, honey, wax and potash – all goods that were slight of bulk yet costly, and which could therefore bear relatively high transport costs. During the second half of the fourteenth century, however, principally as a result of Dutch commercial zeal, the export by sea of bulky low-unit-value goods such as cereals and timber from the Baltic ports of Poland and Russia began to expand. To transport these goods economically, it was essential to avoid the costly transhipments at Hamburg and Lübeck. Accordingly, the sea route through the Sound and round Jutland came to be used more and more frequently. At this point, technological circumstances intervened.

Advances in shipping technology, and especially in the construction of higher tonnage vessels, encouraged the ever more frequent use of the sea route via the Sound. In addition, the development of artillery (the first cannons appeared in Europe at the beginning of the fourteenth century) enabled whoever controlled the coasts of the Sound to pose a credible threat from the land to any vessel attempting to pass through the strait, especially as they entered the narrow strip of water between Elsinore and Hälsingborg.

At the beginning of the sixteenth century, both Zealand and Skåne were in Danish hands. The Danes were not slow to draw the logical conclusions. They installed artillery in the mighty coastal fortress of Kronborg at Elsinore and, using the menace posed by their cannons, forced all passing ships in whatever direction they were sailing to stop and pay a toll. Until the eighteenth century, the proceeds from this toll remained the King's and did not figure among state revenues. At the fortress of Kronborg, visitors can still see the cylindrical slot leading from one of the ground-floor rooms down to a windowless subterranean strong room into which the sacks of money collected from passing ships were emptied.

The saying that 'where there are taxes there are statistics' applies as usual. The toll was introduced in 1429. The earliest surviving registers date from 1497, 1503 and 1528. An almost unbroken series of surviving registers begins in 1536. In 1660 Skåne was annexed by Sweden but the island of Zealand and the fortress of Kronborg remained in the hands of the Danes, who continued to collect the toll. Finally, under the convention of March 1867, Denmark agreed to forgo collection of the toll in exchange for an indemnity of 96 million Danish krone.

Initially the toll was levied on the vessels themselves, and the earliest registers therefore show only the name and country of origin of the captain and the toll paid. From 1536 onwards, the tonnage of the ships was entered in the registers, and from 1557 the nationality of the vessels and their port of departure were also noted. Then, in the 1660s, a duty was levied on the merchandise itself, and the registers began to give detailed descriptions of the cargoes.

From the 160 years between 1497 and 1657, registers have survived for 110 years. Over these 110 years, 403,902 vessels, 59 per cent of them Dutch, sailed through the Sound in one direction or the other. 520,885 vessels, 35.5 per cent of them Dutch, sailed through between 1661 and 1783. The vessels that used the Sound between 1661 and 1783 had a higher average tonnage than those that used it between 1497 and 1657. The Sound registers supply a massive amount of information on these ships and their cargoes. Nina Ellinger Bang and Knud Korst went to the considerable trouble of publishing in tabular form all the information that can be derived from the registers. The result is six fat quarto volumes, with a total of about 3,200 pages (Bang and Korst, 1906–53).

As we saw in Part I, chapter 4, the Sound registers, like the English export registers, confront the historian with complex and at times insoluble problems of interpretation. Yet the historian of North European trade from 1497 onwards would be much the poorer without the mass of information compiled by the servants of the King of Denmark, backed by the threat of the cannons of Kronborg.

The third great series of documents on maritime traffic is Spanish. Christopher Columbus discovered America in October 1492, and the following year Pope Alexander VI sought to mediate between Portuguese and Spanish interests. For about a hundred years, Portugal had been exploring the western coast of Africa, aiming to establish direct contacts with India and the East by circumnavigating the African continent. Spain, on the other hand, having joined the race to open up new trade routes later than her Iberian neighbour, had stumbled on the Americas by accident. Portugal staked its claim to a trading monopoly with those territories its seafarers had discovered. Spain reacted by demanding monopoly control over the American continent. Alexander VI proved a skilled mediator. He traced an imaginary meridian passing 100 leagues to the west of the Cape Verde islands (25°N 15°W, 500 miles west of Dakar), slicing the world into two equal portions. To Portugal the Pope assigned the lands east of the meridian, and to Spain the lands to the west. It did not occur to any of the three parties to this arrangement that other nations might decline to respect their cosy carve-up. Indeed, Spain and Portugal bickered over the Pope's solution until finally, on 7 June 1494, they signed the Tordesillas Treaty, whereby they agreed to shift the demarcation line separating their two spheres of influence to a position 370 leagues to the west of the Cape Verde islands.[10]

From the outset of its American adventure, the Spanish Crown manifested two clear-cut and closely correlated aims: to secure for Spain a trading monopoly with the Americas, and to secure for the Spanish Crown tight control over all movements of persons, ships and merchandise to and from the New World. To this end, an order was issued in 1503 setting up in Seville a 'casa para la contratación' (literally a 'house for the negotiation') for trade with 'the Indies, the Canaries, and with the other islands'. The Casa de la Contratación was conceived as the nerve centre of the administrative organization designed to control traffic with the Americas. To make this traffic easier to control, all goods bound to and from the New World had to pass through Seville (Girard, 1932, ch. 1; Chaunu and Chaunu, 1955, I).

Every ship departing or arriving from the Americas had to be inspected by officials of the Crown. Following each inspection, a register was compiled in the form of a file of documents stating where the ship had come from or where it was bound, what its name was, what its captain's name was, what stores, ammunition and artillery it possessed, what cargo it was carrying, what the value of the cargo was, and what duties were payable on that value. This information was gathered for fiscal reasons and, in the case of ships returning from the Americas, in order to monitor the flow of American silver into Spain. However, unlike the English Particular Accounts and Port Books or the Sound registers, the Spanish *registros* were not compiled for exclusively fiscal reasons. The Spanish state, as Huguette and Pierre Chaunu have pointed out,

> also had a political, legal and theological purpose. It claimed to be safeguarding the minds of the Indian Americans . . . this entailed keeping a check on such potentially subversive merchandise as books [which had to be accounted for in the *registros*] as well as a check on people. . . . The checks that the state conducted applied therefore not only to merchandise, but also to everything that was bound for the West Indies: objects, animals, negroes and passengers. (1955, I, p. 70.)[11]

[10] Since the demarcation line that ran 370 leagues to the west of the Cape Verde islands cut across a section of South America, Portugal was able legitimately to claim sovereignty over Brazil when Pedro Alvares Cabral discovered that country in 1500.

[11] On the passengers see the *Libros de asientos de pasajeros* in the Archivo General de Indias: twenty-three volumes covering the entire period from 1508 to 1701, giving the name, father's name, place of residence and destination of all those who left for the Americas. This information should, however, be treated critically.

Between 1505 and 1787, tens of thousands of *registros* were compiled, forming a wonderful source for the history of the movements of people and goods to and from America. Much of this material has, however, been lost: fewer than 2,000 *registros* appear to have survived. Indeed, were it not for the fortuitous survival of another related source, there would be no way of knowing the size of this loss. From the early sixteenth century, perhaps from the same year as that in which the Casa de la Contratación was founded, the contador (auditor) of the Casa kept a *libro de registros* (book of registers) in which an entry was made for each register compiled or received. The complete series of nine *libros de registros*, covering the period from 1504 to 1783, has come down to us. As Huguette and Pierre Chaunu have commented (1955, I, p. 54), the *libros* were not compiled by the employees of the Casa de la Contratación in order to measure the traffic through the port of Seville, or even, more modestly, to monitor the number of ships arriving and departing. The only purpose of the *libros* was to keep track of the *registros* filed in the archives of the Casa. Even if the *libros* were compiled merely 'for the record', they none the less came to represent, following the loss of a great many *registros*, a precious source for economic historians. Unfortunately, the *libros* do not reproduce all the information on cargoes contained in the *registros*, or the data on ships' stores and artillery. They do however record the name of each ship registered, the name of its captain and, from 1544–8 onwards, its port of destination. A careful study of the nine *libros* thus provides a skeleton outline of the movements of ships bound to and from America in the sixteenth, seventeenth and eighteenth centuries.

Not all the documents produced by the Casa de la Contratación (located in the east wing of the Alcazár in Seville) remained at the Casa itself. Reports, information, statistics and dispatches were regularly forwarded to the Consejo de las Indias (Council of the Indies), attached to the court in Madrid. The royal edict issued on 30 June 1564, however, ordered that 'all the writings and items touching the state and Crown of the Indies' kept at the Consejo were to be transported and stored at the archive fortress of Simancas. This order was reiterated and reinforced in December 1567 and in October 1568.

In 1771 the Casa de la Contratación was transferred from Seville to Cádiz. Documents 'touching the state and Crown of the Indies' were thus housed in three different places: Seville, Simancas and Cádiz. But it was then that the ambitious and rational decision was taken to bring all the material relating to the Americas together in a single archive to be created especially for that purpose. In 1785 steps were taken to put this plan into effect. The Casa Lonja in Seville, situated between the Alcazár and the Cathedral, and built by Philip II in 1598 as a place where merchants could meet and trade, was earmarked for the new archive. And so the famous Archivo General de Indias came into existence. The Casa de la Contratación sent its papers to the new archive in 1786 and 1791, and the Consejo despatched its documents in 1786 (the Contaduria papers), in 1788 (the

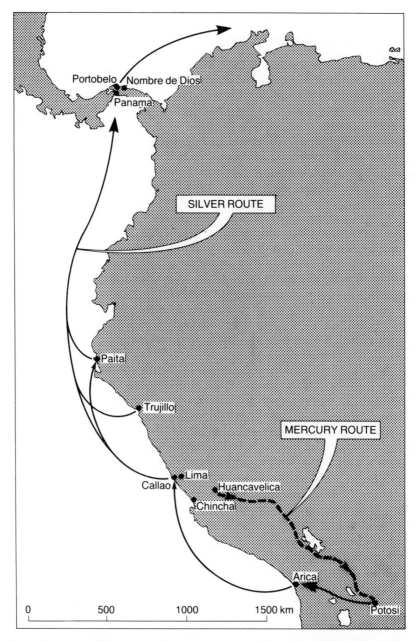

Figure 5 Coast of South America, showing route followed by the *Armada del Sur*. From Huancavelica, where the most important mines were situated, mercury, essential to the extraction of silver, was transported to Potosí. From Potosí the silver was carried to the coast and loaded onto the galleons of the *Armada del Sur*, which shipped it to Panama. From Panama it was carried overland to Portobelo, where it was reloaded onto galleons bound for Spain.

Secretería del Perú papers) and in 1790 (the papers of the Secretería de Nueva España). It is estimated that this excellently arranged and organized archive now contains documents running to a total of more than 14 million sheets (de la Pena y Camara, 1958).

The contents of this archive make it possible to study with a reasonable degree of accuracy the movement of people, goods and ships between Spain and America from the beginning of the sixteenth century right through to the end of the eighteenth century.[12] For the sixteenth century, this by and large coincided with the movement of people, goods and ships between Europe and America, since Spain managed throughout this period to maintain its trading monopoly with its colonies. The only other trans-atlantic trade was between Portugal and Brazil, and this was relatively small-scale. In the early seventeenth century, however, Spain gradually began to lose its grip on trade movements to and from its colonies. Dutch and English smugglers became increasingly numerous and daring, and the Spanish colonies themselves began to seek greater independence from the mother country. As a result, the evidence supplied by the Archivo General de Indias becomes steadily less representative of developments on the Atlantic sea routes. A telling example is provided by figures for the amounts of precious metals imported into Spain from America during the sixteenth and seventeenth centuries. In 1934, on the basis of Spanish archive material, Earl J. Hamilton produced the series of figures set out in table 2. These figures illustrate the dramatic explosion in American silver production during the mid sixteenth century. Throughout the second half of that century the torrent of silver flooding into Spain (and thence into the rest of Europe) continued to rise. The silver was produced principally at Zacatecas in Mexico, and in the last quarter of the century at Potosí – then in Peru but now in Bolivia (see figure 5). From Potosí the silver was transported overland to Arica. From Arica, the galleons of the *Armada del Sur* (Southern Armada), hugging the west coast of South America, took it north to Panama, where it was unloaded and carried across the isthmus to Portobelo. In Mexico, silver from the mines of Zacatecas was transported overland to Vera Cruz. Galleons sailing from Vera Cruz, loaded with Mexican silver, and from Portobelo, loaded with Peruvian silver, met in Cuba. Then, proceeding in convoy, the fleet would make for Seville by way of the Bahamas and the Bermudas (figure 6).

On the evidence produced by Hamilton, imports of American silver began to decline in 1601–10, and then plummeted from 1631–40 onwards. Originally this drop was interpreted as signifying a collapse in American silver production, but the analysis carried out by Brading and Cross in 1972, based on the consumption of mercury used in the refining of silver, as well as the subsequent research by M. Morineau, based on the study of Dutch gazettes, has led to the conclusion that there was no drop

---

[12] The most important work on this matter is Chaunu and Chaunu, 1955. Regrettably the authors are rather prolix and tend to indulge in frequent and unnecessary digressions.

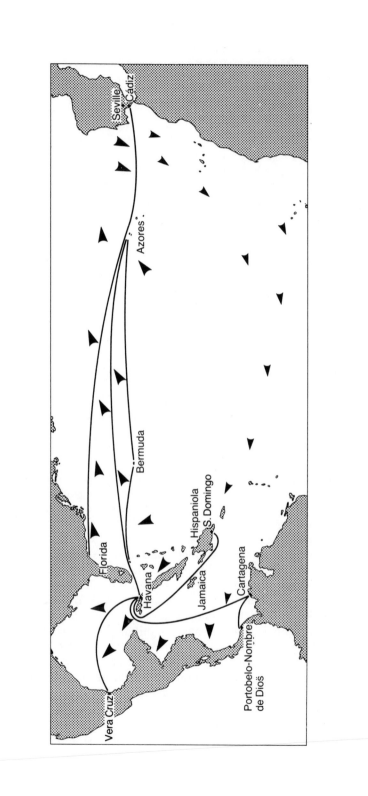

Seville
Cádiz
Azores
Bermuda
Hispaniola
S. Domingo
Florida
Havana
Jamaica
Cartagena
Vera Cruz
Portobelo-Nombre
de Dios

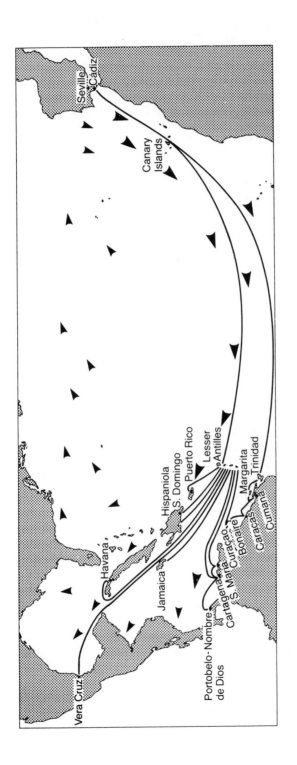

Figure 6 Routes followed by Spanish fleets sailing to and from the Americas, sixteenth–eighteenth centuries. The arrows indicate prevailing winds.

Table 2   Imports of gold and silver into Spain
from the Americas (in metric tons)

Years	Gold	Silver
1503–10	5	–
1511–20	9	–
1521–30	5	–
1531–40	14	86
1541–50	25	178
1551–60	43	303
1561–70	12	943
1571–80	9	1,119
1581–90	12	2,103
1591–1600	19	2,708
1601–10	12	2,214
1611–20	9	2,192
1621–30	4	2,145
1631–40	1	1,397
1641–50	2	1,056
1651–60	0.5	443

Source: Hamilton, 1934, p. 42.

whatsoever in American silver production during the seventeenth century. What happened was that Spain's grip on American production weakened and, as Brading and Cross observed, 'the catastrophic decline in silver imports was a Spanish rather than a European phenomenon' (1972, p. 576).[13] The implications of this conclusion are more far-reaching than might at first appear. The new assessment of silver imports into Europe in the seventeenth century dispels the mystery of the otherwise inexplicably massive development of European trade with the Far East during the seventeenth century: trade that was characterized by a continual massive transfer of silver from Europe to Asia to offset a chronic and severe trading imbalance in Asia's favour. Information on this trade between Europe and Asia is relatively abundant, thanks to surviving documents produced by the English and Dutch East India Companies. But more will be said about those sources in chapter 6.

OTHER FISCAL SOURCES

In addition to the duties outlined in the previous section, European states occasionally levied special taxes on the production, consumption or

[13] See also Morineau, 1985, pp. 42–119 and 551–655. According to Morineau (p. 570), 150 tons of gold and 7,500 tons of silver were imported into Europe from the Americas during the sixteenth century, and 158 tons of gold and 26,168 tons of silver during the seventeenth century.

possession of particular goods. One need only think of the tax levied in Great Britain in 1797 on the possession of clocks (Smith, 1921, pp. 296–7) or of the taxes on soap consumption and brick-manufacturing. Documents resulting from the imposition of such taxes as those on clocks and soap provide economic historians with clues regarding the standard of living of the general population. Similarly, the data generated by the tax on bricks has enabled H. A. Shannon (1934) to compile an index of building work in England and Wales from 1785 to 1849.

Mints are naturally rich sources of data for economic historians in general and for numismatists and historians of money in particular. Given that the state collected a tax (seigniorage) on coinage, one is justified in classifying the resulting documents under the heading of fiscal sources. Yet it would be a mistake to think that all documents produced by mints relate to the collection of seigniorage. Much of the documentation that mints produced was in response to administrative requirements: minting coins is after all a delicate business, dependent on thoroughness and precision. Mints operated mainly with metal delivered to them by private dealers (usually money-changers and bankers), who sought to obtain minted coins: hence the need for regular records of all the metal arriving at the mints, whether in the form of pigs, ingots, or foreign, counterfeit or clipped coins, and of all metal leaving the mint in the form of legal tender. Mint documents also normally report the decisions taken by the competent authorities on the weight, alloy and design of the various types of coin. For historians, such information provides useful clues to the monetary policy of the different states. Naturally it is impossible to find out everything one would like to know, but the sources available on the mints of mediaeval and modern Europe arouse the envy of money historians and numismatists specializing in classical antiquity, for which little documentation exists other than the evidence of the coins themselves.

The two classic ways for states to rake in money were levying taxes and debasing the coinage.[14] In the twelfth century the Italian city states invented a third method: public debt. The earliest public loan for which there is evidence was taken out by the Venetian Republic in 1167 (see plate 8). In Genoa in 1407, at a time when the public debt had climbed to approximately 3 million lire, the state's creditors joined together to form an organization called the Casa di San Giorgio. This took over the administration of state revenues on behalf of the state, with a view to protecting the interests of its private creditors. The public debt of the state of Florence rose from around 50,000 gold florins in 1303 to around 600,000 florins in 1343, then to around 1.5 million florins in 1364, reaching about 3 million florins by 1400. In 1345 all the state's public debts were consolidated in the so-called *monte comune* (common heap). For a long

---

[14] Since the mints generally coined money on behalf of third parties, any devaluation provided an incentive to private individuals or companies to bring metal to the mint, since they would receive a greater nominal value of coins in exchange. The state gained from the devaluation in an indirect way, i.e. through the 'seigniorage' (a tax on the minting of coins), which automatically increased as more coins were minted.

Plate 8   The Venetian Republic's public-debt office

time the Papal State resisted recourse to the expedient of public debt because of scruples over the payment of interest. By the beginning of the sixteenth century, however, the financial circumstances of the Papacy had become so critical that in 1526 Pope Clement VII (one of the Florence Medicis) reached the heroic decision to issue a public loan for the sum of 200,000 gold ducats at an interest rate of 10 per cent. From then on the Papal State's public debt showed a long-term upwards trend. By 1592 the debt had reached approximately 5.6 million scudi; by 1604 roughly 9 million, by 1616 15 million, and by 1657 28 million. In 1599 the payment of interest accounted for approximately 35 per cent of the state's total expenditure. In general, the Papacy's public debt was very well managed; indeed, many foreigners chose to invest their savings in papal bonds.[15]

Loans could be voluntary or exacted by governments from individual citizens according to their income or wealth. In either case the loans were remunerated with the payment of interest. At different dates the titles of the public debt were declared negotiable. By the mid fourteenth century in Venice, Genoa and Florence there had developed a lively market in such titles.

The techniques that the Italians had invented were subsequently exported to the rest of Europe, and public-debt management became one of the most import aspects of the financial operation of the various states. A

---

[15] On the history of the public debt in Venice, Genoa, Florence and Rome see, respectively, Luzzatto, 1929a; Sieveking, 1906–7; Barbadoro, 1929; and Piola Caselli, 1988. There remains, however, a vast amount of unexplored material in the archives.

Plate 9 Archive of the Casa di San Giorgio, Genoa (Genoa State Archive)

vast amount of relevant documentation has survived. On its own, the archive of the Casa di San Giorgio in Genoa consists of more than 33,000 items, occupying a floor and a half of a spacious building, and filling well over a milé and a half of shelves (see plate 9).[16]

From this mass of documents, economic historians can draw a great deal of precious information on the history of state finances, the financial consequences of political and military events, and the distribution among the population of investments in the form of claims on the public debt. Moreover, by comparing returns on the loans with their market price, it is possible to throw light on the level and fluctuations of the interest rate (see for example Cipolla, 1952, repr. 1988).

Our consideration of sources of a fiscal origin may be brought to an appropriate close by turning to documents relating to the financial management of the various city and nation states: for example, the books of public revenue and expenditure, and the records of public budgets. In the case of Italy, one may mention the *Biccherna* series of books, detailing the revenues and expenditure of the City of Siena, and dating back to the middle of the thirteenth century. But even this series pales by comparison with the Pipe Rolls of the Exchequer of London. It is a curious paradox of mediaeval European history that England, which, with its peripheral economy (peripheral not only in geographical terms), was an underdeveloped country compared with northern Italy, Flanders or the Rhineland, none the less equipped itself with such an efficient centralized public administration that it was able to produce documents and document series unparalleled on the continent not only for their complexity and their exhaustiveness (witness the *Domesday Book*) but also for their continuity. The Pipe Rolls are statements of the traditional revenues and expenses of the Crown. One of them dates back to 1130, to the time of Henry I. But the continuous series begins in 1156, during the reign of Henry II, and proceeds almost unbroken for about seven centuries, until 1830.

The earliest Pipe Rolls account for the greater part of the total revenue and expenditure of the English Crown (see for example Poole, 1912). The revenues specified include income from Crown manors, proceeds from timber concessions, taxes of feudal origin levied on landowners (*scutagium*, *donum*, tallage), income deriving from legal proceedings, and proceeds from the sale of effects belonging to convicted prisoners. Most prominent among the expenditures are charitable offerings, tithes paid to churches and religious orders, wages paid to serving people and public officials, and *terrae datae* (gifts of land). Also featured are expenditures for which a special royal authorization was required, and expenditure on public building work. With the passage of time, the sources of Crown revenue multiplied and became more diverse. So did the Crown's expenditures. But, with that traditionalism that had always been a feature of English history, the Pipe Rolls continued to show only those types of revenue and expenditure that had been registered

---

[16] On this archive see Chiaudano and Costamagna, 1956; and Felloni, 1984.

at the times of Henry I and Henry II. Consequently, the information supplied by the Pipe Rolls relates to a steadily decreasing fraction of the overall revenue and expenditure of the English Crown. The series is none the less a continuous source spanning several centuries, and it remains extremely rich in both financial and economic information, including evidence on wages and salaries, prices, court hospitality, food and drink, the construction of public buildings, and so forth.

The first four Pipe Rolls were published by Joseph Hunter in 1833 and 1834. Also in 1934, a roll dating from the first year of the reign of Richard I was published. From 1884 the privately founded Roll Society devoted itself to the publication of the whole series.

LEGISLATIVE SOURCES

We have so far concentrated on public documentary sources of a fiscal origin. There are, however, other sources originating in legislation. For example, for the Middle Ages and the beginning of the Modern Age, town and village by-laws, issued to regulate local life, yield a wealth of information on the organization of production, on consumption, commerce, fairs, weights and measures, money, and so on.

Among other sources of a legislative origin or character, one could hardly overlook the countless ordinances intended to control prices and wages. We have already noted the edict of Diocletian (see Part II, chapter 1), and in mediaeval and modern times these run from Charlemagne to the world wars. Mention should also be made of the innumerable ordinances that have always and everywhere been issued regarding types of money permitted to circulate, exchange rates, exchange controls, and exports of currency and capital. Of great significance for research into the power relations between social classes and groups of workers are the ordinances that, at specific periods and in specific countries, prohibited clearly identified groups of workers from forming corporate associations.

Lastly, economic historians can gather a great deal of useful information from legislation passed by the various different states on the liability of company members, bankruptcy and insolvency, farming contracts, exchange contracts and marriage settlements. Ranging from the writings of twelfth-, thirteenth- and fourteenth-century glossarists and commentators of the Law School of Bologna, to nineteenth-century English Acts of Parliament regarding the structure of the banking system or the extent of liability of business partners or company members, there is a huge mass of material that economic historians can use to throw light on the institutions that hedged around and conditioned the play of purely economic variables.

3 Statistics and their Forerunners

GOVERNMENT CURIOSITY

As time went on, investigations and surveys of demographic, social and economic phenomena became increasingly widespread and frequent, thereby creating for historians an important supplement to public documentary sources of fiscal and legislative origin. Conducted by public authorities, these investigations and surveys were in effect fact-finding activities, even if the quest for knowledge almost always concealed a practical purpose. This trend emerged against a background of cultural developments that successively heightened the 'curiosity' of government. In chronological order, these cultural developments included the Renaissance, the 'Scientific Revolution' of the seventeenth century, the eighteenth-century Enlightenment and the nineteenth-century 'Statistical Movement'.

The Renaissance distinguished itself in this respect mainly by its increased interest in problems of population. In Florence in 1450, the Guild of Doctors and Chemists was given the task of keeping registers of deaths in the city. The purpose of this was to carry out a financial check on claims advanced by the city gravediggers. In 1485 the officials of the Grascia (Victuals Board) were ordered to keep regular records of deaths within the city. On this occasion, the stated purpose was to 'ascertain the number of people at present living in the city of Florence and to ensure the provision of victuals'. Thus, from 1485 onwards, there were two deaths registers in Florence. In Venice, at the end of the fifteenth century, the office of the Avogaria began to keep a record of deaths, its declared purpose being to act as a general registry. In 1504 the local Health Office also began to keep a regular record of deaths in the city. The fact that it was the Health Office that maintained this second register is itself a clear indication of its purpose: to identify rapidly all cases of death by plague, with a view to a swift deployment of emergency preventive measures. In Milan and Mantua the regular registration of deaths was begun in 1452 and 1496, respectively. In both cases the insistence that for each death a medical certificate should be presented declaring the cause of death (and in Mantua even the duration of the illness) clearly shows that the principal aim of this registration was to safeguard public health.

Except in Italy, states did not conduct surveys of births, marriages and deaths, but rather left general registry work to the clergy. But in England and in France, by order respectively of Thomas Cromwell in 1538 and of Villers Cotterêts in 1539, central government took action to ensure that parish priests kept their registers of baptisms, marriages and burials regularly and diligently up to date. Thus was created an extremely precious source of demographic history, of which more will be said in chapter 5.

Northern Italy distinguished itself in sixteenth-century Europe in yet another area: it was the first part of Europe to introduce genuine censuses, conducted not for fiscal reasons but purely for demographic and fact-finding purposes. The first official city census by the Venetian Republic probably dates from 1443, though the relevant documentation has been lost. Censuses were certainly conducted in Venice in 1509 (for which records have survived) and in 1540 (for which they have again gone astray). In the Grand Duchy of Tuscany, censuses of the whole of the Florentine state (i.e. excluding the Siena area) were carried out in 1552, 1562, 1622, 1632 and 1642, and the whole Duchy was covered in 1674. (See Comitato Italiano per lo Studio della Demografia Storica, 1971–2; and Del Panta, 1974, pp. 140–6.)

In the 1570s, when Spanish imperial power was at its zenith, a unique series of documents was produced in Spain. The appearance of this material, gathered essentially out of curiosity, has to be related to the personality of Philip II, a modern, bureaucratically minded centralizing monarch, who was also an indefatigable administrator and a tireless producer of red tape. During Philip's reign (1575–8) an economic–demographic–financial–sociological investigation was launched 'para honra y ennoblecimiento de los pueblos de España' ('for the honour and ennoblement of the communities of Spain') in the villages of New Castile. This inquiry was based on a uniform and very detailed questionnaire, the aim of which was systematically to collect, from every village and town, information on the legal organization of the community, its climate, its population, whether or not its population was thought to be increasing or decreasing, migrations, agricultural and craft production, stock-farming, commerce, shortages of particular goods, the community's sources of income, its tax burden, its social classes and their relative size, landed property and its distribution. The results of this inquiry were collected in documents entitled *Relaciones historico-geográficas de los pueblos de España* (or, more simply, *Relaciones topográficas*). Other investigations were conducted occasionally after 1578 and during the seventeenth century, but the most important group of *Relaciones* to have survived is that resulting from the inquiries of 1575 and 1578. Preserved in the library of the Escurial, the documentation in question is bound in eight volumes, comprising more than 4,000 closely written sheets.

At about the same time, in 1577 to be precise, a similar investigation focusing on the huge Spanish colonial possessions in the Americas was launched. The documents resulting from this inquiry are now known as the *Relaciones de Indias*.

Paradoxically, for centuries the fruit of all this labour remained buried under dust in the archives of Spanish bureaucracy. Its existence was well known but the huge amount of material collected may have discouraged anyone from using it. In 1866 Fermín Caballero, in the speech he delivered on his investiture as a member of the Real Academia de la Historia (Royal Academy of History), informed the scholarly world of the importance of the material, but it was not until 1949 that a critical edition of the *Relaciones* began to appear.[1]

POLITICAL ARITHMETICS AND PROTO-STATISTICS

Simplifying matters to an extreme, the seventeenth century has been termed the century of the 'Scientific Revolution'. It has received this label because it was during this period (roughly speaking that of Galileo, Newton, Harvey, Descartes, Huygens and Leibniz) that the foundation of the experimental scientific approach and of modern science were laid. From then on, it was increasingly unusual for scholars to pose weighty but unanswerable questions regarding, for example, the ultimate purpose of life, the essence of human happiness or the nature of angels. Ever more frequently, and in increasingly precise terms, they instead raised problems of a more prosaic kind, but to which some answer backed by experimental proof might eventually be found – regarding the laws of motion and gravity, for instance. There emerged at that time a mechanistic conception of the universe, a marked preference for mathematics as a tool for formulating and resolving scientific problems, and a widespread recourse to experiment as the only acceptable test of the validity of a theoretical hypothesis. To put it succinctly, it was then that the scientific method came into being.

Something was lost in this process. Fontanelle, writing in 1686, related an interesting conversation:

'It seems to me', said the Countess, 'that philosophy has assumed a decidedly mechanistic character.' 'It is so mechanistic,' said I, 'that I am afraid we shall soon have cause to be ashamed of it; they will see to it that the universe becomes on a large scale what a clock is on a small scale: an exact mechanism that depends merely on the correct arrangement of its different moving parts. But tell me, madam, did you not have a more sublime idea of the universe?'

[1] On the volumes kept in the library of the Escurial see Miguélez, 1917; and Salomon, 1964. The *Relaciones* were published in a critical edition by Vinas y Mey and Paz (1949). In 1561 Philip II initiated another extraordinary documentary enterprise: he commissioned Anton van den Wyngaerde, the most distinguished European topographer of his time, to produce a series of views of the principal cities of Philip's empire. See Kagan, 1989.

The English playwright Thomas Shadwell (1642–92) echoed Fontanelle in his comedy *The Virtuoso*, written in 1676, where he described the new type of scholar as someone who spent his time and wealth trying to find out 'the nature of eels in vinegar, mites in cheese and the blue of plums . . . one who has broken his brain about the nature of maggots, who has studied these twenty years to find out the several sorts of spiders and never cares for understanding mankind'.

I have quoted these passages to draw attention to the conflict that arose, at the inception of the scientific approach, between it and the humanistic tradition. Be that as it may, in the field of what are now pretentiously termed the 'social sciences' the seventeenth century saw the birth and development of new interests and curiosities and above all the emergence of a mania for measurement. In England, for so long the laggard of Europe, but now in the forefront of change, there existed a profusion of learned people, mainly amateur scholars, known generally as 'virtuosi'. Those who were keen to investigate the body of society and to measure demographic, economic and social phenomena were referred to as 'political arithmeticians', and their discipline as 'political arithmetics'. This term stood for a field that is nowadays covered by economics, statistics and demography, terms not then in use.[2] The political arithmeticians still handled numbers with considerable naïveté (see Landes, 1972, p. 55), but must be given the credit for having set out on a path that would lead far. Writing in 1701, John Arbuthnot well expressed their credo:

> arithmetics is not only the great instrument of private commerce, but by it are (or ought to be) kept the public accounts of a nation; I mean those that regard the whole state of a commonwealth, as to the number, fructification of its people, increase of stock, improvement of lands and manufactures, balance of trade, public revenues, coinage, military power by sea and land, etc. (Quoted in Clark, 1938, p. xiii)

The following political arithmeticians gained particular distinction: William Petty (1623–87); John Graunt (1620–84), who founded demography practically single-handed with his studies of the Bills of Mortality of London; Gregory King (1648–1712), who produced level-headed estimates of English national income and slightly less level-headed estimates of French national income; Charles Davenant (1656–1714), who argued the importance 'of the art of reasoning on the basis of figures in subjects pertaining to government'; and Edmund Halley (1656–1742).

On the European continent, political arithmetics took hold above all in Germany, thanks largely to Hermann Conring (1606–81) a 'virtuoso' who had studied medicine. In Germany, the new discipline was given the more cumbersome name of *Staatsmerkwürdigkeiten* and accorded a place

---

[2] It appears that the term 'political arithmetics' was used for the first time by William Petty in 1672 in a letter sent to Lord Anglesea (see C. H. Hull, 1989, I, pp. 239–40n).

on the university curriculum. In France, although developments were less formal, governments from Richelieu to Colbert repeatedly called for reports on trade, manufacturing and finance. In Spain, the spectacular decadence of the country had the effect of stimulating the production of a plentiful series of reports on the economic conditions of the realm and on its economic and financial relations with foreign countries. These were produced by *arbitristas*, a term used to denote people to whom we would now refer as economists. The most renowned *arbitristas* were Gonzáles de Cellorigo, Sancho de Moncaba, Francisco Martínes de Mata, Miguel Alvarez Osorio y Redín, Pedro Fernández de Navarrete and Miguel Caxa de Leruelo.

But it was principally in the eighteenth century, after the deep wounds inflicted by the Thirty Years War (1618–48) had begun to heal, and with the coming-of-age of that complex and profound political and cultural movement generally labelled the Enlightenment, that a spate of investigations, inquiries and reports were undertaken on questions of population, foreign trade, money and poverty. In general, there was a major shift from documentation compiled for fiscal purposes to documentation gathered for the sake of inquiry. During the previous century, the work of political arithmeticians had already prepared the ground, but with increasing mercantilist worries over the trade balance, and the need for better information on foreign trade, this step had become urgent. This is apparent in, for instance, the innovations introduced into the collection of English trade statistics.

The Exchequer Enrolled Customs Accounts for 1275–1547 and the Port Books series from 1565 have been mentioned in the previous chapter. The former series only reflected trade in goods subject to customs duty. In the view of Donald Woodward (1973, p. 156), the Port Books too 'in essence were customs records and not records of trade or shipping'[3] even if the entry and exit of goods free of duty were also frequently registered. In July 1696, however, a specially appointed commission, 'takeing into consideration the Great usefulness of keeping a Distinct accompt of the Importation and Exportation of all Commodities Into and Out of this Kingdom', advocated the creation of the office of Inspector General of Exports and Imports to oversee the collection of data relating to the import and export of all kinds of goods, whether or not they were subject to customs duty, 'in Order to make a Ballance of the Trade' (quoted in Clark, 1938, p. 3). Thus began the Ledgers of the Inspector General of Imports and Exports, also known to historians as the 'Customs 3' series, which ran parallel to the Port Books, and covered the period 1697–1780.[4] The

---

[3] Andrews too acknowledges that the 'purpose of the Port Books was not to provide trade or shipping statistics but rather to prevent customs fraud' (1956, p. 118).
[4] The registers of this series are kept at the Public Record Office in London, with a shelf-mark of Customs 3/1–82 – hence the practice of referring to the series as 'Customs 3. On it see Carson, 1977; E. B. Schumpeter, 1960 (which reviews all the data); and Scholte, 1938. The Port Books were compiled each year until 1799.

Ledgers are the main source of evidence regarding English foreign trade in the eighteenth century.

In 1664 Colbert unsuccessfully attempted to complete a large-scale general inquiry into the economic and social conditions of contemporary France, including foreign trade. But, where Colbert failed, those who followed him succeeded. General inquiries, reaping a wealth of data on French economic, financial, demographic and social conditions were conducted in 1697, 1724, 1730, 1745 and 1764 (although many of the reports produced as part of the 1724 and 1764 inquiries have either gone astray or are lying neglected somewhere in French government archives). Over the same period of time, special investigations focused on the country's population (1709, 1726, 1745, 1784), on the mines (1741, 1764, 1783), on the steel industry (1772, 1774, 1788), on tanneries (1733, 1745, 1759, 1788) and on various aspects of agriculture (for further details see Gille, 1964).

For foreign trade in the seventeenth century, data are partial and intermittent, but for the eighteenth century France can boast three series of official statistics:

(1) those compiled annually by the Chambers of Commerce and forwarded to the Secretary of State for the Navy;
(2) those produced by the Direction des Fermes for the period 1725–78;
(3) those compiled by the Bureau de la Balance du Commerce for the period 1716–72.[5]

None of these series is complete, but the worst problem is that the figures presented by the three series do not tally. Indeed, it has been asserted that the figures produced by the Direction des Fermes 'are so manifestly inaccurate that one wonders how they could have been taken seriously' (Masson, 1911, p. 408n). This is all the more surprising in view of the fact that the three offices depended on one another for the collection and processing of the statistics. All merchants importing or exporting goods were obliged to make a declaration to the Direction des Fermes, whether the goods in question were liable to customs duty or not. The Direction des Fermes then passed on a summarized version of these import–export data to the Bureau de la Balance du Commerce. The Bureau, in its turn, called upon the Chambers of Commerce to provide the current prices of goods imported and exported, before proceeding to assess the overall trade surplus or deficit (see Romano, 1957, pp. 1282–9).Obviously, with all this paper being shunted from one office to the next, many an error and misunderstanding could creep in, and this may help to account for the disagreements between the three series.

During the seventeenth century, the countries that excelled in the collection of data on demographic, economic, financial and social phenomena were France, England, Brandenburg and Spain.

[5] On this series see Gille, pp. 95–7; and Romano, 1957, pp. 1282–9. The data of the Bureau de la Balance du Commerce for 1716–72 was published by Bruyard, director of the Bureau from 1756 to 1781.

In the case of Brandenburg, one can overlook neither the impact of the enlightened despotism of Frederick the Great, nor the fact that the state was politically organized along bureaucratic and military lines that did much to assist the work of government officers charged with the collection of information.[6]

Spain, in spite of its progressive and long-term decline, distinguished itself in the second half of the eighteenth century by a series of initiatives that resulted in sources of considerable importance to economic historians. A nationwide land register bearing the name of the Marqués de la Ensenada was compiled between 1749 and 1754: an exceptional achievement for that time. Then, in 1787, for exclusively demographic purposes, a general census of the population was conducted that bore the name of the Conde de Floridablanca. This census (*Censo español*, 1787) was a model of its kind. The whole population of 10,409,879 inhabitants was analysed by gender, age, civil status, social class and occupation, and separate statistics were compiled for the religious population (monks, nuns and so on), the hospital and prison populations, and the military. The censuses conducted only a few years later in the United States (1790) and England (1801) were technically and qualitatively much inferior: the French censuses of 1801, 1806, 1821, 1831, 1836, 1841 and 1846 did not register the age of the population; and the numeration of the Swedish population in 1749 was not, properly speaking, a census at all, even if it is usually cited as one.[7] Also in Spain, an agricultural and industrial census entitled *Censo de frutos y manufacturas de España e islas adjacentes* was conducted in 1799.[8]

As for Italy, gone were the days when the country was a leader in commerce, finance, accounting, technology and public health. The economic crisis that overwhelmed the country from 1620 to 1680 had turned Italy into a backwater. In the eighteenth century, in both northern and southern Italy, there were a few individuals who sought to keep abreast of developments north of the Alps: the Verri brothers, Cesare Beccaria, Gian Rinaldo Carli, Pompeo Neri, Antonio Genovesi and Abbot Galiani, to name but the most illustrious. Most of the country, however, was sunk in torpor, and there were no structures or institutions equipped to gather economic and social data. This became clearly apparent at the end of the eighteenth and beginning of the nineteenth century, following the occupation of the peninsula by the French armies. The imperial government in Paris bombarded local-government officers throughout Italy with requests for data on population, agriculture, manufacturing, trade, finance, and so on, that they were accustomed to obtaining for

---

[6] On what was achieved in Brandenburg–Prussia up until the foundation of the central statistical institute see the important work by Behre (1905).

[7] The Swedish 'census' simply lumped together information contained in parish registers, but is often mentioned along with the first United States, French and English censuses as one of the earliest national censuses.

[8] On developments in statistical surveys in Spain during the eighteenth century see, among others, Sanz Serrano, 1956.

France. Under such pressure from Paris, the local offices in Italy managed to produce a considerable quantity of data and to complete a number of inquiries. Much of the information, however, they simply invented to humour the French. And to many of the requests for information the Italians merely pleaded ignorance. Writing to Prince Eugenio on 25 February 1806, Napoleon angrily remarked, 'I have in my possession no evidence whatsoever and know less about the affairs of my kingdom of Italy than I do even of those of England' (quoted in Tarlé, 1950, p. 16).

During the revolutionary and imperial period, France was indeed overtaken by a frantic tide of statistical research (see Landes, 1972, p. 71ff; and Perrot and Wolf, 1984). In the forefront of this movement were N. L. François De Neufchâteau (1750–1828) and J. A. C. Chaptal (1756–1832). Following the reorganization of the administration in October 1795, and the consequent re-establishment of the ministries, the Minister of the Interior gained control of economic and statistical affairs. On 8 April 1800, Lucien Bonaparte created a special bureau to house both the library and the archives of the Ministry. On 22 November, Chaptal, who was undertaking a review of the Ministry's organization, turned this bureau into a fully-fledged Bureau de Statistique. In 1802 the Bureau was placed under the direct control of the General Secretary of the Ministry for the Interior and allotted the task of producing *grands mémoires statistiques*. Between 1801 and 1805, 'the bureau's enthusiastic attempt to complete and publish a massive descriptive topography of France turned statistics into one of the major affairs of state' (Woolf, in Perrot and Woolf, 1984, p. 115). A combination of difficulties and of resistance from certain quarters prevented the new office from producing the keenly awaited general statistical overview of the country, and this failure may have been one of the causes of the Bureau's temporary abolition in September 1812. But the mass of documentary material that the office had collected and had placed at the disposal of scholars paved the way for the publication of such works as Alexandre de Ferrière's *Analyse de la statistique générale de la France* (1803–4), Herbin de Halle's *Statistique générale et particulière de la France et de ses colonies* (7 volumes, 1803), J. Peuchet's *Statistique élémentaire de la France*, and J. Peuchet and P. G. Chanlaire's *Description topographique et statistique de la France* (1810).

Other countries soon followed the French example. Central statistical offices were created in Bavaria in 1801, in Prussia in 1805, in Austria in 1810, in Belgium in 1831 and in Russia in 1857. In Russia at the beginning of the eighteenth century the Blizhniaia Kantselariia compiled lists of people liable to military service and to taxation. In 1811 a statistical department was created within the Ministry of Police, entrusted with the collection and analysis of reports submitted by provincial governors, and with the preparation of demographic statistics based on these reports. In 1834 a statistical department was created within the Ministry of the Interior. In 1852 this department was abolished and the Minister of the Interior was given the job of defining the structure and the task of a newly founded statistical office. In March 1857, the office became the Central Statistical Office and was split into two separate departments: the statistical department and the provincial department.

In Austria, the collection of economic and demographic data had taken root in the second half of the eighteenth century under the administration of enlightened sovereigns such as Maria Theresa and her son Joseph II, and of equally or more enlightened ministers such as Kaunitz. The effects of Austrian administrative efficiency made themselves felt beyond the borders of Austria itself, throughout the dominions of the Crown. In Lombardy, for example, a land register was completed in 1760 and the *Sommari generali della popolazione trovatasi nella Lombardia austriaca* (General summaries of the population of Austrian Lombardy) were produced from 1771 to 1796.

The central statistical office established in Vienna in 1810 was initially called the Königliche-kaiserliche Direction der administrativen Statistik, but in 1863 it was reorganized and renamed the Statistische Zentral-Kommission. Each year from 1829 onwards, this institute published the *Tafeln der österreichischen Monarchie* (the first volume of which covers the year 1828). These *Tafeln* (tables) are of particular interest in that they cover all the different regions within the hugely varied, multilingual and multinational empire, and thus reflect the strikingly different stages of development that those regions had attained. The wealth of statistics contained in the *Tafeln* make possible a number of interesting comparisons between areas at vastly different stages of development. For example, in 1900 the illiteracy rate (to take a fairly significant index of development) ranged from 1 per cent in the Vorarlberg region to 73 per cent in Dalmatia.[9] The *Tafeln* for 1841 (actually published in 1844) contain one of the earliest attempts to estimate the gross national product.

Paradoxically, England, whose political arithmeticians had led the field in the use of statistical information in the seventeenth century, did not establish a Statistical Department until 1832. Ambitions for this department, which was attached to the Board of Trade, were far-reaching. It was expected 'to obtain and systematically arrange returns upon the Wealth, Commerce, and Industry of the United Kingdom', and the Parliamentary Select Committee on Public Documents, in its report of 1833, made the recommendation that the Statistical Department of the Board of Trade should rapidly be turned into a Central Statistical Office. Most of these expectations, however, were disappointed. The Department encountered considerable difficulties in the collection of economic information, especially outside London, but was inundated with statistics on health and 'morality' (relating, that is, to crime, alcoholism and schooling). The acute interest that the English were taking at the time in 'moral' statistics can be related to the fact that the country was caught in the throes of the Industrial Revolution, with all the problems that

[9] On Austrian Italy see Zaninelli, 1965; and Faccini, 1980.

resulted from a massive exodus from the countryside to the squalid slums of industrial towns, hotbeds of crime, prostitution and drunkenness, places where children were sent to toil in factories instead of attending school. As late as 1839, the yearbook of the Statistical Department, which bore the promising title *Tables of the Revenue, Population, Commerce, etc. of the United Kingdom and its Dependencies Compiled from Official Records* contained 114 tables of criminal statistics and seventy-nine tables on hospitals. The yearbook for 1845 was packed with information regarding the amount of money confiscated by the police from drunks and returned to them when sober, and the number of public houses licensed to keep billiards and bagatelle tables. Unfortunately, the cornucopia of material of this type was not matched by an abundance of economic statistics.[10] On more than one occasion, Sir Robert Peel was moved to lament the impossibility of obtaining information of the type required for rational decision-making, and, as Lucy Brown has written, 'there is no sign that the Government had a firmer knowledge of the economic situation in the provincial centres than it had ten years previously' (1958, p. 88). Things certainly got no better after 1849, when George Richardson Porter, who, albeit with frustrating results, had run the Department with energy and competence, was promoted to a more elevated position. Albany Fonblanque, his replacement, was described by Disraeli as 'an imbecile as a man of business' (quoted in Cullen, 1975, p. 25). In 1850 the President of the Board of Trade admitted that the Statistical Department was 'susceptible of a great deal of improvement' and it was clear that the department had completely failed to become a central statistical office (ibid.).

However, not everything in England was destined to go awry. In 1801 the first national census was completed. Its results, according to the estimates of present-day scholars, have an error margin of no more than 5 per cent.[11] In 1837 the General Register Office was established, the primary task of which was to oversee the regular and continuous collection by the Civil Service of vital statistics (births, deaths, marriages and divorces). Previously this job had been left to the parish clergy. Thanks to the efforts and vision of William Farr, the General Register Office broadened its collection and publication of data to include health statistics. As a result, the quality and methodology of this work soon showed a marked improvement.[12]

---

[10] On the preceding discussion see Cullen, 1975, pp. 20–1, 25.

[11] On the history of English censuses see Interdepartmental Committee on Social and Economic Research, 1951.

[12] The work involved in producing and publishing statistics was considerably assisted in England by the creation, on local private initiative, of statistical societies such as the Manchester Statistical Society, founded in 1833; the Statistical Society of London, founded in 1834; the Statistical Society of Glasgow, founded in 1836; and the Bristol Statistical Society, founded in 1838. The journals produced by these and similar societies are mines of statistical information.

MODERN STATISTICS

The term 'statistics', employed with the sense now attributed to it, seems to have made its appearance in Germany during the eighteenth century. Before that one talked, as has been seen, of 'topography' (France and Spain),[13] of 'political arithmetics' (England) or of *Staatsmerkwürdigkeiten* (Germany). This last term was a clear reflection of the obsession of German scholars with the role and importance of the state. In the German-speaking countries, those who studied and surveyed demographic, economic, financial and social phenomena mainly did so with a view to describing the organization and operation of the various organs of the state. It therefore comes as no surprise that the term *Statistik* – the root of which is evidently the word *Staat* (state) – was coined in Germany. G. Achenwall employed the term in a work published in 1748, but without indicating that he was coining a new word. When W. Hopper introduced the term 'statistics' into England in 1770 in the translation of a work by J. F. von Bielfeld, statistics was defined as the discipline that 'provides information of the political organization of all the modern states'. And in 1797 the *Encyclopaedia Britannica* defined the term as 'a word lately introduced to express a view or survey of any kingdom, a county, or parish'. In Germany the study of statistics as a science of state found its way onto university curricula during the eighteenth century and, in a manner familiar in German cultural history, a heated dispute about aims and methods soon followed. Some viewed statistics as above all a presentation of quantitative data in tabular form (*Tabellenstatistik*), while others opposed any such purely quantitative conception of the discipline.[14]

The use of graphs and other visual representations was a relatively late development. One of the first scholars to make extensive use of them was William Playfair in his *Commercial and Political Atlas*, published in London in 1786. This chiefly illustrated the movements and structure of the contemporary English and Scottish import–export trade (see Gray Funkhouser and Walker, 1935; Tilling, 1975; and Tufte, 1983, p. 32ff). The example set by Playfair, however, aroused no particular enthusiasm. Indeed, in the first fifty volumes of the *Journal of the Statistical Society of London* (founded in March 1834), graphs appear on only fourteen occasions (Gray Funkhouser, 1937, p. 292).

The point is that, despite the growing interest in measurement and the use of numbers in economic and social analysis, the 'proto-statistics' stage lasted right into the second half of the nineteenth century. It was only with

[13] The adjective *topographique* was widely used in France as late as the early nineteenth century to indicate 'statistical'. Woolf's statement in Perrot and Woolf, 1984, p. 85, that the term originated in eighteenth-century Germany and that it was later imported into France and England therefore has no basis: Woolf was obviously unaware of the existence of the *Relaciones topográficas* produced under Philip II.
[14] On the history of statistics see, from among the many works available, John, 1894; Koren, 1918; Westergaard, 1932; and Stigler, 1986.

Table 3   Collections of historical statistics

FRANCE Institut National de la statistique et des études économiques, *Annuaire statistique de la France*:
   vol. 57 (1946) *Résumé rétrospectif*
   vol. 66 (1961) *Résumé rétrospectif*
   vol. 72 (1966) *Résumé rétrospectif*

GERMANY
Statistisches Bundesamt, *Bevölkerung und Wirtschaft 1872–1972* (Stuttgart, 1972)

GREAT BRITAIN
B. R. Mitchell and P. Deane, *Abstract of British Historical Statistics* (Cambridge, 1962)

ITALY
Istituto Centrale di Statistica, *Sommario di statistiche storiche italiane, 1861–1955* (Rome, 1958)

NETHERLANDS
Central Bureau voor de Statistiek, *75 jaar statistiek van Nederland* (The Hague, 1975)

NORWAY
Statistik Sentralbyrå, *Historisk Statistikk* (Oslo, 1969)

SWEDEN
Statistika Centralbyrån, *Historisk Statistik för Sverige* (Stockholm, 1955)

---

the work of the Belgian L. A. J. Quetelet (1796–1874) that numbers were accepted as the natural language for statistics, and that a mathematical-probabilistic technique was adopted. Only then could the age of statistics really be said to have dawned.[15]

The refinement of survey and analytical techniques, and the setting-up of central statistical offices and statistical societies combined to create an explosion in statistical and economic information. As Joseph Schumpeter observed in his classic *History of Economic Analysis*, 'All types of information about facts have increased beyond the boldest dreams of past generations but our epoch has been particularly characterized by an increase of statistical information which was so great as to open up quite new possibilities for scientific research' (1954, p. 1141). In more melodramatic terms, Jean Stengers wrote that 'the historian who studies contemporary history, and in particular history from about 1850 onwards, sees rising before him a mounting tide of statistical data. This stream soon turns into a torrent: figures flood in from every corner of the horizon (1970, pp. 427–8). A short list of collections of historical statistics for European countries is presented in table 3.

Despite this tidal wave of data and statistics, over the last two centuries (and in Britain the last three) the legislative bodies of West European states

---

[15] In 1853 the first international congress on statistics was held in Brussels and in 1885 the International Statistics Institute was founded in The Hague.

have often felt it necessary to gather further documentary evidence before taking decisions on economic and social matters. Thus originated a fresh outpouring of *paperasserie* crammed with first-hand accounts, statistics and general information. In Britain the results of these inquiries are published in Parliamentary Papers, a term loosely employed to indicate any official publication relating to Parliament and its proceedings. These papers range from accounts of sittings and debates to reports of parliamentary committees or outside agencies (Ford and Ford, 1972, p. 1). In general, those that have contributed the most new information are the reports of Select Committees, the reports of Royal Commissions, the ministerial returns, the departmental papers, the Advisory and Consultative Committee reports, and the working-party reports.[16] These papers touch on a huge range of economic and social issues. For the nineteenth century alone, there are at least thirty-six volumes of Parliamentary Papers on agriculture, more than 200 on the colonies, more than seventy on education, thirty or so on emigration, over twenty on banking problems, and so on. Fortunately there is no shortage of guides and indexes to help scholars find their way around this forest of material (see for example Ford and Ford, 1972; *Catalogue of British Parliamentary Papers*, 1981; Bond, 1971; and Di Roma and Rosenthal, 1967), but to master its mass of documents an entire lifetime might not suffice.

The states of continental Europe followed the example set by Britain and on more than one occasion a common experience gave rise to parallel parliamentary inquiries in different countries. The long-term agricultural crisis that hit Europe as a consequence of American competition in the second half of the nineteenth century prompted parliamentary investigations into the state of agriculture in France in 1865–6, in Britain in 1881–2 and in Italy in 1881–4. Cases of this kind open the way for interesting international comparisons, even if different approaches were used in different investigations.[17]

The drawback with this documentation is that its sheer abundance may discourage potential researchers. The 'Jacini inquiry' into Italian agricultural conditions (1881–94) ran to twenty-two fat large-format volumes, each several hundred pages long.[18] Years earlier, again in Italy, a parliamentary investigation into the country's first steps towards industrialization produced three volumes of written depositions (about 2,000 pages), two volumes recorded from oral depositions (more than 1,500 pages), four volumes of reports from the Chambers of Commerce (600 pages), and two volumes of special reports (another 400 pages).[19] Jean Stengers was right when he talked of a 'deluge' of statistical information.

[16] For a clear description of the background to this complicated web of papers and reports, and of the relations between the various committees and commissions, see Ford and Ford, 1972.
[17] On the British agricultural inquiry of 1881–2 see the interesting report by the Italian Ministry of Agriculture, Industry and Trade (Ministero dell'Agricoltura, Industria e Commercio, 1884).
[18] On the Italian Agricultural inquiry of 1881–4 see Caracciolo, 1958.
[19] On the Italian industrial inquiry of 1871–4 see Are, 1963; and Abrate et al., 1970.

4   Foreign Intelligence Reports

So far we have concentrated on sources produced by cities and states with reference to their own affairs. Yet it would be a mistake to overlook an important type of source that does not fall within this category. As early as the Middle Ages, the various European states and princes showed a keen interest in information bearing on the military strength, the population and the financial resources of other states with which they were or might become involved. Whenever they deemed it advisable, they would dispatch their diplomatic representatives or even special secret informers to collect the information that they desired. Over the centuries, the reports sent back by Venetian ambassadors accredited to the various European States enjoyed particular notoriety, owing to their regularity, their clear structure and their shrewdness.[1]

As early as 1268, the Grand Council of Venice issued a regulation directing every ambassador to present within fifteen days of his return to Venice a report setting down 'in writing the answer that he received in response to his mission as well as any other thing he might have learnt during the journey and that in his opinion might be to the advantage and honour of Venice'. On 31 May 1425 the Senate decreed that reports should be delivered in writing and registered at the Chancellery 'in a book specially for that purpose', judging that it was 'good and useful' for Venice to have a ready supply of intelligence on foreign states.

At the start of the sixteenth century a *Traité du gouvernement de Venise* defined in the following terms the typical structure of a Venetian ambassador's report:

---

[1] As early as the sixteenth century, a number of reports submitted by Venetian ambassadors were (somewhat carelessly and patchily) published. But it was not until well into the nineteenth century that systematic publication of the reports began. From a philological viewpoint, even these nineteenth-century publications leave a great deal to be desired. See, among others, the collections edited by Barozzi and Berchet (1863) and by Alberi (1860). In contrast, the collection edited by Firpo (1961) is exemplary for its rigorous scholarship. Many of the reports have gone astray, especially the earliest ones, owing in part to two disastrous fires in 1574 and 1577 that destroyed papers and furnishings in the Doge's Palace.

the ambassador speaks first of what he has done and negotiated during his ambassadorship, then of the personality of the prince, of his wife and of any children they have, then of the propensities and intentions that the said prince harbours both towards Venice and towards other states. He also tells of [the prince's] ordinary and extraordinary revenues, his expenses in times of peace and of war, his counsellors, the notables who enjoy some authority over him or who are his favourites. The ambassador also reports on the other persons who are the prince's subjects.

As can be inferred, these reports also contained economic information, but this aspect was clearly considered of secondary importance. Economic information was normally confined to references to the prince's revenues and expenditure, and the figures cited were usually based on hearsay. Since no particular critical effort was deployed, one has to use such figures with caution. For the economic historian the importance of these Venetian reports lies less in the information they contain than in the example they set. For gradually the various other European states followed the Venetian example, until the diplomatic, and above all the consular, reports of the more advanced states supplied a rich fund of economic information collected with care and critical intelligence.

In France, for instance, following the institutionalization of the consular service (provided with a legal framework by an ordinance of 1681),[2] Colbert ordered that consular reports should no longer be delivered only at the end of a mission, but instead should be dispatched to France annually. Moreover, Colbert expected these annual reports to provide detailed information on the trade, shipping and manufactures of the countries concerned. During the Revolution the French consuls became rather lax about dispatching their reports. Talleyrand intervened with his *Instruction générale du 8 août 1814 pour les consuls de France en pays étrangers,* urging the maximum care and punctuality in the composition and dispatch of the *mémoires.* He emphasized the importance of such information 'as was most likely to secure for our commerce and shipping the benefits and expansion of which they are capable'.

The surviving mass of French consular reports is so huge that no inventory of them has yet been produced. The reports have been summarily ordered, divided up and scattered throughout the Archives Nationaux and the records office of the Ministry of Foreign Affairs. They constitute an important source of information for economic historians. Suffice it to say, by way of example, that, long before the Piedmontese government

---

[2] In 1681 Colbert issued his *Ordonnance sur la Marine,* which centralized the consular service, removed it from the control of the Chamber of Commerce of Marseille, and placed it under the authority of the French Admiralty. This arrangement continued until 1761, when the Bureau des Consulats was attached to the Foreign Ministry; but, as consuls still had to correspond with the Admiralty on navy matters, such utter confusion resulted that in 1766 the Bureau was returned to the control of the Admiralty. There matters rested until the Revolution.

established the statistical commission of King Carlo Alberto, the French consuls posted in Sardinia and in the mainland dominions of the House of Savoy were already, despite all the difficulties that beset them, compiling and regularly dispatching statistical tables on conditions in the provinces (Nitti, 1963, p. 16).[3]

British consular reports were not as important and did not play as significant a role as French ones. It should not be forgotten that the Victorian Consular Service was divided into the General Service, the Far Eastern Service (covering China and later Japan, Siam and Korea) and the Levant Service; each of these three branches was allocated different aims and given different instructions. Regarded as the poor relation of the Diplomatic Service, the Consular Service neither commanded respect nor enjoyed prestige. As late as 1842 Disraeli commented that 'the Consular establishment is considered a refuge for the destitute. All who are broken in fortune or reputation are made consuls' (quoted in Platt, 1963, p. 497). Moreover, throughout the nineteenth century the collection of economic information was not considered one of the major functions of a British consul. In 1898 Lord Curzon remarked that 'it is not possible and would not be desirable for every Consul to devote the whole of his official time to the furtherance of British trade in which there is still some opening left for private initiative and enterprise (quoted in Platt, 1963, p. 494). There can be no doubt, however, that in the course of the nineteenth century, especially under the pressure of competition from France and Germany, whose businessmen profited greatly from the reports submitted by their consuls, British consular reports improved considerably. Still, as late as 1904, Mr Cockerell in a Foreign Office memorandum noted that out of 188 consular officers from whom annual trade reports were expected only seventeen had sent in their reports and only eight others had written to explain the cause of delay (Platt, 1963, p. 500).

The quantity of economic information available in the mass of consular reports (especially those dating from the latter part of the nineteenth century and those of the twentieth century) was on the whole underestimated by the commercial community. In the opinion of D. C. M. Platt,

the responsibility for the comparative neglect of consular services in the last century rests principally in the fact that British manufacturers already enjoyed the advantage of a considerable network of commercial agencies abroad. Rival trading nations could not call on anything like so broad a representation and the use that their traders made of national consuls reflected their lack of alternative private resources. (1963, p. 511)

---

[3] Prior to the Revolution (1789), there were French consulates in Italy at Ajaccio, Ancona, Bastia, Cagliari, Calvi, Civitavecchia, Finale, Florence, Genoa, Leghorn, Malta, Messina, Naples, Nice, Palermo, Pesaro, Rome, Trieste, Turin and Venice. See Nitti, 1963, p. 10.

Present-day economic historians can, however, find in the British consular reports an abundance of useful information. To cite but one illustration: a Spanish historian who recently wanted to estimate the volume of exports of grapes from Andalusia found the information of the British consuls more reliable than the official data reported by the 'registros oficiales de Comercio Exterior y de Cabotaje' (Morilla Critz, 1989, p. 159).

The published series of Diplomatic and Consular Reports started in 1855. From then until 1915, they were published as Parliamentary Papers. After 1915 they appeared as reports of the Department of Overseas Trade, and after 1946 as reports of the Export Promotion Department of the Board of Trade.

5 'Semi-Public' and Church Sources

'SEMI-PUBLIC' SOURCES

The sources somewhat infelicitously and vaguely defined here as 'semi-public' are those relating to bodies such as guilds and hospitals. These two kinds of institutions, which otherwise had nothing in common, both possessed a legal character that strikes present-day observers as ambiguous inasmuch as they belong fully neither to the public nor to the private domain.

From the middle of the twelfth century onwards, people living in the emerging or re-emerging towns and cities of Europe increasingly strove to band together. This resulted in a mushrooming of associations, which in England were called 'guilds', in France *corporations*, in Germany *Zünfte*, in Italy *corporazioni*, *arti* or *università*, and in Spain *gremios*. These associations were formed not only to defend common economic interests, as Adam Smith was to argue many centuries later, but also for other purposes. At that time, towns and cities were entering a new world of economic and social development, and people venturing into the unknown feel more than most the need to stick together in order to secure their defence, to assert their identity, and to construct the institutions needed to regulate life in a new and rapidly changing world. Economic historians are interested chiefly in the documentary material produced by merchants' and trade guilds. Judged a cumbersome legacy from the Dark Ages and an obstacle to the social progress and economic liberalization advocated by the proponents of the Enlightenment, the guilds were abolished during the course of the eighteenth century. But from the twelfth to the eighteenth century they played a vital role in the creation of oligopolies and oligopsonies; in warding off the claims of particular groups of workers and preventing them from creating their own corporate organizations; in monitoring the quality of products; in professional training through apprenticeship; and in providing their members with various forms of assistance and social security. Much of the documentary material generated by such guilds was lost when they were abolished in the eighteenth century. Many documents were destroyed even earlier, either because they were deemed useless or by sheer accident. As one would expect, however, particular care was taken to preserve the guild regulations and membership registers, on which the continued existence of the organization depended, and these are mostly what have survived. Economic historians can extract a vast amount of information on social and economic matters from the guilds' regulations but they have to take great care not to fall into the trap of believing that everything was always done by the book.

As for hospitals, it should be borne in mind that the hospital as an institution was introduced to the West in the twelfth and thirteenth centuries, at the time of Europe's rebirth, and that it was modelled on similar institutions existing in the Byzantine Empire and throughout the Arab world. From its first appearance in the West until the end of the nineteenth century, the hospital was something utterly different from what it is today. In Europe until the First World War, not only the well-off but also those of modest means were treated at home. Only paupers went into hospital; and they were often glad to be admitted, even when they were not ill at all, simply to find a bed (however filthy and cramped) and a bowl of soup. It is worth remembering that the root of the word 'hospital' is the same as that of 'hostel', 'hotel' and 'hospitality'.

Hospital administration papers contain much that is of interest to social and economic historians. Such documents may

(1) provide information on the administration of a particular hospital and its running costs;
(2) make it possible to chart the movement of wages, salaries and the prices of consumer goods in periods when there were no statistical offices to record such information;
(3) supply information on the type of food and drink consumed by the poor (as opposed to the better-off, whose diets are usually much better documented);
(4) provide evidence (where the hospital admitted infants) on the extent of infant abandonment and the life expectancy of such foundlings;
(5) provide information on the kinds of illness (as identified by contemporary diagnosis) prevalent among the poor, and the relative mortality rates;
(6) supply information on the prices of the medicines and herbal remedies used at the time.

Most hospitals owned land and buildings other than those occupied by the hospital, and in such cases this property was their main source of income. Documents relating to such property, where they have survived, supply information on when and how the property was acquired and the relative contributions made by different social classes. Moreover, documents relating to the management of individual farms belonging to the hospital provide documentary material for the study of the history of agriculture.

A number of hospital archives have preserved a considerable mass of documentary material, extending over several centuries. More often, however, hospital administrators considered it 'useful' to preserve only those documents, such as deeds of gift or purchase, that proved the ownership of property. In such cases a good deal of information that would have been of value to the economic historian has been destroyed.

CHURCH RECORDS

Economic historians take a particular interest in documents of ecclesiastical origin because until recent times the Church, despite all its homilies condemning riches and praising poverty, was a leading economic and financial power. Moreover, parish records of baptisms, marriages and burials are a source of primary importance for European demographic history.

The organizational structure of the Church underwent a complex evolution over the centuries. The ecclesiastical sources of interest to economic historians are therefore diverse and widely scattered. In this short survey we shall start at the top of the hierarchy, with papal documents, and then proceed to diocesan and monastic records and parish registers.

The quantity and quality of papal documents naturally reflects the evolution of the internal organization of the Church (on the Vatican archives see especially Renouard, 1952, repr. 1968). For the early Middle Ages, the papal records consist of a few simple series of documents. From the end of the thirteenth century, however, and especially following the transfer of the papal seat to Avignon in March 1309, papal administration and revenue collection were centralized, producing a greatly expanded bureaucracy and hence a huge increase in documentation. In 1881, when Pope Leo XIII opened the Vatican archives for research, the first scholars that ventured out onto that ocean of documents did so in order to investigate the spiritual, liturgical, dogmatic, political and diplomatic aspects of the Church's history. But it was soon realized that most of the surviving documents contained information of an economic and financial nature. A single example will suffice: of the eight large series of documents relating to the fourteenth century, no fewer than four concern the financial affairs of the Holy See.[1] The scale of these financial affairs, furthermore, was enormous: not only in terms of the sums involved, but also in terms of the geographical area to which they related, stretching from Iceland to Cyprus and from Poland to Portugal. From every corner of this huge area, the Pope received an annual tribute known as Peter's pence. In

---

[1] The eight series (1) *Registra Vaticana*; (2) *Registra Avenionensia*; (3) *Archivi di Castel Sant'Angelo*; (4) *Instrumenta Miscellanea*; (5) *Collectoriae*; (6) *Introitus et Exitus*; (7) *Obligationes et Solutiones*; (8) *Suppliche*. The economic and financial series are (4), (5), (6) and (7).

addition, in times of need he could exact contributions from holders of benefices, and from abbeys, monasteries and dioceses. From John XXII (d. 1334) onwards, the Pope also claimed the assets of all the principal holders of benefices upon their death. Parallel to the registers relating to revenues there were of course the registers of papal outgoings: subsidies for the Crusades, and expenditure on military expeditions, embassies, journeys by papal legates, building work and the upkeep of the papal court – including the purchase of food, wine (which had to be of good quality), fabrics, and so forth. This extraordinary mountain of documentation not only helps us chart the fluctuations in papal finances, but also supplies valuable information on the currencies circulating in the various countries of Europe, on exchange rates, on rates of interest paid and received, on the costs and times involved in transporting goods and in moving people and money, on the dealings and operations of the Florentine and Sienese banks entrusted with the transfer of funds from one part of Europe to another, and on prices, wages and salaries. The Pope also minted his own currency; the relevant accounts and other information relating to this important economic activity are contained in the series of documents entitled *Introitus et Exitus*.

By 1902 the Görresgesellschaft had begun publishing the papal financial documents in a series entitled *Vatikanische Quellen zur Geschichte der päpstlichen Hof- und Finanzverwaltung* (Vatican sources for the history of the administration of the papal court and finances). Despite its many shortcomings, this series opened the door to an inexhaustible stream of investigations of the greatest interest for the economic and financial history not only of the Church but of Europe in general.

The importance of papal documentation for economic historians declines steadily with the approach of the twentieth century, in line with the diminishing importance of the Church within the overall framework of the European and world economies. The nineteenth-century documents are really only of interest for the economic and social history of the Papal State, which, as the century progressed, shrank away until it was confined to Vatican City.

The diocesan and monastic documents of interest to the economic historian are mostly concerned with the management of farms belonging to the diocese, abbey or monastery in question: material that relates above all to the history of agriculture. In the case of diocesan documents, records of the bishop's pastoral visits also deserve mention, since in many cases they contain rough estimates of the population of the parishes visited, supplied by the parish priest. Early in the Middle Ages many abbeys acted as financial institutions, lending money whenever the opportunity arose. The records relating to this form of activity provide economic historians with precious information on the evolution of credit prior to the appearance and development of private banks in the eleventh and twelfth centuries.

Many monastic archives also contain registers of the community's expenditure. These registers provide a basis for the analysis of patterns of consumption of food and drink in monastic communities; they also supply series of prices and wages that span centuries. Giuseppe Parenti's classic work *Prime ricerche sulla rivoluzione dei prezzi in Firenze* (Initial Inquiries into the Price Revolution in Florence) which relates to the sixteenth century, is based on information gleaned from registers of expenditure compiled at the monastery of S. Maria Regina Coeli. But, after the papal documents, from the sixteenth century onwards the most important Church documents for economic historians in general, and for historians of population in particular, are the mass of parish registers in which baptism, marriages and burials were entered.[2]

To gain a clearer understanding of the importance of these documents, one must remember that no European state succeeded in establishing a central registry of births, marriages and deaths until the nineteenth century. As we saw in Part II, chapter 3, during the fifteenth and sixteenth centuries a number of Italian cities organized the collection of information on deaths. But this was achieved only at town and city level: rural areas remained outside the net. In the first half of the sixteenth century both France and England turned their attention to the collection of vital statistics, but the best that they could do was to exert pressure on the parish clergy to gather the relevant data with diligence and regularity. In the Grand Duchy of Tuscany during the sixteenth and seventeenth centuries, a census of the population was conducted every ten years, but the state never attempted to collect information on births, marriages and deaths as they occurred. The somewhat paradoxical reason for this situation was straightforward: the Church, with its network of parishes, possessed the local organization that the state lacked.

The Church's motives for keeping parish registers had nothing to do with demography. It began and continued this practice for an eminently pastoral reason: to prevent marriages between people who were close relatives. The earliest pastoral ordinance on this matter, issued by the Bishop of Nantes on 3 June 1406, is quite explicit.

Parish registers reaching back to the fourteenth and fifteenth centuries are rather few and far between. Parish priests really only began to maintain up-to-date registers in the sixteenth century. In England, Thomas Cromwell issued an ordinance in 1538 ordering the priests of the country's more than 10,000 parishes to register accurately and regularly 'every baptism, marriage, and burial' (see Cox, 1910). The fact that the Crown, in the person of Henry VIII, had just made itself head of the new Anglican Church gave this ordinance added weight. Although there were some cases of laxness and negligence, it has been rightly observed that 'no other

---

[2] I have deliberately written 'baptisms' and 'burials' rather than 'births' and 'deaths'. Parish priests did not record the births of babies who died before they could be baptized, just as they did not record births of non-Christians (e.g. Jews) who were not baptized. Similarly, parish priests recorded the deaths only of those who were buried in their church or its grounds. Those who were sentenced to death, belonged to the Jewish faith or died of plague could not be buried in church grounds and consequently did not appear in parish registers.

Table 4   Dates of the earliest registers of baptisms, marriages and burials in selected Italian dioceses

	Date of earliest registers of		
Dioceses	Baptisms	Marriages	Burials
Acqui	1566	1569	1533
Agrigento	1550	1550	1550
Aosta	1475	1570	1553
Arezzo	1314	1565	1373
Asti	1570	1564	1570
Bari	1498	1564	1500
Benevento	1604	1618	1617
Bergamo	1502	1562	1571
Biella	1553	1570	1571
Bologna	1459	1564	1565
Borgo S. Sepolcro	1475	1522	1377
Brescia	1533	1564	1567
Casale Monferrato	1564	1564	1494
Catania	1588	1564	?
Como	1560	1564	1564
Cortona	1517	1565	1537
Crema	1521	1586	1540
Cremona	1369	1569	1604
Cuneo	1468	1575	1602
Empoli	1482	1564	1476
Faenza	1594	1565	1593
Florence	1428	1480	1385
Foggia	1571	1575	1629
Forlì	1553	1562	1550
Genoa	1554	1558	1558
Gubbio	1571	1559	1609
Imola	1547	1563	1564
Ivrea	1473	1583	1606
Mantua	1547	1581	1496
Messina	1561	1585	1591
Milan	1460	1560	1452
Naples	1525	1559	1564
Novara	1553	1564	1574
Orvieto	1515	1597	1597
Padua	1564	1564	1565
Palermo	1499	1499	1499
Parma	1459	?	?
Pavia	1459	1544	1564
Perugia	1476	1564	1463
Pescia	1487	1560	1508

Continued

Table 4   *(Continued)*

Dioceses	Baptisms	Date of earliest registers of Marriages	Burials
Pistoia	1471	1543	1457
Prato	1482	1585	1557
Ravenna	1492	1565	1594
Rome	1540	1560	?
Salerno and Acerno	1590	1590	1590
Saluzzo	1560	1581	1595
S. Miniato	1523	1525	1522
Sassari	1576	1585	1609
Savona	1530	1564	1546
Siena	1381	1500	1500
Spoleto	1537	1623	1615
Syracuse and Ragusa	1542	1556	1556
Todi	1582	1567	1591
Trapani	1528	1564	1562
Trento	1548	1565	1581
Treviso	1398	1566	1585
Trieste and Capodistria	1527	1604	1670
Turin	1551	1577	1577
Udine	1369	1566	1281
Urbino	1526	1610	1610
Venice	1563	1563	1543
Verona	1533	1511	1529
Vicenza	1564	1564	1584
Volterra	1525	1550	1550

Source: Corsini, 1971–2, pp. 651–4.

country possesses such a considerable number of registers of fair quality from such an early date' (Wrigley and Schofield, 1981).

In France, and above all in Italy, the situation was much more varied. In France in 1539, Villers Cotterêts issued an ordinance that was similar to Cromwell's but that proved less effective. As for Italy, C. A. Corsini drew up a table (a simplified version of which appears here as table 4) showing that matters here took their usual chaotic course. The fact is that the Catholic Church in France, Italy and Spain was very slow to take clear and precise measures. More than forty diocesan synods and provincial councils turned their attention to the question of parish registers between 1406 and 1558 without managing to come up with a definite policy. The Council of Trent (1563) was unwilling to place the three kinds of registers (baptisms, marriages and burials) on the same footing: registers of baptisms were referred to as documents already in use; the keeping of registers of marriages was prescribed; and registers of burials were completely overlooked. It was not until the *Rituale Romanum* of 1614 that the Catholic Church made it compulsory for all parish priests to keep all three kinds of register.

In other countries such registers were begun even later. In the Netherlands very few parish registers were kept before 1650. In Estonia they began to be generally maintained in 1660, and in Poland not before 1700.

Altogether, an enormous quantity of registers was produced in Europe, and although many were lost through neglect, carelessness or accident, many others survived. The major problem is how to make use of this material. Historians face two main problems. First, there is the geographical dispersion of the material itself: as we have already noted, in sixteenth-century England there were more than 10,000 parishes, and in France and Italy the number was considerably higher. The task of collecting and collating data scattered across tens of thousands of parishes and covering several centuries is one of gigantic proportions, enough to keep battalions of scholars busy for generations. Secondly, the lack of information on the size of the population and its age structure severely limits the use to which all the data on births, marriages and deaths can be put.

The Swedish Church after 1628, but more generally from 1686 onwards, supplemented its annual registration of baptisms, marriages and burials with an annual registration of the parish population by household, noting changes of address and assessing the literacy and religious education of the inhabitants. These registers or *husförhörslängder* (a kind of improved version of the *status animarum*, or lists of souls, of the Mediterranean parishes) were not always preserved, but from 1749 onwards the information that they contained was passed on to state officials, who used them to compile a nationwide record. This initiative gave Sweden the most fully developed system of demographic registration and documentation anywhere in Europe at that time.

There were no comparable developments anywhere else on the European continent, but following the end of the Second World War a growing number of historians took an increasingly active interest in the use that might be made of parish registers. The French were among the first to stress the extreme irregularity over time in the numbers of baptisms and especially of burials: these were used as evidence of the frequency and gravity of the so-called *crises de mortalité* of pre-industrial times, highlighting the extent to which humanity was still at the mercy of untamed nature (see especially Meuvret, 1946; and Goubert, 1960). This was an intelligent piece of interpretation, but technically still very elementary: all that was involved was the aggregation of registered baptisms and burials for successive periods of a week, a month, six months or a year. In the meantime, however, a surprise was being prepared.

In 1956 Michel Feury and Louis Henry published a slim and modestly entitled booklet, *Le Manuel de dépouillement et d'exploitation de l'état civil ancien*, which introduced a completely new methodology called 'family reconstruction'. Based on the information contained in parish registers, this approach enabled scholars to work out rates of birth, marriage and death, average age at marriage, spacing of births, average age of the mother at the birth of the last child, with a degree of sophistication that had previously only been achieved for contemporary industrial societies through the use of the demographic material provided by modern censuses and registers of vital statistics (Fleury and Henry, 1956; 1965). The new methodology was rightly called 'revolutionary' by M. W. Flinn (1981, p. 1) and its introduction paved the way in France for a long phase of enthusiastic study of parish registers. This work, of which Flinn (1981) has provided an excellent summary, considerably advanced our knowledge of demographic trends in the sixteenth, seventeenth and eighteenth centuries.

The enthusiasm generated by Fleury and Henry's work was contagious. In England, a working group on demographic history was formed under the direction of E. A. Wrigley, R. S. Schofield and Peter Laslett. This group, the Cambridge Group for the History of Population and Social Structure, launched a nationwide movement. Up and down the country, volunteers from across the class spectrum and from a variety of social groupings – from pensioners to school-teachers to chemists – took on the task of collecting, in accordance with a predetermined framework, the data contained in surviving parish registers. These data were then sent to Cambridge to be processed at national level by the working group. Everyone expected the project to culminate in the appearance of a history of the English population founded on the family-reconstruction method. When, however, an outline of the demographic history of England was published (Wrigley and Schofield, 1981), it was found that a third method, developed by the Cambridge Group itself, had been used. This method, known as 'back projection' (or 'inverse projection'), operated, as its name indicates, by working backwards: starting with the censuses available for the nineteenth century, and relying on data from parish registers processed using the aggregative technique, it sought to reconstruct for earlier dates hypothetical totals and demographic structures to which the data on baptisms, marriages and burials contained in the registers could be related.

Each of the three methods has its own strengths and weaknesses. Family reconstruction is technically the most sophisticated method, yet it is terribly time-consuming and cannot be applied to parishes with a mobile population (emigration and/or immigration). It is therefore not suitable for urban parishes and is most usefully applied to relatively isolated rural parishes.

6 Private Sources

Private documents of interest to economic historians come in all shapes and sizes, from servants' shopping lists to the accounts of multinational companies. The scope and variety of this material means that there is little point in attempting to provide representative examples of different types. If, in defiance of the dictates of prudence and good sense, mention is made here of some of the more important types of private document available to economic historians, it is to give the reader an idea, however vague and partial, of the material that economic historians consult in their effort to reconstruct the economies of the past.

Private sources reflect, even more eloquently than public, semi-public or ecclesiastical ones, the level of development attained by the society in which they were produced. In this respect, a comparison of Italian, English and Russian sources for past centuries is revealing. Among the various mediaeval Italian sources available to economic historians, there is a plentiful supply of registers of accounts and commercial letters from merchant and banking companies: this is at once an index and a reflection of the high degree of mercantile development achieved by northern Italy during the Middle Ages. For mediaeval England, there is an abundance of documents referring to manorial management, but only a few private sources documenting the activity of merchants; the only sizable body of documents of this type is the collection of papers relating to the Cely family, staple merchants at the end of the fifteenth century (Malden, 1900; Hanham, 1985). This lack of documentation reflects the slow development of trade and banking in mediaeval England. As regards Russia, it is worth quoting A. Kahan's remarks:

> for Russian history before the nineteenth century most of the surviving documents concern activities in one way or another connected with the government rather than with private contractual relationships or other dealings among the citizens themselves. . . . There are relatively few private collections of documents that would provide quantitative materials for historical studies. The surviving documents pertain mostly to large landed estates and for the nineteenth century to business firms. There

146

is a conspicuous scarcity of documentation left by social groups, by the urban merchants and artisans and by the peasants who wrote only with the plough on the soil. (1972, p. 361)

To impose some kind of order on the following account, it seems advisabe to categorize the available forms of private documentation as follows: (1) family sources; (2) notarial sources; (3) company sources; (4) travel accounts; (5) gazettes and newspapers; and (6) miscellaneous sources.

FAMILY SOURCES

Of the various kinds of family sources, registers that keep a running account of the expenditures of single families are of particular interest. Such documents provide a mass of reliable information on prices and wages; patterns of nutrition and other kinds of consumption; the availability of domestic service; expenditure on education, health, and travel; and investments in land, urban property and public debt. In short, they provide information on the level and structure of demand. Unfortunately, up till the end of the eighteenth century almost all such documents refer to families of the nobility (and in England the gentry), or to those of the well-to-do merchant and professional classes. Very few families of artisans[1] and practically no labouring or peasant families, kept such accounts. In order to reconstruct the typical budget of a group of common people prior to the eighteenth century, Brown and Hopkins (1956, p. 297) had to make do with the accounts book of a community comprising two priests and their servant in Bridport (Dorset) spanning the years 1453–60. It was not until the end of the eighteenth century that the scholars and philanthropists D. Davies and P. Eden, who took an interest in poverty, surveyed the family budgets of sixty families of ordinary people in the villages and small towns of southern England (Davies, 1795; Eden, 1797).

NOTARIAL SOURCES

Notarial sources are only available for Southern Europe. There have always been two Europes: one of butter, beer and open fields, and one of olive oil, wine and closed fields. The former was also the Europe of the seal, the latter that of the notary. At the beginning of the fourteenth century, Baumgartenberg, a German, wrote in his *Formularius de Modo Pensandi*, 'in Lombardy and in Tuscany, public deeds are written out by

---

[1] One interesting survival is the expenses book of the painter Lorenzo Lotto (*Libro di spese diverse*), which contains material of interest to both economic history and art history.

Plate 10 Notarial protocol of Oberto Scriba de Mercato, a Genoese notary (Genoa State Archive)

public notaries. Seals are not affixed to such documents, but the notary inscribes his own sign and that is enough . . . this doesn't happen in, Germany' (quoted in Rockinger, 1863, p. 766). In England, the legate Otto, addressing the Council of the Church of England and Wales held in London in April 1237, explicitly stated that 'publici notarii non existunt' ('public notaries don't exist') in England and, again, 'tabellionum usus in regno Anglie non habetur' (in the Kingdom of England they don't make use of notaries'). Canon 32 of the Council states 'tabellionum usus in regno Anglie non habetur propter quod magis ad sigilla recurri auctentica est necesse' ('in the Kingdom of England there is no use of notaries because it is necessary to have recourse to official seals'). (Cheney, 1972, p. 12; Powicke and Cheney, 1964, pt I, p. 257.) In other words, in Southern Europe the notary was a *persona publica*, and the notarial deed was (and still is) deemed to constitute legal proof of the facts certified. In Northern Europe, to be accepted as probative, documents had to bear the official seals rather than notarial certification.

Italian-style notaries made their first appearance in Lombard Italy in the late seventh and early eighth century, and by the eleventh century were widely accepted (Petrucci, 1958, pp. 7–25). Around this time the use of notaries spread from the Italian peninsula into south-eastern France. In Lyon around 1260, public notaries were still rather rare, but during the 1280s their number multiplied rapidly (Fédou, 1964, pp. 142ff). Their northward progress, however, went no further, and northern France, along with the other countries of Northern Europe, remained seal territory.

The registers on which notarial deeds were written were called in Italian *protocolli* (see plate 10) and the deeds entered on these 'protocols' were termed *imbreviature*, since they reported only the brief essentials of the transaction. As Armando Sapori (1955a) has written, visits to the notary proceeded as follows. The client or clients set out the nature of their business in the presence of witnesses. The notary wrote down the particulars in his notebook and then asked if his clients wanted a fully drafted document, i.e. a deed written out on a strip of parchment and authenticated by the inscription of the notary's name and capacity and his mark (a personal symbol used in place of a signature). Mostly, and especially in minor cases involving persons not belonging to the merchant class, the party or parties would forgo a full draft in order to avoid too great an expense. For, unlike the straightforward *imbreviatura*, which was relatively inexpensive, the full document, owing to the cost of the material and to the scribe's fee, was very costly.

Mediaeval notarial protocols are important to economic historians principally because throughout the Middle Ages people in Southern Europe regularly reported to notaries for a great number of transactions, including trifling ones that nobody today would dream of making the object of a legal document. Notarial protocols contain inventories of craft workshops, chemists' stores, libraries, country and town dwellings and their furnishings and fittings; loan and pawn contracts; deeds of sale for goods, slaves, animals, work implements, houses, workshops, land; contracts of sale on credit; lease and rent agreements on houses, land, workshops, work implements; labour and service contracts; promises of marriage; marriage settlements; promises of peace between enemies or feuding families; deeds founding trade companies and manufacturing firms; contracts of commenda,[2] of exchange, of insurance; commissions for labour, and for works of art; transport contracts; and so on. The readiness of people in the Middle Ages to call on the notary even for transactions involving small amounts of money means that, if one now surveys the surviving notarial protocols, one encounters all the characters of mediaeval society, from the noble, the rich tradesman and the doctor to craftsmen, the labourer, the poverty-stricken widow and the wretched peasant: all captured in the act of completing a transaction, of taking a decision. The introductions to these notarial deeds are themselves powerfully evocative, conveying a concrete sense of the situation: 'In nomini Domini amen. On such a day of such a year of such an indiction, at the well in the great square or on the church steps, at the hour of vespers, in the presence of the following witnesses. . . .'

Of the numerous surviving notarial protocols from mediaeval Italy, southern France and Catalonia, the Genoese protocols are deservedly the most famous, both for their antiquity and for their contents, which reflect the feverish economic activity of a city that at the time was at the forefront of European economic development. Thanks to close Italian–American co-operation, the protocols of the notaries Giovanni Scriba (1186–90), Guglielmo Cassinese (1190–2), Bonvillano (1198), Giovanni di Guiberto (1200–11) and Lanfranco (1202–26) have been saved from a state of neglect that endangered their survival, and published (see Chiaudano, 1938–40; Hall et al., 1939; Eierman et al., 1939; and Part I, chapter 3).

To appreciate the full importance of these sources, it should be borne in mind that prior to the mid thirteenth century most private deeds relate to ecclesiastical bodies and to the fortunes that they had amassed. Furthermore, these documents refer mainly to rural properties. By contrast, some 90 per cent of the deeds registered in the Genoese cartularies refer to transactions between secular persons or bodies, and, although many have to do with land and buildings, the majority relate to commercial or banking operations. This affords a view of the birth and development of mediaeval mercantile capitalism, and makes it possible to study the earliest phases in the development of trade between the Mediterranean and Northern Europe, whose economic centre of gravity was located in Flanders and whose point of contact with the South was the Champagne fairs.

---

[2] In a commenda agreement one party entrusts capital to another party, who is to use it in an overseas commercial venture and to return it together with a previously agreed share of the profit. Any loss on the capital is borne exclusively by the investor; the travelling party, in turn, loses the reward for his labour if no profit is made. See Lopez and Raymond 1955, pp. 174ff.

COMPANY SOURCES

In relation to company documents, a distinction has to be drawn between sources that relate to farms and sources that relate to merchant, manufacturing and banking companies.

We have already seen (Part II, chapter 5) that many of the surviving documents relating to farms come from diocesan, monastic or hospital archives. There are two reasons for this: first, religious bodies and hospitals generally owned large amounts of landed property; and, secondly, the continuity of these institutions' existence favoured the survival of their deeds and administrative documents. There are far fewer sources on secularly owned farms, and they tend to refer to much later dates, although England is an exception in this respect. The sources of greatest interest to economic historians tend to be inventories of property and accounts books. As regards the latter, it should not be forgotten that, in England at least, fully fledged manorial book keeping was introduced at the end of the twelfth and the beginning of the thirteenth century. The most ancient example of manorial book-keeping to have survived is provided by the accounts of the bishops of Winchester, dating from 1208-9. In the following decades this new and more detailed type of farm accounting spread rapidly.

Overall, however, it has to be said that the inventories of farm property and the farm accounts that have survived refer as a rule to large and medium-size properties, whether ecclesiastical or secular in ownership. Unfortunately, there is very little we know about the operation and economics of peasant smallholdings.

A very early set of non-agricultural accounts comes from Pompeii. In July 1875, in house 26 of region V of insula 1, beneath a layer of plaster and earth, among the remains of what must once have been a wooden strongbox, were discovered 151 originally waxed tablets, measuring 12-15 by 10-12 cm, on which accounts had been engraved using a stylus. The tablets may be dated at around AD 50-60. Careful study has revealed that the accounts refer to 153 operations carried out by an *argentarius* named L. Caecilius Jucundus. The closest modern-day equivalent of the *argentarius* of Roman times would be the banker, but the equation is far from exact, owing to the enormous institutional and material differences between financial markets then and now. Be that as it may, to judge by the accounts recorded on the tablets, most of L. Caecilius Jucundus's transactions were based on advances of money to persons wishing to purchase goods at the public auctions in Pompeii (Andreau, 1974). To my knowledge, these Pompeiian tablets are the only example of private business accounts referring to non-farming activities to have survived from the Roman world.

In the primitive world of the early Middle Ages, allusions to trading and manufacturing activities appear on the *polyptyques* discussed in Part II,

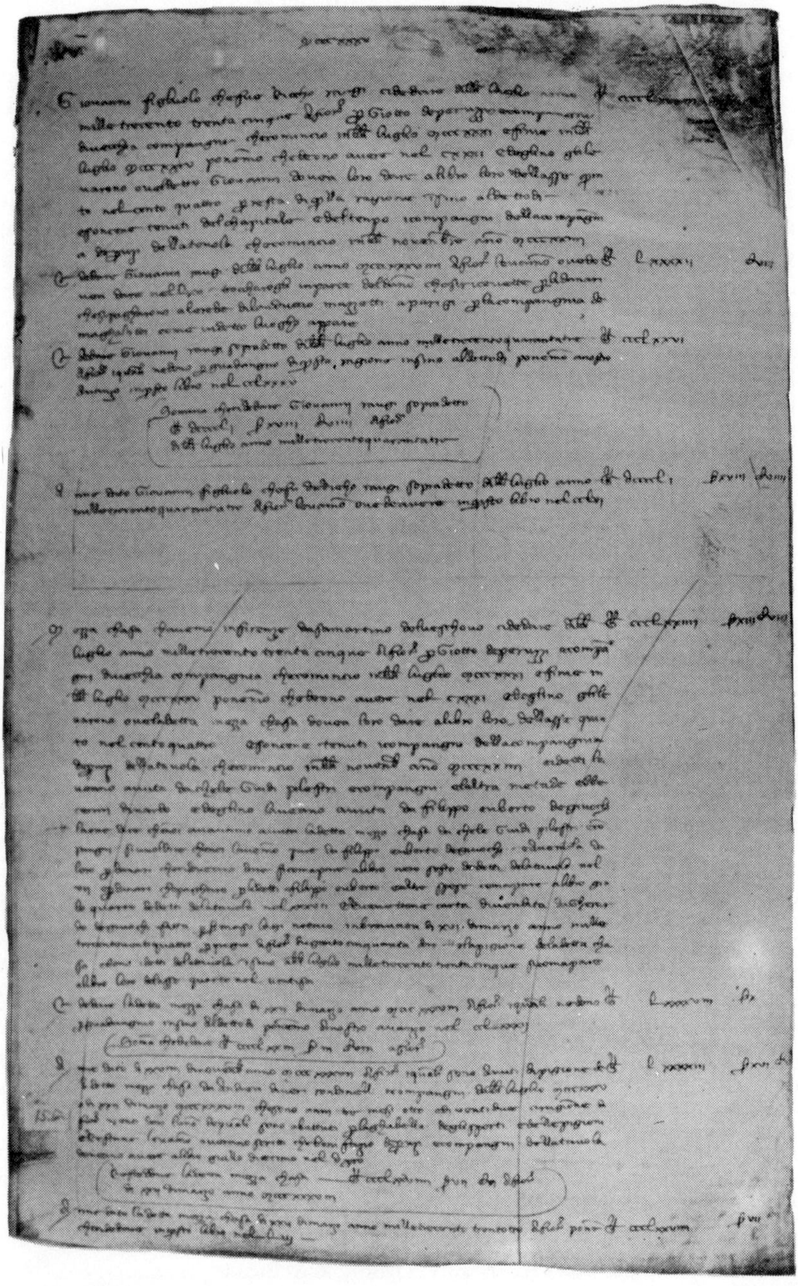

Plate 11 Page of an account book kept by the Peruzzi company, from Sapori (ed.), 1934

chapter 1. This suggests that the activities in question were largely conducted within the framework of the manorial economy. Outside the manors, there were a few *homines duri*[3] who, travelling in convoy for self-defence, ventured to travel through Europe for trading purposes; but heaven only knows if and how they kept accounts.

Fully developed systems of private documentation for trading, banking and manufacturing operations only emerged in the thirteenth century. Before that century drew to a close there appeared with increasing frequency the new figure of the stable 'merchant', operating from a single base and using agents, correspondents and branches. This more modern type of business-man began to force out and replace the traditional wandering merchant who travelled with his wares. Tuscany was at the forefront of this development.

Typically, the records of a medium- or large-scale Tuscan company would comprise correspondence; private papers (i.e. deeds relating to company contracts, contracts of commenda, limited partnership contracts, hire agreements, insurance, and so on); account registers;[4] reference and instruction manuals, abacus books, and maritime maps known as *portolani* because they showed the location of the main ports.

A lot of this documentation has survived, but much has been lost or destroyed. From the fourteenth century, the main sources to have survived are the accounts books of large companies such as the Peruzzi (a contemporary giant with a capital of 103,000 gold florins; fifteen branches, scattered right across Europe from London to Cyprus; and a staff of ninety *fattori* or agents), the Alberti, and the Gianfigliazzi. The accounts books of these firms (see plate 11) were published several decades ago by Armando Sapori (1934; 1952; 1946). In the case of the Medici bank, accounts books covering without a break a period of more than half a century – from 26 March 1397, the year in which the bank was founded, to 24 March 1451 – have survived. The few fragments of correspondence available from this period are, however, wholly inadequate. This is particularly unfortunate in so far as a more ample correspondence might have clarified and made greater sense of the figures contained in the accounts books. After 1450 the situation was reversed: surviving correspondence of the Medici bank is much more plentiful, but the accounts books are in extremely short supply (De Roover, 1970).

The importance of the Datini archive in Prato, which dates from the second half of the fourteenth century, derives from its exceptional

---

[3] The expression *homines duri* was used by Alperto di Metz to describe the merchants of the early Middle Ages; see Vercauteren, 1970.

[4] Accounts registers generally included the *memoriale*, a kind of diary; the 'secret book' or 'company book'; the 'book of incomings and outgoings' or cash book; the book of inventories; miscellaneous other books. The 'secret book' included the 'founding deeds' of the company, accounts of capital sums allocated to branches, accounts of members and of depositors, accounts of interest paid on deposits, accounts of salaries, and profit and loss accounts. The 'secret book' was considered the most important book and would be jealously guarded by one of the company members.

completeness. Francesco di Marco Datini da Prato's company was of medium proportions, small in comparison with giants such as the Bardi, Peruzzi, Acciaiuoli, Alberti and Medici concerns. Francesco di Marco[5] was a tireless worker who spent all night as well as all day writing letters, perusing his firms' correspondence, and taking decisions. And he wouldn't throw away a single scrap of paper with writing on it. Lacking an heir, he left his considerable fortune to an institution that he had founded – the Ceppo – devoted to providing support for the needy of Prato. He also left his archive, consisting of more than 120,000 commercial letters (as well as 11,000 personal letters), over 600 books of accounts, a variety of reference books, and miscellaneous documents (see Sapori, 1955; and Melis, 1972). This mass of documents stands out from other, similar collections for its extraordinary completeness: books of accounts, all company and personal correspondence, and even the reference books. That it has all survived practically intact is something of a miracle. In 1560 a certain Alessandro Guardini testified that he had managed to retrace books from the Datini archive previously believed lost, and that he had rearranged in 'their cabinets in Francesco di Marco's Ceppo all the papers he possessed in Italy and outside Italy'. Subsequently, however, to make room for the administrative papers of Datini's charitable institution, the registers and the papers of Francesco di Marco were removed from the archive and cast into a stair cupboard, where they were accidentally rediscovered in 1870 (Bensa, 1928, pp. 1–3).

North of the Alps, company accounting for a long time remained much less developed than in Italy. In the first half of the sixteenth century, Matthäus Schwarz (plate 12), head of accounting at the mighty Fugger company, wrote,

> book-keeping is comparable to a money box; it is a practical, sophisticated, well-ordered, precise, entertaining, beautiful and succinct art applied to the work of merchants, and it was invented by the Italians. But this art that makes people rich is little appreciated by us Germans and especially by those who think they can make do without it. (Quoted in Weitnauer, 1981, p. 174)

It appears, besides, that the Italians were not particularly keen to teach foreigners a technique that gave them an unquestionable business advantage. Schwarz put it thus:

> I, Matthäus Schwarz, citizen of Augsburg, when as a young man I was in Italy in the years, 1514, 1515, 1516, I first stayed with reputable merchants in Milan and heard of their writings and of their book-keeping, but when they talked about book-keeping I did not know what the term meant. When I realized that it was something of use to merchants I sought to investigate the subject, but I found the world treacherous and I was badly directed. I began my quest for information in Milan

---

[5] On Francesco di Marco see the delightful biography by Origo (1957).

but I did not succeed in finding any teacher there, and I was told that good teachers might be found in Genoa. I went in search of them but I was ill served. I was then advised to go to Venice. I went and found a teacher, Antonio Mariafior, who had a great reputation. Despite this, when I later left him, I deemed him shallow. But, as I was convinced that I possessed a good knowledge of the art, in September 1516 I left Venice for the Fuggers in Augsburg, where everybody considered me an expert. But, when it came to the point, I realized I knew little or nothing. (Quoted in Weitnauer, 1981, pp. 183–4)

Plate 12 Portrait of Matthäus Schwarz, chief book-keeper of the Fugger company, by Christoph Amberger (Thyssen-Bornemisza collection, Lugano)

When Schwarz wrote this, things were, however, already changing rapidly. It is almost impossible for any group to maintain indefinitely an absolute monopoly over a particular body of technical knowhow. On the initiative of Schwarz, a number of important innovations were in fact introduced into the Fugger company's book-keeping practices. Jacob Fugger also paid particular attention to commercial correspondence. He achieved such results in this area that on more than one occasion Emperor Maximilian turned to the Fugger company to forward urgent dispatches.

Current economic theories stress the role and importance of information in business decisions and in economic affairs in general. For mediaeval and Renaissance merchants, the letters they received from agents, colleagues and other correspondents constituted the principal source of up-to-date information: these letters touched on business, rates of exchange, currencies, prices, market conditions, political news, economic predictions, the reliability of communication channels, and general items of news and gossip on the country, the princes and the court. It is not hard to understand the attention merchants paid this correspondence, the continual effort they made to ensure that letters were forwarded promptly, or their jealous zeal to prevent their correspondence from falling into the hands of competitors and rivals. These letters, the main source of information for merchants of the time, are now a precious and reliable source of information for present-day historians. This accounts for the interest that economic historians take in this type of documentation. Ugo Tucci (1957) has published the letters of the Venetian merchant Andrea Berengo spanning the period 1553–6. Felipe Ruiz Martín (1967) has published 476 trading letters of the Ruiz de Medina del Campo company of Spain, representing correspondence between the head office and the company's agent in Florence. V. Vazquez de Prada (1960–4) has published 1,638 letters from the correspondence of the same company with Antwerp. Approximately 10,500 trading letters relating to the Maresco and David families have survived. Of these, Henry Roseveare (1987) has selected and published 480, spanning the period 1664–80. But all the letters that have been published – indeed, all those that are known to us – represent only a tiny part of that vast mass of trading correspondence still kept in public and private archives.

As a store of basic everyday information and for use in the training of new agents and employees, mediaeval merchants relied on internal company manuals. These brought together information on products from particular areas, on transport costs, on customs duties, on exchange rates, currencies, weights and measurements used in different markets, and so forth. The introduction to the most famous of these manuals, the *Pratica della mercatura* (The practice of trade), by Francesco Balducci Pegolotti, an agent of the powerful Florentine de' Bardi company, runs as follows:

In nomine Domini amen. This book is called the book of detailed information about countries and measures of merchandises and about other things that merchants from different parts of the world and with different knowledge must know as they practice trade and monetary exchange. The book provides information on the different prices of commodities in different countries and one will learn how a merchandise can be better than another, where commodities come from, and we will show how to preserve them for as long as possible. (Tr. A. Evans, 1936)

Some of these handwritten manuals from the fourteenth and fifteenth centuries have been published. Most of them are Italian (see Orlandini, 1925; F. Borlandi, 1936; Pegolotti, 1936 edn; A. Borlandi, 1963; Ciano, 1964; Dini, 1980), but a few hail from other parts of Europe (for instance, Müller, 1934). Following the invention of printing, similar manuals were compiled, printed and put on sale with considerable success. Between 1589 and 1640, John Browne's *The Merchant Avizo* went through six editions, and J. De Savary's *Le Parfait Negociant*, published at the end of the seventeenth century, was also frequently reprinted. These manuals too are a useful source of information for economic historians, especially as regards weights, measures, currencies and rates of exchange.

On 22 September 1599, 101 London merchants held a meeting at which they undertook to pay sums totalling £30,133 6s. 8d. 'to venter in the pretended voiage to the Easte Indies'. On 31 December 1600, letters patent bearing the signature of Queen Elizabeth recognized the creation of a trading company called the Governor and Merchants of London Trading into the East Indies. The new company's first convoy of ships set sail from London in February 1601. Thus was born that giant of intercontinental commerce that later became famous under the name of the East India Company. In Holland in 1602, hundreds of merchants, under the leadership of Johan van Oldenbarnevelt, put together a starting capital of 6.5 million guilders (at least ten times the value of the £30,133 raised by the English company) and founded the Vereinigde Oostindische Compagnie (see plate 13), later the chief rival of the London East India Company. The archives of these two colossi have come down to us and are an extremely rich source of qualitative and quantitative information on the history of economic and commercial (but also political, naval and military) relations between Europe and the East during the seventeenth, eighteenth and nineteenth centuries.

Each of these companies had a head office in its home country and a local headquarters in Asia, entrusted with the execution of directives from head office and with the organization and monitoring of the company's trade within Asia itself. As a result, records have survived in two separate collections. In many respects these two collections duplicate one another: for example, the original dispatches sent from the Bombay office of the East India Company to the company's head office in London are now kept in the London archive, while copies of them are housed in the archive in Bombay; and vice versa for dispatches sent from London to Bombay. This means that gaps owing to losses at the one office can often be remedied by consulting the archives of the other. For example, in the 1930s

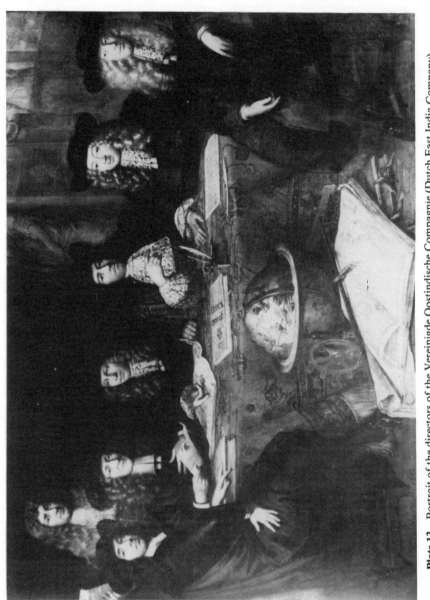

Plate 13 Portrait of the directors of the Vereinigde Oostindische Compagnie (Dutch East India Company), by Jan de Baen (Westfries Museum, Hoorn)

some overzealous employees at the London archive decided when reordering the records to get rid of material they deemed insignificant. Luckily, there were copies of most of this material in Bombay.

'The documentation relating to the administration of the East India Company in India is probably the best historical material in the world.' This view, expressed by James Grant Duff in 1826, is an overstatement, yet there is not the slightest doubt that the historical material kept in the European and Asian archives of the East India Company and the Vereinigde Oostindische Compagnie is a source of exceptional importance for economic history.

The London archive of the East India Company is divided into five sections:

(1) a section relating to the activities of the London head office;
(2) a section on the offices in India (Bengal, Agra, the North-Western Provinces, Punjab, Madras, Bombay);
(3) a section on countries other than India;
(4) a section on shipping;
(5) a section on staff.

The first and second sections consist of minutes of meetings and committees (or, in the case of the second section, councils), correspondence, accounts, and miscellaneous documents (Foster, 1919, repr. 1966). In all, there are approximately 175,502 registers, files and document envelopes, including roughly 10,000 log books and account books relating to 4,348 voyages made between 1660 and 1834 by 1,403 ships (India Office Library, 1986).

The Company's Bombay archive comprises 98,000 registers and more than 300,000 document files, subdivided as follows:

(1) Factory and Residency records;
(2) Bombay Presidency records;
(3) documents relating to missions and committees;
(4) dispatches;
(5) miscellaneous material. (Dighe, 1954, Introduction).

The European archive collection of the Vereinigde Oostindische Compagnie is housed in the Algemeen Rijksarchief in The Hague, and the Asian collection in the Batavia archive.

In the fourteenth century, large- or medium-scale Tuscan trading companies did not specialize. They operated in the trading sector, but also in banking and manufacturing. As late as the sixteenth century, companies such as the Fuggers of southern Germany, the Ruiz de Medina del Campo of Spain, and the Capponi and the Salviati of Tuscany maintained the same tradition of operating on a broad front. Specialization was introduced by the large trading companies of the seventeenth century, but was slow to spread.

As we saw in Part II, chapter 2, state creditors in fifteenth-century Genoa joined together to form a consortium that came to operate as a banking institution called the Banco di San Giorgio. In England at the end of the seventeenth century, at a time when public finances were in a disastrous state, the government had a pressing need for liquid assets to defray wartime expenses. Noting the examples set by the Banco di San Giorgio and, above all, the Bank of Amsterdam, a group of businessmen devised a project for a bank, the capital of which would be wholly invested in public loans. This plan won the approval of the authorities with the condition that the capital (and hence the loan to the government) should not fall short of £1.2 million. Subscriptions were opened on 21 June 1694. London, by that time, had become a major centre of commerce and finance. On the first day alone, subscriptions were collected totalling £300,000, and within twelve days the full quota had been met. Accordingly, on 27 July the government authorized the setting-up of the bank. The decree in question granted the bank authority to accept deposits, to settle bills of exchange, to issue banknotes (although they were not declared legal tender until 1833), and to trade in letters of exchange and precious metals. At the same time, the bank was forbidden to deal on the commodities market or to grant loans to the Crown without obtaining prior authorization from Parliament.

Thus was born the Bank of England. Slowly and gradually, but especially during the nineteenth century, the Bank assumed the character and role of a central bank. Indeed, it came to serve as a prototype for the central banks subsequently created in other countries – albeit with certain variations regarding the degree of independence from political power.[6]

It is generally held that the Bank of England's documentary records have suffered neither dramatic accidental losses nor drastic deliberate thinning. Documentary material was traditionally kept in the relevant department of the Bank. It was not until the 1930s that someone had the idea of founding a small public museum to chart the history of the bank. A section equipped with several of the most representative documents relating to the history of the Bank and its activities was created as an annexe to the museum. This section was incorrectly called an archive, but it formed the nucleus around which a genuine historical archive gradually developed. In 1972 the post of archivist was created. After 1978 the transfer of documents from the various departments of the Bank to the archive was speeded up. Today the archive comprises approximately 20,000 files and about 70,000 bound volumes. The latter consist mainly of records of transactions arising from the management of customers' accounts or from the Bank's function as registrar of government stock issues.

---

[6] Among other works, see Andreades, 1901, repr. 1966; and Clapham, 1944, I. On the creation and development of central banks, see Ciocca, 1983 (Eng. tr. 1987).

Central-bank archives, and in particular those of the Bank of England, contain documents that are full of information regarding not only the monetary, banking and financial history of the home country, but also the history of international financial relations. The Bank of England records, for example, include around seventy files concerning financial relations with Italy and a much higher number on financial relations with France.

In the course of the nineteenth century there emerged such banking colossi as the Rothschild and the Hambro banks, Credit Mobilier and the Deutsche Bank. Although technically involved chiefly in financial activities, these institutions played a leading role in industrial ventures such as the construction of the railways and, in the case of Deutsche Bank, the establishment of electrical and chemical industries. The banks clung on to much of their documentation and this now forms an important source of information for economic historians of the nineteenth century. For example, the Archives Nationaux in Paris and the Centre des Archives Contemporaines in Fontainebleau house the Rothschild archives (to consult them one needs written permission from Européenne de Banque). The Rothschild archive takes up approximately 800 m of shelving, spans the entire period from 1811 to 1940, and is organized in three sections: *dossiers d'affaires* for the period 1811–1945; copies of letters sent between 1849 and 1944; and correspondence received by the House of Rothschild and its branches between 1838 and 1940 (see Gille, 1965–7).

Large manufacturing companies employing large workforces in their factories began to appear during the Industrial Revolution. Industrial firms were slow to create their own archives. One exception to this rule was the St-Gobain Pont-à-Mousson company, which has records reaching right back to the seventeenth century.

It was in the United States and in Germany that industrial companies first began to create genuine company archives. In the United States, the effort to order and catalogue company archives really began in the 1920s, with the direct participation of Harvard University. The University's Baker Library, annexed to the School of Business Administration, now holds approximately 1,400 collections of documents relating to American financial, trading and industrial companies, dating back to the beginning of the seventeenth century.

In Germany, Krupp created its own company archive in 1905. This example was followed by Siemens and Bayer in 1907, by Bosch in 1933, by Gutehoffnungshütte in 1937, and by Thyssen and Mannesmann in 1938.

Nowadays many industrial firms have good company archives. Other than those just cited, one might list: DuPont in the United States, Imperial Chemical Industries (ICI) and British Petroleum (BP) in Great Britain, Renault in France, and Ansaldo and Terni in Italy. (See *Lingotto*, 1984, including the bibliography.)

For modern and contemporary times, as for the Middle Ages, the company documentation available to economic historians relates almost exclusively to large companies, though occasionally also to medium-size companies. Small family-owned trading and manufacturing companies largely remain shrouded in obscurity. This gap in our knowledge is particularly serious inasmuch as it distorts our vision of the past. This can best be appreciated when, by accident, some isolated exceptional document unexpectedly emerges from the recesses of history. The following account provides an example.

A few years ago, while working in the Florence State Archive on papers of the Arcispedale di S. Maria Nuova, John Muendel of the University of Wisconsin at Waukesha came upon three small notebooks of accounts kept by a small family firm consisting of two blacksmiths, Deo di Buono and his son Giovanni, both of whom worked at Stia in the Casentino area, about 30 miles from Florence. These accounts, for the period 1458–97, revealed on analysis that between January 1468 and April 1472 only 25 per cent of debts owing to Deo and Giovanni were paid in cash. The remaining 75 per cent were settled in kind. (See Muendel, 1985, pp. 32–4.) In other words, in the second half of the fifteenth century, not many miles from Florence, where De Roover's examination of documentary evidence relating to the Banco de' Medici has laid bare clear signs of a highly advanced capitalism and of sophisticated business, commercial, financial and credit techniques, there existed a rural society where the use of money was still the exception and barter-based trade the rule. This speaks volumes of the sort of biased view that can result from treating the surviving sources as typical.

There is, however, one type of document available for large, medium and small companies alike: company inventories drawn up on the owner's death or on a change of ownership. For large companies, the classic example is the 1527 inventory of the Fugger company, published and studied by J. Strieder (1905). For small companies mention may be made of the 1456 inventory of Giovan Pietro's tiny pottery works in Pavia, the 1492 inventory of Giovan Antonio Beretta's printworks, also in Pavia (Cipolla, 1944, pp. 12–13), and the inventories of numerous chemists' shops of every time and place. If more attention were paid to such sources, the result could be a more balanced view of the business world from the Middle Ages onwards.

TRAVEL ACCOUNTS

Accounts of journeys, including missionaries' reports, are an important and precious source of information for economic and social historians. There are a huge number of travel accounts, of every degree of quality: from the famous work by Marco Polo on his journey and stay in China to an insignificant little book by a certain John Dale, published in London in 1894 and entitled *Round the World by Doctors' Orders* – though the precise nature of these mysterious 'doctors' orders' is not clarified anywhere in the book. To give a rough idea of the abundance of this material, suffice it to say that the Tursi collection of travel reports at the Marciana Library in Venice includes several thousand items; that the Turin-based international centre for research into the history of travel in Italy lists in its index more than 100,000 articles, pamphlets and books; and that the Hakluyt Society in London, founded in 1846 with the express purpose of publishing in critical editions all accounts of journeys deemed worthy of such treatment, included in its first series 100 volumes, published between 1847 and 1898. The second series, begun in 1899, had reached 165 titles by 1984 and continues to grow. (On the Hakluyt Society and its publications see Lynam, 1967; and Quinn, 1974.)

In this brief sketch of the available material we shall concentrate on four types of travel report. First, there are the accounts written by mediaeval travellers, who jumble together factual information and legendary material. Among the main exponents of this genre were Liutprando da Cremona, sent to Byzantium in AD 949 as legate to Emperor Otto; al-Maqaddasi Ahsan al-Tagasim (c. 910 AD), who travelled widely throughout the Islamic Empire; Marco Polo (1254–1324), who has already been mentioned and to whom we shall return; Fra Giovanni dal Pian del Carpine (d. 1252), whom Pope Innocent IV sent as his legate to the Great Khan of the Tartars in 1245; and Fra Oderico da Pordenone (1286–1331), who was sent into Armenia and Persia, and who later journeyed to China, where he remained for three years in Peking.

A second category would cover the memoirs of all those who ventured forth on perilous voyages during the wave of European overseas expansion from the fifteenth to the seventeenth centuries. This would include the memoirs of the Florentine Francesco Carletti, who went round the world in the years 1594–1606; those of J. H. van Linschoten, Fernão Mendes Pinto, Ludovico de Varthema, C. Fryke, and C. Schweitzer; and also those of missionaries such as the Jesuit Matteo Ricci, who left a collection of profound observations on early-seventeenth-century China.

A third category is that of the memoirs of genteel travellers, most of them English, who in the sixteenth and seventeenth centuries undertook 'grand tours' of continental Europe. Most notable are the memoirs of M. Eyquem de Montaigne, J. Evelyn, R. Dallington, T. Coryat and F. Moryson. The manuscript of F. Moryson, still housed in Corpus Christi College Library in Oxford, has not yet been published in a critical edition worthy of its content. Part of the manuscript was published in 1903 by C. Hughes, but without any critical commentary. This edition included the more descriptive chapters, in which the author, who had on several occasions visited the Netherlands, Germany, Switzerland, Italy and Turkey, sketched the character of the inhabitants and provided information on the customs, political institutions, military and naval forces, and state revenues and expenditures of these countries. The more diary-based part of the manuscript, containing day-to-day records of journeys, and therefore information on expenses for board and lodging, on tolls, transport, travelling times, currency, exchange rates, and so on, was published anonymously in Glasgow in 1907, again without any critical commentary. The more readable and entertaining section of the manuscript is that published by Hughes in 1903, but the macro-economic information given is all second-hand, based on hearsay. The more arid material published in Glasgow, however, contains much first-hand data of interest to the economic historian.

Our fourth category is the writings of eighteenth- and nineteenth-century travellers, many of whom adopted a highly systematic – one might even say, scientific – approach. Daniel Defoe's *Tour thro' the Whole Island of Great Britain* (1724–6) was a pioneering work of its kind, and Arthur Young's accounts of his journeys in Ireland, England, Wales, France and Italy include observations of particular importance for the history of agriculture.

To conclude this section, it is worth mentioning a recent hypothesis regarding the origins and composition of Marco Polo's work. Tradition has it that Marco Polo, captured by the Genoese during a naval conflict between Genoese and Venetian forces, was locked up for some time in a prison in Genoa along with Rustichello da Pisa, and that while in prison he dictated to Rustichello (who translated Polo's account into French, the language of the court) the text that later became famous under the title of *Milione*. However, following a careful analysis of the text's language and content, F. Borlandi (1962) advanced the convincing hypothesis that Rustichello's text was not the product of Marco Polo's dictation, but, rather, a free and somewhat fanciful literary reworking by Rustichello of a text written by Polo. This text, Borlandi argued, was nothing other than a *pratica della mercatura* (trading manual) that Polo still had with him when taken prisoner by the Genoese near Laiazzo in 1296. If this thesis is correct, Marco Polo's text gains even greater importance in the eyes of economic historians.

GAZETTES AND NEWSPAPERS

As we have seen, mediaeval and Renaissance merchants gained their information in part from trading manuals but above all from commercial correspondence, to which they paid particular attention. Such correspondence contained information on market conditions and forecasts, economic and monetary policy, exchange rates and bankruptcies, and also on political developments, military and naval conflicts, shipwrecks, acts of piracy, events and gossip at court, and so on. The trading companies sought to ensure that correspondence was forwarded promptly and that it did not fall into the hands of their competitors. After all, the success of many of their dealings depended on the speed at which they reacted to changing market conditions and on their ability to keep one step ahead of their competitors.

Following the invention of movable-type printing, but especially from the second half of the sixteenth century onwards, various enterprising individuals with commercial experience compiled trading manuals containing information on products, weights, measures, currencies, exchange rates and trading practices in the major markets of Europe. These they had printed and placed on sale. This process was extended to commercial correspondence. An information network was organized; letters were compiled containing the latest news on economic, commercial and political matters; and the finished news-letters were distributed among those subscribers who were willing to pay a fixed price to receive them. Thus, for example, in sixteenth-century Augsburg there was an agency, run first by a certain Jeremias Crasser and later by a Jeremias Schiffle – self-styled *Nouvellanten* – that supplied its subscribers with periodical letters containing a range of information gleaned from a variety of sources.[7]

This kind of letter, produced by a growing number of *Nouvellanten* or gazetteers, became increasingly popular and sought-after. For a long time such letters were distributed in handwritten copies, thus respecting their original form, but printed letters began gradually to appear. Thus were born the ancestors of our newspapers, at that time referred to as 'news-letters', 'gazettes', *Zietungen*, *avvisi* or *notizie*. The frequency of their appearance varied from case to case, but daily publication was rather a late development.

Among the earliest gazettes were the Frankfurt fair gazettes published from 1588 onwards under the title *Calendarium Historicum*. The first printed gazette seems to have been the *Aviso Relation oder Zeitung* published weekly in Augsburg by Johann Carolus from 1609 onwards. Preceded by loose-leaf papers and occasional sheets, the *Tydinghe nuy verscheyde Quartieren* made its appearance in Holland in 1618. The same year, the *Nieuwe Tydinghen* began publication in Antwerp, and in 1658 the *Weekelyke Courante van Europa*, a Dutch weekly published on Saturday, emerged. London's first gazette, entitled the *Weekly News*, appeared in 1626. The first French newspaper was Dr Théophraste Renaudot's *Gazette de France* (1631 onwards), which Cardinal Richelieu promptly exploited as a vehicle for propaganda.

The first London daily newspaper, the *Daily Courant*, appeared in 1702. In 1704 Daniel Defoe, author of *Robinson Crusoe*, began publishing *Review*, a paper containing a great deal of commercial news. At first published weekly, from 1705 onwards *Review* came out three times a week. The *Daily Universal Register*, first published in 1785 and renamed *The Times* in 1788, also carried a large amount of commercial news and economic announcements. Indeed, until May 1966, the paper's front page

---

[7] The agency of Crasser and Schiffle was employed by Count Philip Edward Fugger (1546–1618) to make fair copies of his company's business correspondence. See Matthews, 1959, pp. 17–18

THE Universal DAILY Register

Printed Logographically — DIEU ET MON DROIT — By His Majesty's Patent

NUMB. 1.] SATURDAY, JANUARY 1, 1785. [Price Two-pence Halfpenny.

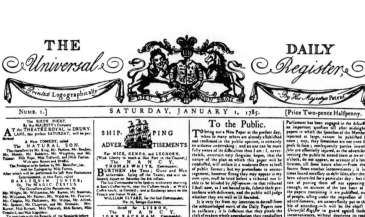

The SIXTH NIGHT.
By His MAJESTY's Company
AT the THEATRE ROYAL in DRURY-LANE, this present SATURDAY, will be performed
A New COMEDY, called
The NATURAL SON.
The characters by Mr. King, Mr. Parsons, Mr. Bensley, Mr. Moody, Mr. Baddeley, Mr. Wrighten, and Mr. Palmer. Miss Pope, Miss Tidswell, and Miss Farren.
With new Scenes and Dresses.
The Prologue to be spoken by Mr. Bannister, jun.
And the Epilogue by Miss Farren.
After which will be performed the last New Pantomime Entertainment, in two Parts, called
HARLEQUIN JUNIOR;
Or, The MAGIC CESTUS.
The Characters of the Pantomime, by
Mr. Wright, Mr. Williamson, Mr. Burton, Mr. Staunton, Mr. Williames, Mr. Palmer, Mr. Waldron, Mr. Fawcett, Mr. Chaplin, Mr. Phillimore, Mr. Wilson, Mr. Alfred, Mr. Spencer, Mr. Chapman, and Mr. Grimaldi. Mrs. Burnet, Miss Burnett, Miss Tidswell, Miss Barnes, Miss Cranford, and Miss Stageldoir.
To conclude with the Repulse of the Spaniards before
The ROCK of GIBRALTAR.

To-morrow, by particular desire, (for the 4th time) the revived Comedy of the DOUBLE DEALER, with the favorite Masque of ARTHUR and EMMELINE.
On Tuesday the Tragedy of VENICE PRESERVED. Jaffier by Mr. Brereton, Pierre by Mr. Bensley, and Belvidera, by Mrs. Siddons: And on Friday the Carmelite. Massinger's Play of the MAID of HONOUR, (with alterations and Additions) is in Rehearsal and will soon be produced.

NINTH NIGHT. FOR THE AUTHOR.
AT the THEATRE-ROYAL, COVENT-GARDEN, this present SATURDAY, January 1, 1785, will be performed, a New Comedy, called
The FOLLIES of a DAY,
Or, The Marriage of Figaro.
With new Dresses, Decorations, &c.
The principal characters by Mr. Lewis, Mr. Quick, Mr. Edwin, Mr. Wilson, Mr. Wewitzer, Mr. Bonnor, Mr. Thompson, and Mrs. Martyr; Mrs. Bates, Mrs. Webb, Miss Wewitzer, and Miss Younge.
With a new Prologue, to be spoken by Mr. Davies.
To which will be added, for the the sixth time,
A new Pantomime, called,
The MAGIC CAVERN,
Or, VIRTUE's TRIUMPH.
With new Scenery, Machinery, Music, Dresses, and Decorations.
The Scenes chiefly designed by Mr. Richards, and executed by him, Mr. Carver, Mr. Hodgins, and Assistants.
The Overture, Songs, Choruses, and the Music of the new Pantomime, and composed by Mr. Shield.
Nothing under full Price will be taken.
The Words of the Songs, &c. to be had at the Theatre.

MR. WALTER returns his thanks to his Friends and the Public for the great encouragement and generous support he has already received from them to his new improvement in Printing, by the readiness with which they have subscribed to his intended publication of the works of some eminent Authors; and whilst he solicits a continuance of their favours, begs leave to acquaint them that by
The middle of January will be published,
In One Volume 12mo,
MISCELLANIES IN VERSE AND PROSE,
Intended as a Specimen of his Printing Types at the Logographic Office, Printing-House Square, Blackfriars.—And by the beginning of February, his first volume, containing Watts's Improvement of the Mind, with an Introduction written on the occasion, will be ready to be delivered to the subscribers.

This Day is published, Price 6d.
PLAN of the CHAMBER of COMMERCE, King's-Arms Buildings, Cornhill, London, which is open every day, for Consultation, Opinion, and Advice (verbal or in Writing) Mediation, Assistance, Arbitration, &c. in all *Commercial, Maritime,* and *Insurance* Affairs, and matters of *Trade* in general, and the *Laws* and *Usages* relating thereto.——The Address is, To the Director of the Chamber of Commerce, as above.
To be had of Richardson and Urquhart, Royal Exchange; J. Sewell, Cornhill; T. Whieldon, Fleet-street; W. Flexney, Holborn; and at the aforesaid Chamber.
Where may also be had, in one Volume Folio,
Mr. Weskett's COMPLETE DIGEST of the THEORY, LAWS and PRACTICE of INSURANCE; an entire new and comprehensive work, including all the adjudged Cases extant, with several never before printed; Extracts from the Statutes, foreign Ordinances, and marine Treaties; accounts of all the Insurance Companies, the MaritimeCourts, the commercial and maritime Laws, the Law of Nations, &c. the whole forming (alphabetically) a new *Lex Mercatoria.*
☞ "This Work has been compiled with great Care and Industry, by one who is evidently a Master of the Subject. It abounds with Proofs of extensive Reading, as well as mature Reflection, and judicious Remarks; and if the completest System of Insurance that has hitherto been composed be entitled to Praise, the present useful Digest must meet with the Approbation of the commercial World." Crit. Rev. Vol. 51, p. 443.—All the other Literary Journals speak in similar Terms of this Book; which had already been translated abroad.

This Day is published, in 3 Vols. Price 9s. sewed.
By the LITERARY SOCIETY,
MODERN TIMES: or The ADVENTURES of GABRIEL OUTCAST. A Novel, in Imitation of Gil Blas.
"Qui capit ille facit."
Printed for the Author, and sold by J. Walter, Printing-house Square, Black-friars; where may be had, gratis, the Plan of this Society, associated for the Encouragement of Literature, who propose to print and publish at their own Risk and Expence such original Works as they may approve of, and give their Authors all Profits arising from the same.

MRS. KING begs leave to acquaint her Friends she opens her SCHOOL at CHIGWELL in ESSEX, on Monday, the 10th of January, for the EDUCATION of YOUNG LADIES: as she has always been accustomed to watch and improve the opening mind, hopes to give satisfaction to those who trust her with so important a charge.
Till the 10th of January Mrs. King may be spoke with at Mr. Kerr's, Kit-maker to his Majesty, in the Mews, Charing-cross.
N. B. Wanted an Apprentice and Half-boarder.

SHIP-PING ADVER-TISEMENTS

For NICE, GENOA, and LEGHORN,
(With Liberty to touch at One Port in the Channel,)
The NANCY.
THOMAS WHITE, Commander,
BURTHEN 160 Tons; Guns and Men answerable. Lying off the Tower, and will absolutely depart on Saturday the 8th instant.
The said Commander to be spoken with every morning at Sam's Coffee-house, near the Custom-house; at Will's Coffee-house, in Cornhill; and at Exchange hours on the French and Italian Walk, or
WILLIAM ELYARD, for the said Commander,
No. 16, Savage-Gardens.

Direct for LISBON,
The NANCY.
JOHN RACKHAM, Commander,
BURTHEN 300 Tons, Men answerable. Lying off Horslydown Chain; Seven-eighths of her Cargo absolutely engaged, and is obliged by Charter-party to depart on Saturday the 8th instant.
The said Commander to be spoken with every morning at Sam's Coffee-house, near the Custom-house; at Will's Coffee-house, in Cornhill; and in Exchange hours in the French and Italian Walk; or
WILLIAM ELYARD, for the said Commander,
No. 16, Savage-Gardens.

For NICE, GENOA, and LEGHORN.
(With Liberty to Touch at One Port in the Channel.)
The LIVELY,
ROBERT BRINE, Commander,
BURTHEN 109 Tons, Guns and Men answerable. Lying off Iron Gate.
The said Commander to be spoke with every Morning at Sam's Coffee-house, near the Custom-house; at Will's Coffee-house in Cornhill; and in Exchange Hours in the French and Italian Walk; or
WILLIAM ELYARD, for the said Commander,
No. 16, Savage-Gardens.

For CONSTANTINOPLE and SMYRNA, or SMYRNA and CONSTANTINOPLE,
(With Liberty to Touch at One Port in the Channel,)
The BETSEY,
ROBERT LANCASTER, Commander,
BURTHEN 200 Tons, Men answerable. Lying at Iron-Gate. Two-thirds of her Cargo engaged, and is obliged to depart by Charterparty, in all the present Month of January.
The said Commander to be spoke with every Morning at Sam's Coffee-house, near the Custom-house, at Will's Coffee-house in Cornhill; and in Exchange Hours in the French and Italian Walk; or
WILLIAM ELYARD, for the said Commander,
No. 16, Savage-Gardens.
N. B. No Goods to be taken on Board the Vessel without an Order from the Broker.

NEW NOVELS.
This Day are published, (in two Volumes, price 5s. sewed,)
THE YOUNG WIDOW; or, the HISTORY of Mrs. LEDWICH.
The HISTORY of Lord BELFORD and Miss SOPHIA WOODLEY, 3 vol. 9s. bound.
Printed for the Editor, and sold by F. Noble, in Holborn;
Where may be had lately published,
St. Ruthin's Abbey, a Novel, 3 vols. 9s. bound.
The Woman of Letters; or, History of Fanny Belton, 2 vol. 7s bound.
A Lesson for Lovers; or, History of Col. Melville and Lady Richly, 2 vols. 7s. bound.
Literary Amusements, or, Evening Entertainer, 2 vol. 7s. bound
Adventures of a Cavalier, by Daniel Defoe, 3 vols. 9s bound.

T. RICKABY, PRINTER,
No. 15, Duke's Court, Drury Lane;
REspectfully informs his Friends and the Public in general, that the Partnership between him and Mr. Moore being entirely dissolved, he now intends to carry on every branch of the PRINTING BUSINESS upon his own account;—and having purchased a complete assortment of the neatest and best materials, is determined to pursue a Mode of Printing which he hopes will meet with the approbation of his employers.
N.B. Cards, Hand-Bills, Circular Letters, and all articles of the kind, accurately printed at a few hours notice, in a manner particularly neat, and at the lowest prices.
⁂ An Apprentice wanted.

To the Readers of the London Medical Journal.
This day is first published, price 1s.
SYMPATHY DEFENDED; or, the State MEDICAL CRITICISM in London; written to improve the Principles and Manners of the Editor of the London Medical Journal. To which are added the Contents of the Treatise on Medical Sympathy, and a Postscript, on account of a premature Review in a late Number of the London Medical Journal.
By a Society of Faculties;
Friends to the Public and Enemies to Imposition.
"Cum tua non edas, carpis mea carmina, Laeli,
"Carpere vel noli nostra, vel ede tua."
MART. Epig.
This pamphlet has been hitherto distributed gratuitously. The repeated applications for them, particularly from the country, have become so numerous, that the Society feel themselves under the necessity of putting them into the hands of a publisher.
Sold by J. Murray, Bookseller, Fleet-street.

Nondum lingua suum dextra, peregit opus.
MART.
SHORT-HAND, on the latest and most approved Principles taught by J. LARKHAM, No 11, Rose Alley, Bishopsgate Street.
It would exceed the limits of an advertisement merely to mention the various errors either in the *plan* or the *execution* of the different schemes of Short-hand hitherto made public, or to point out the peculiarities and excellencies of the present: Mr. L. therefore only begs leave to observe, that the approbation of many gentlemen well known in the literary world, and well versed in the *Theory* and *Practice* of Short-hand, expressed in stronger terms than delicacy will permit him to repeat, warrants him in saying *his* will be found a system of short and swift writing, more *easy* to acquire and retain, more *expeditiously*, more *legible* and more *regular* than any ever yet offered to the Public.
The terms of teaching *one* Guinea, the usual time of learning *seven* lessons.

To the Public.

TO bring out a New Paper at the present day; when so many others are already established and confirmed in the public opinion, is certainly an arduous undertaking; and no one can be more fully aware of its difficulties than I am: I, nevertheless, entertain very sanguine hopes, that the nature of the plan on which this paper will be conducted, will ensure it a moderate share at least of public favour; but my pretensions to encouragement, however strong they may appear in my own eyes, must be tried before a tribunal not liable to be blinded by *self-opinion*: to that tribunal I shall now, as I am bound to do, submit these pretensions with deference, and the public will judge whether they are well or ill founded.

It is very far from my intention to detract from the acknowledged merit of the Daily Papers now in existence; it is sufficient that they please the class of readers whose approbation their conductors are ambitious to deserve; nevertheless it is certain some of the best, some of the most respectable, and some of the most useful members of the community, have frequently complained (and the causes of their complaints still exist) that by radical defects in the plans of the present established papers, they were deprived of many advantages, which ought naturally to result from daily publications. Of these some build their fame on the length and accuracy of parliamentary reports, which unquestionably are given with great ability, and with a laudable zeal to please those, who can spare time to read ten or twelve columns of debates. Others are principally attentive to the politics of the day, and make it their study to give satisfaction to the numerous class of politicians, who, blessed with easy circumstances, have nothing better to do, than to amuse themselves with watching the motions of ministers both at home and abroad; and endeavouring to find out the secret springs that set in motion the great machine of government in every state and empire in the world. There is one paper which in no degree interferes with the pursuits of its cotemporaries; it looks upon parliamentary debates as sacred mysteries, that cannot be submitted to vulgar eyes without profanation; political investigations it apprehends to be little short of treason, and therefore *loyally* abstains from them; it deals almost solely in advertisements; and consequently, though a very useful, it is by no means an entertaining paper. Thus it would seem that every News-Paper published in London is calculated for a particular set of readers only; so that if each set were to change its favourite publication for another, the commutation would produce disgust, and dissatisfaction to all; the politician would then find nothing to amuse him but long accounts of petty squabbles about trifles in Parliament, or panegyrics on the men and measures that he most disliked; or libels on those whom he most revered. The person to whom parliamentary debates afford unspeakable delight, would find himself bored with political speculations about the measures that the different courts in Europe might probably adopt; or disgusted with whole pages of advertisements, in which he felt no concern;—whilst the plain shop-keeper who wanted to find a convenient house for his business, and the servant who purchased his paper in hopes of seeing in it an advertisement directing where he might find a place to suit him, would have their labour for their pains, in perusing publications, filled with senatorial debates, or political essays and remarks, which would direct them to nothing less than the house or place they wanted.—A News-Paper, conducted on the true and natural principles of such a publication, ought to be the Register of the times, and faithful recorder of every species of intelligence; it ought not to be engrossed by any particular object; but, like a well covered table, it should contain something suited to every palate: observations on the dispositions of our own and of foreign courts should be provided for the political reader; debates should be reported for the amusement or information of those who may be particularly fond of them; and a due attention should be paid to the interests of trade, which are so greatly promoted by advertisements.—A paper that should blend all these advantages, and by steering clear of extremes, hit the happy medium, has long been expected by the public.—Such, it is intended, shall be the UNIVERSAL REGISTER, the great objects of which will be to facilitate the *commercial* intercourse between the different parts of the community, through the channel of *Advertisements*; to record the principal occurrences of the times; and to abridge the account of debates during the sitting of Parliament.

It is no less the interest of the proprietors of News-Papers, than of the public, that every encouragement should be given to advertising correspondents, yet this private interest of the proprietors is frequently sacrificed to the rage for parliamentary debates, to the great injury of trade; for the extreme length of these debates so greatly retards the publication of the New-Papers which are noted for detailed accounts of them, that the advantages arising from this species of intelligence, though highly acceptable in itself, are frequently over-balanced by the inconveniences occasioned to people in business by the delay. These inconveniences are great and many; it generally happens, that when either House of Parliament has been engaged in the discussion of an important question till after midnight, the papers in which the speeches of the Members are reported at large, cannot be published before noon; nay, they sometimes are not even sent to press so soon; consequently parties interested in *sales* are essentially injured, as the advertisements, inviting the public to attend them at *ten* or *twelve* o'clock, do not appear, on account of a late publication, till some hours after.—From the same source flows another inconvenience; it is sometimes found necessary to *defer* sales, after they have been advertised for a particular day; but the notice of putting them off not appearing early enough, on account of the late hour at which the papers containing it are published, numbers of people, acting under the impression of former advertisements, are unnecessarily put to the trouble of attending.—It will be the object of the *Universal Register* to guard against these great inconveniences, without depriving its readers of the pleasure of learning what passes in Parliament.—It is intended, then, that the debates shall be regularly reported in it; but on the other hand, that the publication may not be delayed to the prejudice of people in trade, the speeches will not be given on a large scale; the *substance* shall be faithfully preserved; but all the uninteresting parts will be omitted. I shall thus be enabled to publish this paper at an early hour; and I propose to bring it out *regularly* every morning at *six* o'clock. The *Universal Register* will therefore have this advantage over the *Daily Advertiser*, that, though published as early, it will contain a substantial account of the proceedings in Parliament the preceding night, which is never to be found in that paper; and compared with the other morning papers it will be found to have the merit of containing in substance, what they give in long detail (which men in business cannot well spare time to read) and, nevertheless, of being published much sooner. These circumstances, it is hoped, will give the *Universal Register* at least an *equal* claim to public favour with the parliamentary papers, and the *trading* part of the metropolis, it is presumed, will find it their advantage to give it the preference.

An essential part of the plan of this new paper is, that, for the convenience of advertising correspondents, their favours shall, *to a certainty*, be inserted on the very day that they shall direct; provided they deliver them at the office in due time. For the *strict* observance of this rule, the credit of the paper shall stand pledged; and its pretensions to public countenance will be renounced, if this fundamental principle in its institution shall ever be violated, except in cases of absolute necessity, which human prudence cannot prevent.—And here I beg it may be understood that I do not make use of the word *necessity* as a reserve, under colour of which, I may, whenever I think fit, be released from my engagements; I mean by that word a necessity arising from accidents that sometimes happen in the printing business, and from which, the most careful man cannot, at all times, be secure. But so far from wishing to shrink from my engagements, I intend, whenever the length of the Gazette, Parliamentary Debates, &c. shall render it impossible for me to insert all the advertisements promised for the day, in *one* sheet, to print an additional half sheet, and publish it with the ordinary paper without any additional charge to my customers.—From the difficulty that people experience in procuring the insertion of their advertisements even in the *Daily Advertiser*, and particularly from the impossibility of obtaining an *early* insertion at some periods of the year, it may be presumed that this regulation will greatly recommend the UNIVERSAL REGISTER to public notice, and procure it support.

These, though in my opinion good, are not the *only* grounds on which I build my hopes of success. I flatter myself, I have some claim to public encouragement, on account of a great improvement which I have made in the art of printing. The inconveniences attending the old and tedious mode of composing with letters taken up *singly*, first suggested the idea of devising some more expeditious method. The cementing of several letters together, so as that the type of a *whole word* might be taken up in as short a time as that of a *single letter*, was the result of much reflection on that subject. But the bare idea of cementing was merely the opening, not the accomplishment or perfection of the improvement. The fount consisting of types of words, and not of letters, was to be so arranged, as that a compositor should be able to find the former with as much facility as he can the latter. This was a work of inconceivable difficulty. I undertook it however, and was fortunate enough, after an infinite number of experiments, and great labour, to bring it to a happy conclusion. The whole English language is now methodically and systematically arranged at my fount: so that printing can now be performed with greater dispatch, and at less expence, than according to the mode hitherto in use.

In bringing this work to perfection, I had not my own advantage solely in view; I wished to be useful to the community; and it is with pleasure I see that the public will derive considerable benefit from my industry; for I have resolved to sell the REGISTER *One halfpenny* UNDER the price paid for seven out of eight of the morning

Figure 7 Front page of the first number (1 January 1785) of the *Daily Universal Register* (later renamed *The Times*)

Figure 8 Front page of *The Times*, 1 January 1788

was always given over to classified advertisements, many of which consisted of economic announcements (see figures 7 and 8).

Journals wholly or chiefly devoted to commercial, financial and economic news began to appear during the nineteenth century. *The Economist* was founded in 1843. Italy was out in front on this occasion, with *Il giornale di commercio*, founded in Leghorn by Luigi Nardi in 1822, appearing once a fortnight. Nardi's paper was devoted to reports on market trends, prices of various commodities, rates of exchange, trade passing through the port of Leghorn and other foreign ports, and other matters of a strictly economic nature. The *Corriere mercantile di Genova* started publishing in 1825. *Il Sole*, another economic paper, first appeared in 1865. The *Financial News* of London started publishing in 1884 and was taken over by the *Financial Times* in 1945. The *Financial Times* was founded by Horatio Bottomley in London in 1884. The *Wall Street Journal* was published for the first time on 8 July 1889 by Dow Jones and Co. It began as an afternoon paper, and its first number consisted of four pages.

Obviously, the earliest newspapers did not report distant events as soon as they occurred. The 3 October 1798 edition of *The Times* carried news of Lord Nelson's victory in the Battle of the Nile. The battle had taken place on 1 August of the same year and, according to the report, the news had 'reached the Admiralty on [2 October] at a quarter past eleven, borne by a certain captain Capel who had been kept in quarantine in Naples for an entire day' (quoted in Vincent, 1911, p. 222). The development of telegraph, telephone and radio caused a revolution in communications, and the immediacy of televised information has now substantially undermined the social relevance and impact of print journalism.

Historians generally have a low opinion of newspapers, and are reluctant to treat them as sources of information. Indeed, one of the worst insults that one historian can hurl at another is to call him 'a journalist' – though the 'sociologist' label has also become rather damaging of late. There are many reasons for this attitude: the sensationalism in which newspapers frequently indulge; the partisan character of certain publications; the fact that journalists are always working against deadlines and don't always have time to check their stories as carefully as they ought to; the fact that journalists, because they deal with unfolding events, are unable to assess, except by instinct, the possible long-term consequences of what they report. Yet newspapers are a vitally important historical source, not only because of what they report accurately, but also because of what they report inaccurately or even unprofessionally. Items of news that have been deliberately distorted or suppressed can reveal a great deal about the degree of censorship or the limits imposed on freedom of the press or freedom of thought in a particular country at a particular time. Moreover, information supplied by newspapers, regardless of its accuracy, provides historians with a clue to what the mass of the population knew about a particular event, and helps them understand shifts in public opinion.

MISCELLANEOUS SOURCES

Like detectives, economic historians have to cast their net very wide: they cannot afford to confine their attention to economic sources alone. There are two main reasons for this. First, economic life does not take place in a vacuum, but within a political, social and cultural context. It is essential that economic historians gain an awareness and a thorough understanding of the nature and characteristics of this context, but this they can only do through a careful examination of sources relating to the various different sectors of society. Secondly, many precious items of economic and social information are to be found in non-economic sources. The following account provides a good example of this.

In 1700 Bernardino Ramazzini (1633–1714), a physician and Professor of Medicine at the University of Modena, appointed that very year to the University of Padua, published a book that was to become a classic of medical literature: *De Morbis Artificum Diatriba*. This was a treatise in what today would be termed 'occupational medicine', i.e. it investigated illnesses associated with particular occupations.

Illnesses contracted on the job by workers were not a new subject. In 1472 Ulrich Ellenbog wrote eight pages on ailments affecting goldsmiths. In 1556 Georg Agricola published an important book on the mining technology of his time, devoting a chapter to miners' illnesses. Then, most important of all, in 1567 the Swiss scholar Theophrastus Bombastus von Hohenheim (better known as Paracelsus) published a book dealing with the aetiology, pathogenesis, prevention, diagnosis and treatment of miners' illnesses.[8] But nobody had ever thought of writing a general and systematic treatise covering all professions and trades, examining the link between illnesses and the often dangerous and insanitary conditions in which people were expected to work. Moreover, it should not be forgotten that in the seventeenth century physicians belonged to the upper classes and as a rule had little or no interest in the conditions of health of ordinary workers, whom they considered little better than beasts of burden – biologically inferior beings brimming with 'very crude and corrupt humours'. By contrast, Ramazzini emerges from his writings as a deeply human and acutely intelligent physician. From a medical and humanitarian viewpoint, he recognized the importance of studying and where possible alleviating the suffering of working people, and, as is clear from his introduction, he also grasped the economic importance for society of workers in good physical shape, making them more productive.

In the first edition of *De Morbis* (1700), Ramazzini covered forty-two occupations (or, to be precise, forty-one groups of workers plus the group of scholars). The second edition, which appeared in 1713, included a

[8] Mention might also be made of S. Stockhausen's *Lithargya fumo noxio mobifico* (1556) and Martin Pausa's *Consilium Perpneumoniae* (1614).

further twelve occupations. Altogether, the fifty-four chapters provide an exceptionally lively picture of the living and working conditions of the working and labouring classes of the time, and are hence a source of primary importance for economic and social historians.[9]

Ramazzini's work was soon translated into other languages, but it was too far ahead of its time to attract imitators. It was not until more than a century later, during the nineteenth century, that major systematic studies of work-associated illnesses appeared, with evidence on the living and working conditions of workers and artisans. Studies by C. T. Thackrah (1831) in England, B. W. McCready (1837) in the United States and L. R. Villermé (1840) in France led the way in this field. Villermé's work merits special consideration.

Louis René Villermé (1782–1863) studied medicine in Paris and in 1804 registered for military service as a surgeon. Following his imperial adventure, Villermé established a private practice, but his main interests were epidemiology and social medicine. In 1820 he published his first paper on social medicine, devoted to 'Prisons, how they are and how they ought to be'. Villermé was particularly well versed in the use of statistics, and his friendship with the great Belgian statistician L. A. J. Quetelet helped him to improve his natural gift. After a number of studies on the distribution of births over the course of the year, on prisons, on epidemics, on marsh fever, on the deficiencies of French censuses, and on alcoholism, in 1840 he published his masterpiece, the *Tableau de l'état physique et morale des ouvriers employés dans les manufactures de coton, laine et de soie*. This gives a detailed picture, grounded on solid statistical foundations, of the living and working conditions of workers employed in the wool, silk and cotton industries, with special reference to the Mulhouse, Lille, Sedan and Lyon areas.

If one compares the work of Ramazzini with Villermé's *Tableau*, one cannot help being struck by the contrast that emerges between the cultures to which they belonged. Ramazzini's work is written in Latin and consists of purely qualitative descriptions. In the whole of Ramazzini's admittedly excellent work there is not a single table of statistics. Villermé, by contrast, wrote his text in French and his pages bristle with numbers and tables.

[9] The book was translated into English in 1713 by W. C. Wright under the title *Diseases of Workers*. The translation was republished by the Hafner Publishing Company (New York and London) in 1964, under the auspices of the Library of the New York Academy of Medicine, with an introduction by G. Rosen. On the importance of Ramazzini's work as a source of economic and social history see Romani, 1942.

7 International Organizations

In Part II, chapter 3, we discussed the considerable advances that were made in Europe during the eighteenth and nineteenth centuries in the collection, processing, publication and use of economic and social statistics. At the end of the chapter we noted Joseph Schumpeter's comment that the information explosion has above all been an explosion of quantitative and statistical data. We have also seen that economic, demographic and social statistics have been collected and produced over the centuries by governments, religious bodies and even by private individuals, such as Dr Villermé.

In the nineteenth century, however, international and supranational bodies began to take their place among the producers of economic, demographic and social statistics. This development became particularly clear following the end of the First World War, when the League of Nations was created. Though this body achieved little in political and diplomatic terms, its feverish activity on the statistical front led to the production of a mass of international statistics on commerce, balances of payment, prices, manufacturing and population. A useful guide through this maze of information is provided by A. C. von Breycha-Vauthier.

After the Second World War, there was a startling proliferation of international and supranational bodies, and by 1987 8,000 such bodies had gained official recognition. These ranged from the United Nations Organization (UNO) to the Belgian–Mediterranean Association for the Struggle against Thalassaemia (ABMIT), all duly listed in the *Yearbook of International Organizations* published in Munich, a work that, owing to the relentless multiplication of the organizations that it lists, becomes more and more unwieldy with every passing year. Among other things, these international and supranational bodies have two features in common: first, they are often referred to by their initials, or acronyms based upon them (table 5 provides a short list of the initials and names of some of the lending organizations); secondly, they publish international statistical yearbooks on the topics with which they are concerned. Thus, whereas economic historians of classical antiquity face a struggle to provide even

Table 5 A selection of leading international organizations

Initials/acronym	Name
AACB	Association of African Central Banks
ACDAC	Asian Pacific Development Administration Centre
AGSIDC	Arab Gulf States Information Documentation Centre
AID	Agency for International Development
AMF	Arab Monetary Fund
BIS	Bank for International Settlements
CACM	Central American Common Market
Comecon, CMEA	Council for Mutual Economic Assistance
ECSC	European Coal and Steel Community
EEC	European Economic Community
Eurostat	European Communities Statistical Office
EFTA	European Free Trade Area
EIB	European Investments Bank
IATA	International Air Transport Association
IDB	Inter-American Development Bank
ILO	International Labour Office
IMF	International Monetary Fund
ISI	International Statistics Institute of the Hague
OAS	Organization of American States
OECD	Organization for Economic Co-operation and Development
OECE	European Organization for Economic Co-operation
OPEC	Organization of Petroleum Exporting Countries
SEAIS	South East Asia Iron and Steel Institute
UN(O)	United Nations (Organization)
FAO	Food and Agricultural Administration
IAEA	International Atomic Energy Agency
IBRD	International Bank for Reconstruction and Development, (World Bank)
ICAO	International Civil Aviation Organization
IFC	International Finance Corporation
IMO	International Maritime Organization
ITU	International Telecommunication Union
UNESCO	United Nations Educational, Scientific and Cultural Organization
UNIDO	United Nations Industrial Development Organization
UPU	Universal Postal Union
WHO	World Health Organization
WIPO	World Intellectual Property Organization

two or three credible figures, economic historians of the contemporary period are submerged in an ocean of quantitative data in which it is hard for them to find their bearings.[1] But all that glitters is not gold. Many of the data are not the result of new surveys, but have simply been copied from other publications. Very often the data published by international bodies are provided by national statistical institutes. The overwhelming majority of such publications fail to give any satisfactory indication of the margins of error affecting the data, or, indeed, any adequate information regarding the methods used to collect them. International bodies are, however, in a position to exert effective pressure on national statistical institutes to improve their collection of statistical information and they do help to bring a certain uniformity to different nations' approaches to data collection.

[1] Useful guides through this forest of international statistics include Pieper, 1978; Wasserman O'Brien and Wasserman, 1986; Union of International Associations, 1969; Dicks, 1981; Jeanneney, 1957; Publications of the European Community 19; Statistical Office of the European Communities, 1961.

8 In Conclusion

The list of sources already cited is long, but it is by no means complete. We have not touched on the huge reserve of trifling and minor documents. We have even passed over in silence a number of documents or groups of documents that are of prime importance. The reason for this neglect is twofold: lack of space coupled with the fact that, because of their exceptional character, many of these documents did not fit into any of the categories discussed. However, the following material has to be mentioned, if only in passing: the Jewish documents of the Cairo Geniza, dating back to the tenth and eleventh centuries;[1] the inventory of compensations paid at the end of the thirteenth century to the victims (above all, workers) of the bullying and cheating of Sire Jehan Boinebroke, a Douai merchant and a champion of the most unscrupulous and avaricious form of capitalism;[2]

---

[1] In the second half of the nineteenth century, in the Geniza (store) attached to the Fustāt synagogue in old Cairo and located near the al-Basatin cemetery, a mass of documents relating to transactions by Jewish merchants trading round the Indian Ocean was accidentally discovered. Most of these documents date from the tenth and eleventh centuries, but a few are earlier and a few date from after 1250. They survived thanks to the Jewish tradition of preserving any written document bearing the name of God (even, for example, in the form of a greeting such as 'May God protect you!'). Solomon Schechter estimates that he has handed over more than 100,000 sheets from the Geniza to the manuscript section of Cambridge University Library, and there are fifteen other collections of documents recovered from the same source.

The documents comprise commercial and private correspondence, contracts of sale and of marriage, rabbis' books of accounts, and so on. It appears from the documents that spices, dyes, medicinal herbs, iron and steel, brass tableware, silk, pearls, Chinese porcelain, tropical fruit and ivory were imported into Egypt from the East. In its turn, Egypt exported to the East fabrics, silver ornaments and tableware, brass, glass, carpets, soap, paper, books, metals, coral, sugar, olive oil, lamp oil, raisins and linen. See Goitein, 1955 and 1967.

[2] Sire Jehan Boinebroke was a patrician and a merchant and manufacturer of fabrics in Douai, where he died in 1285 or 1286. He was a grasping and unscrupulous businessman who bullied, cheated and exploited his workers relentlessly. On his deathbed, obtaining a glimpse of Hell, he repented and ordered the executors of his will to make amends for the many 'wrongs done' and to give back 'that which he had wrongfully taken'. A crowd of people who had been victims of Boinebroke's bullying presented themselves to the executors

174

the archive of the Veneranda Fabbrica of Milan Cathedral;[3] the diary-cum-register of the incomparable procurator Dauvet, who, with the tenacity of a bloodhound, spent the four years from June 1453 to July 1457 tracking and pursuing to every recess and corner of France the business spoils of Jacques Coeur, thereby providing a picture of the variety and huge extent of the business network of the greatest French merchant of the Middle Ages;[4] the English Probate Inventories and their equivalents in the Mediterranean countries, to be found in the relevant notarial cartularies;[5] the *Descrittione dei Paesi Bassi* by Ludovico Guicciardini, which provides a priceless mass of background information on the society and economy of the Low Countries in the second half of the sixteenth century;[6] and the calculations of English national income performed at the end of the seventeenth century by that champion of

---

of his will bearing evidence of the wrongs they had suffered at his hands. The resulting inventory, dated to between February 1286 and February 1287, has been edited and annotated by G. Espinas (1933) and provides vivid testimony of the humiliation and exploitation that mediaeval workers could suffer at the hands of their employers.

[3] The construction of Milan Cathedral began at the end of the fourteenth century and was eventually completed, after various long interruptions, five centuries later. A special body called 'La Veneranda Fabbrica del Duomo' was founded to collect and administer funds for the construction and maintenance of the Cathedral and to direct the work itself. The papers accumulated in its archive (see *Annali*, 1877) contain a wealth of information on prices of building materials, salaries of masons, stone-cutters and artists, building techniques, rates of exchange, and so on. For examples of the use made of these papers see De Maddalena, 1949; and Sella, 1968.

[4] Jacques Coeur was born in Bourges between 1395 and 1400. By the end of the 1440s he had become one of the richest men in France. He was involved in trade, finance and agriculture; he was owed considerable sums of money by the King of France; and he had wide influence at court and in international politics. His ascent, his wealth and his power earned him the envy of many, and above all that of the King, who, being heavily indebted to Coeur, gave orders for his arrest in May 1453. With the aim of appropriating Coeur's assets, the King commissioned the procurator Jean Dauvet to search out and catalogue all the merchant's properties, possessions and credits. Dauvet began his hunt on 2 June 1453, but the more he found the more he realized that there was still more to find. His investigation took him from Paris to Tours, Blois, Orléans, Rouen, Berri, Langres and Lyon. Everywhere he went he found goods or credits in the name of Jacques Coeur, who, it transpired, owned properties in Puisage, Berri and in the Bourbonnais area, mines in the Beaujolais and Lyon areas, warehouses in Tours, salt businesses on the Loire, Rhône and Seine rivers, woollen and fabric businesses at Rouen and La Rochelle, spice businesses at Montpellier and Marseille, a cloth and fabrics business in the Champagne area, toll contracts, and rights to ransoms of English prisoners. Dauvet noted everything down in his journal, which thus came to represent an inventory of the properties and business activities of Jacques Coeur in France. The journal is a quarto register comprising 509 sheets. It is housed at the Archives Nationaux in Paris and has been published in an edition by M. Mollat, (1962).

[5] These inventories provide valuable information about private estates, levels of consumption, house furnishings, the contents of wardrobes and libraries, and so on.

[6] Guicciardini's work is a standard source for economic historians of the Netherlands in the sixteenth century. See Brulez, 1968 and 1970.

political arithmetics Gregory King.[7] For the period from 1750 to 1939, readers wishing to gauge the numerous gaps in the present account might usefully turn to the three hefty volumes of *Documents of European Economic History*, edited by S. Pollard and C. Holmes.

'And there are yet other things that I shall not relate.'

[7] Gregory King (1648–1712), genealogist, engraver and 'political arithmetician', compiled a series of *Natural and Political Observations upon the State and Condition of England*, which he completed in 1692. King sent a copy of this work to the Board of Trade in September 1697, but the text was not published until 1801, when George Chalmers included it in the appendix to the second edition of his *Estimate of the Comparative Strength of Great Britain* (available in an edition of 1969).

King's text and calculations form the best surviving account of the economic conditions in England at the end of the seventeenth century. King based his text on the observations that he had himself recorded during journeys undertaken in the course of his genealogical research. Among others, see Glass, 'Two Papers on Gregory King', in Glass and Eversley, 1965.

Bibliography

Abrate M., Are G., Deichman M., Indovina F., Mori G., Origgi G. C. and Pagani A. 1970: *L'imprenditorialità italiana dopo l'Unità. L'inchiesta industriale del 1870–74*, Milan.

Alberi E. (ed.) 1860: *Relazioni degli ambasciatori veneti al Senato durante il secolo XVI*, Florence.

Allison W. H., Fay, S. B., Shearer A. H. and Shipman H. R. 1931: *A Guide to Historical Literature*, New York.

Alonso W. and Starr P. 1987: *The Politics of Numbers*, New York.

Alterman H. 1969: *Counting People: the census in history*, New York.

American Historical Association 1961: *Guide to Historical Literature*, New York.

Ampolo C. 1979: Oikonomia. *Annali del Seminario di Studi del Mondo Classico. Serie di archeologia e storia antica*, I, Istituto Orientale di Napoli.

Anderson A. 1764: *An Historical and Chronological Deduction of the Origin of Commerce from the Earliest Accounts to the Present Time*, London.

Andreades A. M. 1901, repr. 1966: *History of the Bank of England*, Paris (repr. London).

Andreau J. 1974: *Les Affaires de Monsieur Jucundus*, Rome.

Andrews J. H. 1956: Two problems in the interpretation of the Port Books. *Economic History Review*, 2nd ser., IX.

Annali 1877: *Annali della Fabbrica del Duomo di Milano*, Milan.

Are G. 1963: Una fonte per lo studio della fondazione industriale in Italia: l'inchiesta 1870–74. *Studi Storici*, III.

Ashton T. S. 1962: The relation of economic history. In H. P. R. Finberg (ed.), *Approaches to History*, Toronto.

Aström S. E. 1963/5: From cloth to iron. *Societas Scientiarum Finnica: Commentationes Humanarum Litterarum*, XXXIII and XXXVII.

—— 1968: The reliability of the English Port Books. *Scandinavian Economic History Review*, XVI.

Atti 1871–5: *Atti del Comitato dell'Inchiesta Industriale*, Florence and Rome.

—— 1883–6: *Atti della Giunta Parlamentare per la Inchiesta Agraria sulle Condizioni delle Classi Agricole*. Rome.

Austin M. M. and Vidal Naquet P. 1977: *Economic and Social History of Ancient Greece*, Berkeley, Calif.

Baasch E. 1967: *Holländische Wirtschaftsgeschichte*, Jena.

Bang N. E. and Korst K. (eds) 1906–53: *Tabelle over skibsfart og varetransport gennem Øresund 1497–1783* (with captions in French), Copenhagen and Leipzig.

Barbadoro B. 1929: *Le finanze della Repubblica Fiorentina. Imposta diretta e debito pubblico fino all'istituzione del Monte*, Florence.

Barozzi N. and Berchet G. (eds) 1863: *Le relazioni degli stati Europei lette al Senato dagli ambasciatori veneziani nel secolo XVII*, Venice.

Bates, D. 1988: *Bibliography of Domesday Book*, London.

Battara P. 1935: *La popolazione di Firenze alla metà del Cinquecento*, Florence.

Bautier R. H. et al. (eds) 1964–84: *Les Sources de l'histoire économique et sociale de la France*, Paris.

Behre O. 1905: *Geschichte der Statistik in Brandenburg-Preussen bis zum Gründung der Königlichen Statistischen Bureau*, Berlin.

Beloch K. J. 1886: *Die Bevölkerung der griechisch-römischen Welt*, Leipzig.

Bensa E. 1928: *Francesco di Marco da Prato*, Milan.

Bernareggi E. 1971-2: Notizie sulla produzione della zecca di Milano nel periodo sforzesco in documenti d'archivio. *Annali dell'Istituto Italiano di Numismatica*, 18–19.

Bernheim E. 1903: *Lehrbuch der historischen Methode und der Geschichtes-philosophie*, Leipzig.

Bernocchi M. 1974-8: *Le monete della Repubblica Fiorentina*, Florence.

Beutin L. 1958: *Einführung in die Wirtschaftsgeschichte*, Cologne.

Bland A. E., Brown P. A., Tawney R. H. 1915: *English Economic History. Select Documents (1000–1846)*, London.

Bloch M. 1947: *Apologie pour l'histoire ou métier d'historien*, Paris.

—— 1954: *Esquisse d'une histoire monétaire de l'Europe*, Paris.

Bond M. F. 1971: *Guide to the Records of Parliament*, London.

Borlandi A. (ed.) 1963: *Il manuale di mercatura di Saminiato de' Ricci*, Genoa.

Borlandi F. (ed.) 1936: *El libro di mercatantie et usanze de' paesi*, Turin.

—— 1962: Alle origini del libro di Marco Polo. In *Studi in onore di A. Fanfani*, Milan.

Boulding K. E. 1970: *Economics as a Science*, New York.

Bowden W., Karpovich M. and Usher A. P. 1937: *An Economic History of Europe since 1750*, New York.

Brading D. A. and Cross H. E. 1972: Colonial silver mining: Mexico and Peru. *Hispanic American Historical Review*, 52.

Brakel S. van 1915: Schiffsheimat und Schifferheimat in den Sundzollregistern, *Hansische Geschichtsblätter*.

Braund D. (ed.) 1984: *Augustus to Nero: a sourcebook on Roman history*, London.

Breisach E. 1983: *Historiography: ancient, medieval and modern*, Chicago.

Bresslau H. 1889-1931: *Handbuch der Urkundenlehre für Deutschland und Italien*, Leipzig.

—— 1921: *Geschichte der Monumenta Germaniae Historica*, Hanover.

Breycha-Vauthier A. C. von 1939: *Sources of Information: a handbook on publications of the League of Nations*, London.

Brodnitz G. 1918: *Englische Wirtschaftsgeschichte*, Jena.

Brown E. H. P. and Hopkins S. 1956: Seven centuries of the prices of consumables compared with builders' wage-rates, *Economica*, n.s., XXIII.

Brown L. 1958: *The Board of Trade and the Free Trade Movement 1830–1842*, Oxford.

Brown S. A. 1989: *The Bayeux Tapestry: history and bibliography*, London.

Browne J. 1957: *The Merchant Avizo*, ed. P. MacGrath, Boston, Mass.

Brühl C. R. and Violante C. 1983: *Die Honorantie Civitatis Papie*, Cologne.

Brulez W. 1968: Le commerce international des Pays Bas au XVI siècle: essai d'appréciation quantitative. *Revue belge de philologie et d'histoire*, XLVI.

——— 1970: De economische kaart van de Nederlanden in the 16 eeuw volgens Guicciardini. *Tijdschrift voor Geschiedenis*, LXXXIII.

Brunt P. A. 1971: *Italian Manpower 225 BC–AD 14*, Oxford.

Bücher K. 1893: *Die Entstehung der Volkswirtschaft*, Berlin.

Bullock A. 1977: *Is History Becoming a Social Science?* London and New York.

Butler W. E. 1978: *A Source Book on Socialist International Organizations*, Alphen aan den Rijn.

Caballero F. 1866: *Discurso de recepción en la Real Academia de la Historia: relaciones geográficas escritas en tiempo de Felipe II*, Madrid.

Callu J. P. and Barrandon J. N. 1986: L'inflazione nel IV secolo (295–361): il contributo delle analisi. In A. Giardina (ed.), *Società romana e impero tardo antico*, I: *Istituzioni, ceti, economie*, Bari.

Cantor N. F. and Schneider R. I. 1967: *How to Study History*, Arlington Heights, Ill.

Cantore E. 1972: *Scientific Man*, New York.

Caracciolo A. 1958: *L'inchiesta agraria Jacini*, Turin.

Carbone S. 1962: *Provveditori e Sopraprovveditori alla Sanità della Repubblica di Venezia*, Rome.

Carletti F. 1967: Ragionamento del mio viaggio intorno al mondo (1594–1606). In M. Guglielminetti (ed.), *Viaggiatori del Seicento*, Turin.

Carli G. R. 1754–60: *Delle monete e dell'istituzione delle zecche d'Italia*, Mantua and Lucca.

Carson E. 1977: Customs records as a source for historical research. *Archives*, XIII.

Carus Wilson E. 1941: An industrial revolution of the thirteenth century. *Economic History Review*, XI.

——— 1950: Trends in the export of English woollens in the fourteenth century. *Economic History Review*, 2nd ser., III.

Carus Wilson E. and Coleman O. 1963: *England's Export Trade 1275–1547*, Oxford.

Catalogue of British Parliamentary Papers 1981: *Catalogue of British Parliamentary Papers 1801–1900*, 1000-volume Series and Area Studies Series, Shannon.

Censo español 1787: *Censo español executado de orden del Rey comunicada por el exc. señor Conde de Floridablanca*, Madrid.

Central Bureau voor de Statistiek 1975: *75 jaar statistiek van Nederland*, The Hague.

Chalmers G. 1969: *Estimate of the Comparative Strength of Great Britain*, Liverpool.

Chandaman C. D. 1975: *The English Public Revenue 1660–1688*, Oxford.

Chaudhuri K. N. 1978: *The Trading World of Asia and the English East India Company 1660–1760*, Cambridge.

——— 1987: *Trade and Civilization in the Indian Ocean*, London.

Chaunu H. and P. 1955: *Seville et l'Atlantique (1504–1650)*, Paris.

Cheney, C. R. 1972: *Notaries Public in England*, Oxford.

Chiang M. 1947: *Tides of the West*, New Haven, Conn.

Chiaudano M. (ed.) 1938–40: *Il cartulare di Giovanni Scriba (1186–1190)*, Turin.

Chiaudano M. and Costamagna G. 1956: L'archivio storico del Banco di S. Giorgio di Genova. *Archivi storici delle aziende di credito*, Rome.

Childs W. R. 1986: *The Customs Accounts of Hull 1453–1490*, Leeds.
Christensen A. 1934: Das handelsgeschichtliche Wert der Sundzollregister. *Hansische Geschichtsblätter*, LIX.
—— 1941: *Dutch Trade in the Baltic about 1600*, Copenhagen.
Ciano C. (ed.) 1964: *La pratica di mercatura datiniana (sec. XIV)*, Milan.
Cicero, 1913 tr.: *De Officiis*, tr. W. Miller, London.
Ciocca P. L. (ed.) 1983 (Eng. tr. 1987): *La moneta e l'economia. Il ruolo delle banche centrali*, Bologna: *Money and the Economy: central bankers' views*, London.
—— 1987: *L'instabilità dell'economia*, Turin.
Cipolla C. M. 1943: Profilo di storia demografica della città di Pavia. *Bollettino storico pavese*, V.
—— 1944: Per una storia del lavoro in Italia. *Bollettino storico pavese*, VI.
—— 1952, repr. 1988: Note sulla storia del saggio d'interesse. Corso, dividendi e sconto dei dividendi del Banco di S. Giorgio nel sec. XVI. *Economia internazionale*, V; repr. in C. M. Cipolla, *Saggi di storia economica e sociale*, Bologna.
—— 1956: *Money, Prices and Civilization in the Mediterranean World, Fifth to Seventeenth Century*, Princeton, NJ.
—— (ed.) 1972–6: *The Fontana Economic History of Europe*, London.
—— 1974 (Eng. tr. 1976): *Storia economica dell'Europa pre-industriale*, Bologna; *Before the Industrial Revolution: European Society and Economy, 1000–1700*, London.
—— 1982: *Il fiorino e il quattrino. La politica monetaria a Firenze nel 1300*, Bologna.
—— 1987: *La moneta a Firenze nel Cinquecento*, Bologna.
—— 1988: *La moneta a Milano nel Quattrocento*, Rome.
Clapham J. H. 1921: *The Economic Development of France and Germany 1815–1914*, New York.
—— 1944: *The Bank of England*, Cambridge.
Clark G. N. 1938: *Guide to English Commercial Statistics*, London.
Clément P. (ed.) 1859–82: *Lettres, instructions et mémoires de Colbert*, Paris.
Coale A. J. and Zelnick M. 1963: *New Estimates of Fertility and Population in the United States*, Princeton, NJ.
Cole G. D. H. 1952: *Introduction to Economic History*, London.
Cole W. A. 1958: Trends in eighteenth-century smuggling. *Economic History Review*, 2nd ser., X.
Coleman D. C. 1987: *History and the Economic Past: an account of the rise and decline of economic history in Britain*, Oxford.
Comitato Italiano per lo Studio della Demografia Storica 1971–2: *Le fonti della demografia storica in Italia*, Rome.
Conti E. 1966: *I catasti agrari della Repubblica fiorentina e il catasto particellare toscano (sec. XIV–XIX). La formazione delle strutture agrarie moderne nel contado fiorentino*, Rome.
—— 1984: *L'imposta diretta a Firenze nel Quattrocento (1427–1494)*, Rome.
Cook R. M. 1959: Die Bedeutung der bemalten Keramik für den griechischen Handel. *Jahrbuch der deutschen archäologischen Instituts*, LXXIV.
Corsini C. A. 1971–2: Nascite e matrimoni. In Comitato Italiano per lo Studio della Demografia Storica, *Le fonti della demografia storica in Italia*, Rome.
Coryat T. 1786: *Crudities*, London.

Cossa L. 1892: *Introduzione allo studio dell'economia politica*, Milan.

Court W. H. B. 1962: Economic history. In H. P. R. Finberg (ed.), *Approaches to History*, Toronto.

Cox J. C. 1910: *The Parish Registers of England*, London.

Crawford M. 1980: Economia imperiale e commercio estero (Italian tr.) In *Tecnologia e società nel mondo romano*, Como.

Crawford M., Gabba E., Millar F. and Snodgrass A. 1983: *Sources for Ancient History*, Cambridge.

Crinò A. M. 1957: Documenti relativi al libro di Sir Robert Dallington sulla Toscana. In *Fatti e figure del Seicento anglo toscano*, Florence.

Croce B. 1938: *La storia come pensiero e come azione*, Bari.

Cullen M. J. 1975: *The Statistical Movement in Early Victorian Britain*, Hassocks, Sussex.

Curtin P. D. 1969: *The Atlantic Slave Trade*, Madison, Wis.

Dallington R. 1605: *Survey of Tuscany*, London.

Davies D. 1795: *The Case of Labourers in Husbandry Stated and Considered*, London.

Daviso di Charvensod M. C. 1961: *I pedaggi delle Alpi occidentali nel Medio Evo*, Turin.

Day J. 1981: The question of monetary contraction in late mediaeval Europe. *Nordisk Numismatisk Årsskrift*.

Defoe D. 1713, ed. G. D. H. Cole 1927: *A Tour through the Whole Island of Great Britain*, London.

De la Pena y Camara, J. M. 1958: *Archivo General de Indias de Sevilla. Guia del visitante*. Madrid.

Del Panta L. 1974: Premières recherches relatives aux recensements du Grand-Duché de Toscane du milieu du XVI à la fin du XVII siècle. In C. A. Corsini (ed.), *Pour connaître la population de la Toscane aux XVII, XVIII et XIX siècles*, Florence.

De Maddalena A. 1949: *Prezzi e aspetti di mercato in Milano durante il secolo XVII*, Milan.

Denifle H. 1897–9: *La désolation des églises, monastères et hôpitaux en France vers le milieu du XV siècle*, Paris.

De Roover R. 1970: *Il Banco Medici dalle origini al declino (1397–1494)*, Florence.

De Rosa L. 1970: Vent'anni di storiografia economica italiana (1945–65). *Ricerche storiche ed economiche in memoria di C. Barbagallo*, Naples.

—— 1972a: Tra storia ed economia. L'avventura della storia economica. I difficili inizi. *Rassegna economica*, XXXVI.

—— 1972b: Tra storia ed economia. L'avventura della storia economica. La maturità. *Rassegna economica*, XXXVI.

Diaz F. 1976: *Il Granducato di Toscana*, Turin.

Dicks G. R. 1981: *Sources of World Financial and Banking Information*, Westport, Conn.

Dietz B. (ed.) 1972: *The Port and Trade of Early London*, London.

Dighe V. G. 1954: *Descriptive Catalogue of the Secret and Political Department Series 1755–1820*, Bombay.

Dini B. (ed.) 1980: *Una pratica di mercatura in formazione*, Florence.

Di Roma E. and Rosenthal J. A. 1967: *A Numerical Finding List of British Command Papers Published 1833–1961*, New York.

Domínguez Ortiz A. 1963: *La sociedad española del siglo XVII*, Madrid.

—— 1971: *The Golden Age of Spain 1516–1659*, New York.

Dopsch A. 1922: *Die Wirtschaftsentwicklung der Karolingerzeit*, Vienna.

Doren A. 1934: *Italienische Wirtschaftsgeschichte (Mittelalter und Renaissance)*, Jena.

Dorini V. and Bertelé T. (eds) 1956: *Il libro di conti di Giacomo Badoer (Constantinopili 1436–40)*, Rome.

Douglas D. C. (ed.) 1953: *English Historical Documents*, London.

Duncan Jones R. 1982: *The Economy of the Roman Empire*, Cambridge.

Dupaquier J. 1974: *Introduction à la démographie historique*, Paris.

Eden F. M. 1797: *The State of the Poor or an History of the Labouring Classes in England*, London.

Eierman J. E., Krueger H. C. and Reynolds R. L. 1939: *Bonvillano (1198)*, Genoa.

Elliott J. H. 1986: *The Count-Duke of Olivares*, New Haven, Conn., and London.

Elton G. R. 1967: *The Practice of History*, London.

Erxleben E. 1969: Das Münzgesetz der delisch-attischen Bundes. *Archiv für Papyrusforschung*, XIX.

Espinas G. 1933: *Les Origines du capitalisme. 1. Sire Jehan Boinebroke, patricien et drapier douaisien*, Lille.

Evelyn J. 1674: *Navigation and Commerce, their Origin and Progress*, London.

Faccini L. 1980: Karl Czoernig e la statistica agraria in Lombardia. *Società e storia*, III.

Fanfani A. 1943: *Introduzione allo studio della Storia Economica*, Milan.

Federico G. 1982: Per una valutazione critica delle statistiche della produzione agricola italiana dopo l'Unità. *Società e storia*, XV.

Fédou R. 1964: *Les Hommes de loi lyonnais à la fin du Moyen Age*, Paris.

Feemster R. M. 1954: *The Wall Street Journal*, New York.

Felloni G. 1984: L'archivio della Casa di San Giorgio di Genova (1407–1805) ed il suo ordinamento. *Atti della Società Ligure di Storia Patria*, n.s., XXIV.

Filangeri R. 1946: Danni e perdite negli Archivi di Stato: Napoli. In Commissione Alleata, Sottocommissione per i monumenti, belle arti e archivi, *Rapporto finale sugli archivi*, Rome.

—— 1954: Vicende di guerra dell'Archivio di Stato. *Il Fluidoro. Cronache napoletane*, I.

Finberg H. P. R. (ed.) 1962: *Approaches to History*, Toronto.

Finley M. I. 1982: Le document et l'histoire économique de l'antiquité. *Annales ESC*, XXXVII.

—— 1986: *Ancient History, Evidence and Models*, New York.

Finn R.W. 1963: *An Introduction to Domesday Book*, New York and London.

Firpo L. 1965: *Relazioni di ambasciatori veneti al Senato*, Turin.

First Report 1912: *First Report of the Royal Commission on Public Records*, London.

Fischer W., McInnis R. M. and Schneider J. (eds) 1986; *The Emergence of a World Economy*, Wiesbaden.

Fiumi E. 1956–9: Fioritura e decadenza dell' economia fiorentina. *Archivio storico italiano*, CXV–CXVII.

Fleury M. and Henry L. 1956: *Des registres paroissiaux à l'histoire de la population. Manuel de dépouillement et d'exploitation de l'état civil ancien*, Paris.

—— 1965: *Nouveau manuel de dépouillement et d'exploitation de l'état civil ancien*, Paris.

Flinn M. W. 1981: *The European Demographic System 1500–1820*, Baltimore.

Fohlen C. 1958: Recent research in the economic history of modern France. *Journal of Economic History*, XVIII.

Ford P. and G. 1972: *A Guide to Parliamentary Papers*, Southampton.

Foster W. 1919, repr. 1966: *A Guide to the India Office Records 1600–1858*, London.

Foust C. M. 1986: Customs 3 and Russian Rhubarb. A note on reliability. *Journal of European Economic History*, XV.

Frank T. 1927: *Economic History of Rome*, Baltimore.

Galbraith V. H. 1961: *The Making of Domesday Book*, Oxford.

Ganshof F. L. 1933: Note sur un passage de la vie de Saint Géraud d'Aurillac. In *Mélanges offerts à M. Nicolas Jorga*, Paris.

—— 1958: *La Belgique carolingienne*, Brussels.

Gardiner P. (ed.) 1959: *Theories of History*, Glencoe, Ill.

Géraud H. 1837: *Paris sous Philippe le Bel*, Paris.

Giacchero M. (ed.) 1974: *Edictum Diocletiani et collegarum de pretiis rerum venalium*, Genoa.

Giannantonio P. 1972: *Lorenzo Valla filosofo e storiografo dell'umanesimo*, Naples.

Gies J. and F. 1972: *Merchants and Moneymen: the commercial revolution 1000–1500*, New York.

Gille B. 1964: *Les Sources statistiques de l'histoire de France: des enquêtes du XVII siècle à 1870*, Geneva and Paris.

—— 1965–7: *Histoire de la maison Rothschild*, Geneva.

Girard A. 1932: *Le commerce français à Séville et Cadiz au temps des Habsbourg*, Paris and Bordeaux.

Giuseppi M. S. 1923: *A Guide to the Public Manuscripts Preserved in the Public Record Office*, London.

Glass D. V. and Eversley D. E. C. (eds) 1965: *Population in History*, London.

Goitein S. D. 1955: The Cairo Geniza as a source for the history of Muslin civilisation. *Studia Islamica*, III.

—— 1967: *A Mediterranean Society: the Jewish communities of the Arab world as portrayed in the documents of the Cairo Geniza*, Berkeley, Calif.

Gonzales T. (ed.) 1829: *Censo de la población de las provincias y partidos de la corona de Castilla en el siglo XVI*, Madrid.

Goubert P. 1960: *Beauvais et le Beauvaisis de 1600 à 1730*, Paris.

Gould J. D. 1970: *The Great Debasement*, Oxford.

Gras N. S. B. 1927: The rise and development of economic history. *Economic History Review*, I.

Graser E. R. 1940: The significance of two new fragments of the Edict of Diocletian. *Transactions of the American Philological Association*.

Gray Funkhouser H. 1937: Historical development of the graphical representation of statistical data. *Osiris*, III.

Gray Funkhouser H. and Walker H. M. 1935: Playfair and his charts. *Economic History*, III.

Greenfell B. P., Hunt A. S. and Smyly J. G. 1902: *The Tebtunis Papyry*, London.

Grote G. 1846–67; *History of Greece*, London.

Guasti C. (ed.) 1880: *Ser Lapo Mazzei*, Florence.

Guérard B. (ed.) 1844: *Polyptyque de l'abbé Irminon*, Paris.

Guicciardini L. 1581: *Descrittione dei Paesi Bassi*, Antwerp.

Guillaume P. and Poussou J. P. 1970: *Démographie historique*, Paris.

Hall M. V., Krueger H. C. and Reynolds R. L. (eds) 1939: *Guglielmo Cassinese (1190–1192)*, Turin.

Hamilton E. J. 1934: *American Treasure and the Price Revolution in Spain 1501–1650*, Cambridge, Mass.

—— 1950: Origin and growth of the National Debt in France and England. In *Studi in onore di Gino Luzzatto*, Milan.

Hanham A. 1985: *The Celys and their World: an English merchant family in the fifteenth century*, Cambridge.

Harte W. B. 1977: Trend in publications in the economic and social history of Great Britain 1925–74. *Economic History Review*, XXX.

Hauser P. M. and Duncan O. D. 1959: The data and methods. In P. M. Hauser and O. D. Duncan (eds), *The Study of Population*, Chicago.

Heckscher E. F. 1953: A plea for theory in economic history. In F. C. Lane and J. C. Riemersma (eds), *Enterprise and Secular Change*, London.

Hempel C. 1959: The function of general laws in history. In P. Gardiner (ed.), *The Theories of History*, Glencoe, Ill.

Herlihy D. and Klapisch-Zuber C. 1978: *Les Toscans et leurs familles. Une étude du catasto florentin de 1427*, Paris.

Herodotus, 1972 tr.: *The Histories*, tr. A. de Sélincourt, Harmondsworth.

Hicks J. 1979: *Causality in Economics*, Oxford.

Hildebrand B. 1848: *Die National Ökonomie der Gegenwart und Zukunft*, Frankfurt a. M.

Hinton R. W. K. (ed.) 1956: *The Port Books of Boston 1601–1640*, Hereford.

Hoffman W. G., Grumbach F. and Hesse H. 1965: *Das Wachstum der deutschen Wirtschafts seit der Mitte des 19. Jarhrhundert*, Berlin.

Hopkins K. 1978: Rules of evidence. *Journal of Roman Studies*, LXVIII.

Horn W. and Born E. 1979: *The Plan of St Gall*, Berkeley, Calif.

Horton B. J., Ripley J. and Schnapper M. B. 1948: *Dictionary of Modern Economics*, Washington, DC.

Huet P. D. 1716: *Histoire du commerce et de la navigation des Anciens*, Paris.

Hull C. H. (ed.) 1899: *The Economic Writings of Sir William Petty together with the Observations upon the Bills of Mortality More Probably by Captain John Graunt*, Cambridge.

Hull D. L. 1979: In defense of presentism. *History and Theory*, XVIII.

Hutchins J. G. B. 1958: Business history, entrepreneurial history and business administration. *Journal of Economic History*, XVIII.

Hutchinson T. W. 1977: *Knowledge and Ignorance in Economics*, Oxford and Chicago.

India Office Library, Department of Oriental Manuscripts and Printed Books 1986: *Annual Report 1985–1986*, London.

Institut National de la Statistique et des Etudes économiques 1946, 1961, 1966: *Annuaire statistique de la France*, 57, 66, 72: *Résumés rétrospectifs*.

Interdepartmental Committee on Social and Economic Research 1951: *Guide to Official Sources*, II: *Census Reports of Great Britain, 1801–1931*, London.

Istituto Centrale di Statistica 1958: *Sommario di statistiche storiche italiane 1861–1955*, Rome.

Jeanneney J. M. 1957: *Tableaux statistiques relatifs à l'économie française et à l'économie mondiale*, Paris.

Jeannin P. 1964: Les comptes du Sund comme source pour la construction d'indices généraux de l'activité économique en Europe (XVI–XVIII siècle. *Revue historique*, CCXXXI.

John V. 1894: *Geschichte der Statistik*, Stuttgart.

Jones R. F. 1936: *Ancients and Moderns*, St Louis.

Kaeppelin P. 1908: *La Compagnie des Indes Orientales*, Paris.

Kagan R. L. 1989: *Cities of the Golden Age: the views of Anton van den Wyngaerde*, Berkeley, Calif.

Kahan A. 1972: Quantitative data for the study of Russian history. In V. R. Lorwin and J. M. Price (eds), *The Dimensions of the Past*, New Haven, Conn.

Kahler E. 1968: *The Meaning of History*, Cleveland.

Kendall M. G. (ed.) 1952: *The Source and Nature of the Statistics of the United Kingdom*, London.

Keynes J. M. 1973 edn: *The Collected Writings of John Maynard Keynes*, ed. D. Moggridge, XIV: *The General Theory and After*, London.

Kierkegaard S. 1938 tr.: *Journals*, tr. and ed. A Dru, London.

King G. 1936 edn: *Two Tracts*, G. E. Barnett, London.

Kissinger H. 1979: *White House Years*, Boston, Mass.

Klein P. 1989: Storia quantitativa e teoria economica. In S. Cavaciocchi (ed.), *Metodi, risultati e prospettive della storia economica nei secoli XIII–XVIII*, Florence.

Knies K. 1853: *Die politische Ökonomie vom Standpunkte der geschichtliche Methode*, Brunswick.

Koren J. (ed.) 1918: *The History of Statistics*, London.

Kötzschke R. 1924: *Allgemeine Wirtschaftsgeschichte des Mittelalters*, Jena.

Kowalevskii M. M. 1901–14: *Die ökonomische Entwicklung Europas bis zum Beginn der kapitalistischen Wirtschaftsform*, Berlin.

Krueger H. C. and Reynolds R. L. (eds) 1951–3: *Lanfranco (1202–1226)*, Genoa.

Kula W. 1972: *Problemi e metodi di storia economica*, Milan.

Kulischer J. 1925: *Russische Wirtschaftsgeschichte*, Jena.

—— 1928–9: *Allgemeine Wirtschaftsgeschichte des Mittelalters und der neue Zeit*, Munich and Berlin.

Kyd J. G. (ed.) 1952: *Scottish Population Statistics Including Webster's Analysis of Population 1755*, Edinburgh.

La documentación notárial 1984: *La documentación notárial y la historia*, Salamanca.

Laffemas I. 1606: *Histoire du commerce de la France enrichie des plus notables antiquitéz du traffic des pays estrangers*, Paris.

Landes D. S. 1972: Statistics as a source for the history of economic development in Western Europe. The protostatistical era. In V. R. Lorwin and J. M. Price, *The Dimensions of the Past*, New Haven, Conn.

Laxton P. (ed.) 1989: *London Bills of Mortality* (on microfiche), London.

Layard A. H. 1853: *Discoveries in the Ruins of Nineveh and Babylon*, London.

Le Blanc F. 1692: *Traité historique des monnoyes de France*, Paris and Amsterdam.

Leijonhufvud A. 1981: *Information and Coordination*, New York.

Lingotto 1984: *Lingotto. La memoria dell'industria* (study congress), Turin.

List F. 1841: *Das nationale System der politischen Ökonomie*, Stuttgart and Tübingen.

Lodge R. 1894: *The Study of History in a Scottish University*, Glasgow.

Lopez R. S. 1962: *The Birth of Europe*, New York and Philadelphia.

Lopez R. S. and Raymond I. W. (eds) 1955: *Medieval Trade in the Mediterranean World*, New York.

Lorwin V. R. and Price J. M. (eds) 1972: *The Dimensions of the Past: materials, problems and opportunities for quantitative work in history*, New Haven, Conn.

Lot F. (ed.) 1939: *L'état des paroisses et des feux en 1328*, Paris.

Lotto L. 1969 edn: *Libro di spese diverse (1538–1556)*, ed. P. Zampetti, Venice and Rome.

Lowenthal D. 1985: *The Past is a Foreign Country*, Cambridge.

Lunt W. E. 1939: *Financial Relations of the Papacy with England to 1327. Studies in Anglo-Papal Relations during the Middle Ages*, Cambridge.

Luzzatti L. 1929: *Memorie (1841–76)*, Bologna.

Luzzatto G. 1929a: *I prestiti della Repubblica di Venezia nei secoli XII–XV*, Padua.

—— 1929b: Sull'attendibilità di alcune statistiche medievali. *Giornale degli economisti.*

—— 1932: The study of medieval economic history in Italy: recent literature and tendencies. *Journal of Economic and Business History*, IV.

—— (ed.) 1936: *Storia economica*, Turin.

Lynam E. (ed.) 1967: *Richard Hakluyt and his Successors: a volume issued to commemorate the centenary of the Hakluyt Society*, Liechtenstein.

Malanima P. 1988: *I piedi di legno. Una macchina alle origini dell'industria medievale*, Milan.

Malden H. E. (ed.) 1900: *The Cely Papers Selected from the Correspondence of the Cely Family Merchants of the Staple 1475–88*, London.

Mandelbaum M. 1938: *The Problem of Historical Knowledge*, New York.

Marshall A. 1885: *The Present Position of Economics*, Cambridge.

Masson P. 1911: *Histoire du commerce français dans le Levant au XVIII siècle*, Paris.

Marx K. 1970 edn: *Das Kapital*. In *Marx–Engels ausgewählte Werke*, Berlin.

Matthews G. T. (ed.) 1959: *News and Rumor in Renaissance Europe: the Fugger newsletters*, New York.

Matthews R. C. O. and Feinstein C. H. 1982: *British Economic Growth 1856–1973*, Oxford.

McCready B. W. 1837: On the influence of trades, professions and occupations in the US in the production of disease. *Transactions of the Medical Society of the State of New York*, III.

McCullagh C. B. 1984: *Justifying Historical Description*, Cambridge.

McDonald J. and Snooks G. D. 1986: *Domesday Economy*, Oxford.

Meiggs R. 1975: *The Athenian Empire*, Oxford.

Meiggs R. and Lewis D. M. 1969: *A Selection of Greek Historical Inscriptions to the End of the Fifth Century BC*, Oxford.

Melis F. 1972: *Documenti per la storia economica dei secoli XIII–XVI*, Florence.

Meritt B. D., Wade-Gery H. T. and McGregor M. F. 1939–53: *The Athenian Tribute Lists*, Cambridge, Mass., and Princeton, N. J.

Meuvret J. 1946: Les crises de subsistance et la démographie de la France d'ancien régime. *Population*, I.

Miguélez OSA, Padre 1917: *Catalogo de los codices españoles de la Biblioteca de El Escurial*, I: *Relaciones historicas*, Madrid.

Millar F. 1977: *The Emperor in the Roman World*, London, 1977.

Ministero dell'Agricoltura, Industria e Commercio 1884: L'inchiesta agraria in Inghilterra. *Annali*, 1884.

Mirbt C. 1924: *Quellen zur Geschichte der Papstum*, Tübingen.

Mitchell B. R. and Deane P. 1962: *Abstract of British Historical Statistics*, Cambridge.

Moliné-Bertrand A. 1985: *Au siècle d'or. L'Espagne et ses hommes. La population du royaume de Castille au XVI siècle*, Paris.

Mollat M. (ed.) 1952: *Les Affaires de Jacques Coeur. Journal du procureur Dauvet*, Paris.

Momigliano A. 1974, repr. 1980: Historicism revisited. *Medelingen der Koninklijke Nederlandge Akademie van Wetenschappen*, XXXVII; repr. in Momigliano, 1980 (see below).

—— 1974, repr. 1987: Le regole del giuoco nello studio della storia antica. *Annali della Scuola Normale Superiore di Pisa*, 3rd ser., IV; repr. in *Storia e storiografia antica*, Bologna.

—— 1980: *Sesto contributo alla storia delgi studi classici e del mondo antico*, Rome.

Morazé C. 1943: *Introduction à l'histoire économique*, Paris.

Moresco M. and Bognetti G. P. 1938: *Per l'edizione de notai liguri del secolo XII*, Turin.

Morgenstern O. 1965: *On the Accuracy of Economic Observations*, Princeton, NJ.

Morilla Critz J. 1989: Cambios en la viticultura de Andalucia Oriental. *Revista de historia económica*, 7.

Morineau M. 1985: *Incroyables gazettes et fabuleux métaux. Les retours des trésors américains d'après les gazettes hollandaises (XVI–XVII siècles)*, Paris.

Moryson F. 1903 edn: *Itinerary*, ed. C. Hughes, London.

Moryson F. 1907 edn: *An Itinerary*, Glasgow.

Motta E. 1893–5: Documenti visconteo-sforzeschi per la storia della zecca di Milano. *Rivista italiana di numismatica*, 6–8.

Muendel J. 1985: The Mountain Men of the Casentino during the late Middle Ages. *Science and Technology in Medieval Society*, 441.

Müller K. O. (ed.) 1934: *Welthandelsbräuche (1480–1540)*, Stuttgart and Berlin.

Mullett B. D. 1951: *Index Numbers*, New York and London.

Mullins E. L. G. 1958: *Texts and Calendars: an analytical guide to serial publications*, London.

Murphey M. G. 1973: *Our Knowledge of the Historical Past*, Indianapolis.

Myrdal K. G. 1974: *Il tema dell'uguaglianza nello sviluppo mondiale. Lezioni Nobel di Economica*, Rome.

Nash R. C. 1982: The English and Scottish tobacco trades in the seventeenth and eighteenth centuries: legal and illegal trade. *Economic History Review*, 2nd ser., XXXV.

Nicolet C. 1963: A Rome pendant la seconde guerre punique: techniques financières et manipulations monétaires. *Annales ESC*, XVIII.

—— 1971: Les variations des prix et la théorie quantitative de la monnaie à Rome de Cicéron à Pline l'Ancien. *Annales ESC*, XXVI.

Nielsen A. 1933: *Dänische Wirtschaftsgeschichte*, Jena.

Nilsson M. 1962: *Öresundstullräkenskaperna som källa för frakfarten genom Öresund under perioden 1690–1709*, Gothenburg.

Nitti G. P. 1963: Fonti consolari francesi sull'economia italiana del secolo XIX. Archivio Economico dell'Unificazione Italiana, XII.

Noto A. (ed.) 1950: *Liber Datii Mercantie Communis Mediolani (sec. XV)*, Milan.

Origo I. M. (Marchesa) 1957: *The Merchant of Prato: Francesco di Marco Datini*, London.

Orlandini V. (ed.) 1925: *Tarifa zoè noticia dy pexi e mexure di luogi e tere che s'adovra mercandantia per el mondo*, Padua.

Pagnini G. F. 1765–6: *Della decima e di varie altre gravezze imposte dal Comune di Firenze della moneta e della mercatura dei fiorentini fino al secolo XV*, Lisbon and Lucca.

Palmieri M. 1983 edn: *Ricordi fiscali (1427–1474)*, ed. E. Conti, Rome.

Paoli C. 1942: *Diplomatica*, Florence.

Parenti G. 1939: *Prime ricerche sulla rivoluzione dei prezzi in Firenze*, Florence.

Parker W. N. (ed.) 1986: *Economic History and the Modern Economist*, Oxford.

Parodi E. G. 1887: Illustrazione linguistica a frammenti di un libro di banchieri fiorentini. *Giornale storico della letteratura italiana*, X.

Pascal, 1960 tr.: *Pensées*, ed. L. Lafuma, tr. J. Warrington, London.

Patissier P. 1822: *Traité des maladies des artisans*, Paris.

Patterson G. C. 1972: Silver stocks and losses in ancient and medieval time. *Economic History Review*, 2nd ser., XXV.

Pegolotti, F. 1936 edn: *Pratica della mercatura*, ed. A. Evans, Cambridge, Mass.

Perrot J. C. (ed.) 1975: *Statistical Sources on the History of France: prefect studies under the Empire*, New York.

Perrot J. C. and Woolf S. J. 1984: *State and Statistics in France 1789–1815*, New York.

Petrucci A. 1958: *Notarii*, Milan.

Pieper F. C. 1978: *Subject Index to Sources of Comparative International Statistics*, Barkenham.

Piola Caselli F. 1988: La diffusione dei luoghi di monte della Camera Apostolica alla fine del VI secolo. In *Credito e sviluppo economico in Italia dal medioevo all'età contemporanea*, Verona.

Pirenne H. 1937: *Mahomet et Charlemagne*, Paris and Brussels.

Platt, D. C. M. 1963: The role of the British consular service in overseas trade. *Economic History Review*, 2nd ser. XV.

Playfair W. 1786, 2nd edn 1789: *The Commercial and Political Atlas*, London.

Plutarch, 1916 tr: *Lives*, 10 vols, tr. Bernadette Perrin. London.

Pollard S. and Holmes C. 1968–73: *Documents of European Economic History*, 3 vols (1750–1870; 1870–1914; 1914–39), London.

Poole R. L. 1912: *The Exchequer in the Twelfth Century*, Oxford.

Popper K. 1960: *The Poverty of Historicism*, London.

Porta G. 1976/9: Censimento dei manoscritti delle Cronache di Giovanni, Matteo e Filippo Villani. *Studi de filologia italiana*, XXXIV and XXXVII.

Postan M. M. 1973: *Medieval Trade and Finance*, Cambridge.

Poulton H. J. 1972: *The Historian's Handbook: a descriptive guide to reference works*, Norman, Okla.

Power E. 1934: On medieval history as a social history. *Economica*, n.s., I.

Power E. and Postan M. M. 1933: *Studies in English Trade in the Fifteenth Century*, London.

Powicke F. M. and Cheney C. R. 1964: *Councils and Synods*, Oxford.

Proesler H. 1928: *Wirtschaftsgeschichte in Deutschland, ihre Entwicklung und ihre Probleme*, Nuremberg.

Publications of the European Community: *Catalogue*.

Quinn D. B. 1974: *The Hakluyt Handbook*, London.

Ramazzini B. 1700, 2nd edn 1713 (Eng. tr. 1713, repr. 1964): *De Morbis Artificum*

Diatriba, Modena (2nd edn Padua); tr. W. C. Wright as *Diseases of Workers*, London (repr. New York and London).

Redlich F. 1958: History of German economic historiography. *Journal of Economic History*, XVIII.

Reginald of Durham 1845: *Godrich of Finchale*, London.

Reinhard M., Armangaud A. and Dupaquier J. 1968: *Histoire générale de la population mondiale*, Paris.

Renouard Y. 1952, repr. 1968: Intérêt et importance des archives vaticanes pour l'histoire économique du Moyen Age, spécialement du XIV siècle. *Miscellanea archivistica Angelo Mercati*, Vatican City; repr. in Y. Renouard, *Etudes d'histoire médiévale*, I, Paris.

Riccobono S. et al. (eds) 1945: *Acta Divi Augusti*, Rome.

Rice Holmes T. 1983: *The Roman Republic*, London.

Robbins L. 1932: *An Essay on the Nature and Significance of Economic Science*, London.

Roberts M. J. 1974: On the nature and condition of social sciences. *Daedalus*.

Rockinger L. 1863: *Briefsteller und Formelbücher*, Munich.

Rodenwalt E. 1957: Untersuchungen über die Biologie der venetianischen Adels. *Homo*, VIII.

Romani M. 1942: Rilievi di un medico sulle condizioni dei lavoratori del secolo XVII. *Rivista internazionale di scienze sociali*, XX.

Romano R. 1957: Documenti e prime considerazioni intorno alla balance du commerce della Francia dal 1716 al 1780. In *Studi in onore di A. Sapori*, II, Milan.

Roseveare H. (ed.) 1987: *Markets and Merchants of the Late Seventeenth Century: the Marescoe–David letters, 1668–1680*, Oxford.

Rostovzev M. I. 1926: *The Social and Economic History of the Roman Empire*, Oxford.

Ruiz Martín F. 1965: *Lettres marchandes échangées entre Florence et Medina del Campo*, Paris.

—— 1967: La población española al comienzo de los tiempos modernos. *Quadernos de historia. Anexos a la revista Hispania*, Madrid.

Russell J. C. 1948: *British Medieval Population*, Albuquerque.

Sabbe E. 1934: Quelques types de marchands du IX et X siècle. *Revue belge de philologie et d'histoire*, XIII.

Salmon L. M. 1923: *The Newspaper and the Historian*, Oxford.

Salomon N. 1964: *La Campagne de Nouvelle Castille à la fin du XVI siècle d'après les Relaciones Topográficas*, Paris.

Salvati M. 1978: *Alle origini dell'inflazione italiana*, Bologna.

Sanz Serrano A. 1956: *Resumen historico de la estadística en España. Centenario de la estadística oficial española 1856–1956*, Madrid.

Sapori A. 1929, repr. 1955: L'attendibilità di alcune testimonianze cronistiche della economia medievale. *Archivio storico italiano*, repr. in Sapori, 1955b (see below).

—— (ed.) 1934: *I libri di commercio dei Peruzzi*, Milan.

—— (ed.) 1946: *I libri della ragione bancaria dei Gianfigliazzi*, Milan.

—— (ed.) 1952: *I libri degli Alberti del Guidice*, Milan.

—— 1955a: Saggio sulle fonti della storia economica medievale. In Sapori, 1955b (see below).

—— 1955b: *Studi di storia economica*, Florence.

—— (ed.) 1970: *Libro giallo della Compagnia dei Covoni*, Milan, 1970.

Savary des Bruslons J. 1679: *Le Parfait Négociant*, 2nd edn, Paris.

Schiavone A. 1987: *Giuristi e nobili nella Roma repubblicana*, Bari.

Schlote W. 1938: *Entwicklung und Structurwandlungen der englischen Aussenhandel von 1700 bis zum Gegenwart*, Jena.

Schmoller G. F. von 1879: *Die strassburger Tucher und Weberzunft*, Strasbourg.

—— 1892: *Die Handelspolitik der wichtigeren Kulturstaaten in dem letzten Jarzehnten*, Leipzig.

—— 1901a: *Grundriss der allgemeinen Volkswirtschaftslehre*, Leipzig.

—— 1901b: *Deutsches Städtwesen in älteren Zeit*, Bonn and Leipzig.

Schumpeter E. B. 1960: *English Overseas Trade Statistics, 1697-1808*, Oxford.

Schumpeter J. A. 1947: The creative response in economic history. *Journal of Economic History*, VII (1947).

—— 1954: *History of Economic Analysis*, London.

Séa H. 1930-6: *Französische Wirtschaftsgeschichte*, Jena.

Sella D. 1968: *Salari e lavoro nell'edilizia lombarda durante il secolo XVII*, Pavia.

Shannon A. 1934: Bricks: a trade index 1785-1849. *Economica*, n.s., I.

Shryock H. S., Siegel J. S. et al. 1976: *The Methods and Materials of Demography*, abridged E. G. Stockwell, New York, San Francisco and London.

Sieveking H. 1906-7: Studio sulle finanze genovesi nel medio evo ed in particolare sulla Casa di S. Giorgio. *Atti della Società Ligure di Storia Patria*, XV.

Smith J. 1921: *Old Scottish Clockmakers*, Edinburgh.

Solmi A. 1932: *L'amministrazione finanziaria del Regno Italico nell'alto medioevo*, Pavia.

Solow R. E. 1986: Economics: is something missing? In W. N. Parker (ed.), *Economic History and the Modern Economist*, Oxford.

Sombart W. 1915: *The Quintessence of Capitalism*, London.

—— 1924: *Der moderne Kapitalismus*, Munich and Leipzig.

—— 1929: Economic theory and economic history. *Economic History Review*, II (1929).

Stanford M. 1986: *The Nature of Historical Knowledge*, Oxford.

Statistical Office of the European Communities 1961: *Basic Statistics of the Community*, Brussels.

Statistikk Sentralbyrå 1969: *Historisk Statistikk*, Oslo.

Statistisches Bundesamt 1972: *Bevölkerung und Wirtschaft 1872-1972*, Stuttgart.

Stengers J. 1970: L'historien devant l'abondance statistique. *Revue de l'Institut de Sociologie*.

Stigler S. M. 1986: *The History of Statistics*, Cambridge, Mass.

Strieder J. 1905: *Die Inventur der Firma Fugger aus dem Jahre 1527*, Tübingen.

Stuart Hughes H. 1968: *Consciousness and Society*, New York.

Stussi A. (ed.) 1967: *Zibaldone da Canal manoscritto mercantile del secolo XIV*, Venice.

Swierenga R. P. 1981: Dutch international migration statistics 1820-1860. *International Migration Review*, 115.

Tarlé E. V. 1950: *La vita economica dell'Italia nell'età napoleonica*, Turin.

Tedlow R. S. 1985: Business history in the United States: past accomplishments and future directions. *Annali di storia dell'impresa*, I.

Thackrah C. T. 1831: *The Effects of the Principal Arts, Trades and Professions . . . on Health and Longevity, with a Particular Reference to the Trades and Manufactures of Leeds*, London.

Thirsk J. and Cooper J. P. (eds) 1972: *Seventeenth Century Economic Documents*, Oxford.

Thucydides, 1919 tr.: *History of the Peloponnesian War*, London.

Tilling L. 1975: Early experimental graphs. *British Journal for the History of Science*, VIII.

Tilly L. and C. 1972: A selected bibliography of quantitative sources for French history and French sources for quantitative history since 1789. In V. R. Lorwin and J. M. Price, *The Dimensions of the Past*, New Haven, Conn.

Tucci, V. (ed.) 1957: *Lettres d'un marchand vénitien, Andrea Berengo 1553–1556*, Paris.

Tufte E. R. 1983: *The Visual Display of Quantitative Information*, Cheshire.

Turner H. T. (ed.) 1841: *Manners and Household Expenses of England in the 13th and 15th Century*, London.

Union of International Associations 1969: *Directory of Periodicals Published by International Organizations*, Brussels.

United Nations 1955: Methods of appraisal of quality of basic data for population estimates. *Population Studies*, 23.

US Department of Commerce, Bureau of the Census 1975: *Historical Statistics of the United States*, Washington, DC.

US Government Printing Office 1978: *Legal and Illegal Immigration to the US*, Washington, DC.

US National Archives 1948: *Guide to the Records in the National Archives*, Washington, DC.

Urquhart M. C. and Buckley K. A. H. 1965: *Historical Statistics of Canada*, Cambridge.

Valla L. 1928 edn: *De falso credito et ementita Constantini donatione declamatio*, ed. W. Schwahn, Leipzig.

Vazquez de Prada, V. 1960–4: *Lettres marchandes d'Anvers*, Paris.

Vercauteren F. 1967: The circulation of merchants in Western Europe from the 6th to the 10th century. In S. L. Thrupp (ed.), *Early Medieval Society*, New York.

—— 1970: From the ancient city to the medieval commune. In R. Cameron (ed.), *Essays in French Economic History*, Homewood, Ill.

Vettori F. 1738: *Il fiorino d'oro antico illustrato*, Florence.

Veyne P. 1971: *Comment on écrit l'histoire*, Paris.

Vila Vilar E. 1982: Las ferias de Portobelo: apriencia y realidad del comercio con Indias. *Anuario de estudios americanos*, XXXIX.

Villermé L. R. 1840: *Tableau de l'état physique et morale des ouvriers employés dans les manufactures de coton, laine et de soie*, Paris.

Vinas y Mey C. and Paz R. (eds) 1949: *Relaciones historico geográfico estadísticas de los pueblos de España hechas por inicitativa de Felipe II*, Madrid.

Vincent J. M. 1911: *Historical Research: an outline of theory and practice*, New York.

Visconti A. 1911: Il Magistrato di Sanità nello Stato di Milano. *Archivio storico lombardo*, 4th ser., XV. 38.

Volpe G. 1928: Aziende agrarie medioevali. *Medioevo italiano*, Florence.

Warmington E.H. 1974: *The Commerce between the Roman Empire and India*, London.

Wasserman O'Brien J. and Wasserman S. R. 1986: *Statistics Sources*, Detroit.

Weitnauer A. 1981: *Venezianischer Handel der Fugger nach der Musterbuchhaltung des Matthäus Schwarz*, Munich and Leipzig.

Wells, C. M. 1984: *The Roman Empire*, Glasgow.

Westergaard H. 1932: *Contributions to the History of Statistics*, London.

White L. T. 1962: *Medieval Technology and Social Change*, Oxford.

Will E. 1973: La Grande Grèce, milieu d'échanges. Réflexions méthodologiques. In *Economia e società nella Magna Grecia* (proceedings of the Twelfth Congress of Taranto on Graecia Magna), Naples.

Williams J. B. 1926: *A Guide to the Printed Materials for English Social and Economic History 1750–1780*, New York.

Williams N. 1955: The London Port Books. *Transactions of the London and Middlesex Archaeological Society*, 18, pt 1.

Williams N. J. 1911: Francis Shaxton and the Elizabethan Port Books. *English Historical Review*, LXVI.

Williams S. 1985: *Diocletian and the Roman Recovery*, New York.

Wilson C. and Parker G. 1977: *An Introduction to the Sources of European Economic History 1500–1800*, Ithaca, NY.

Wilson R. G. 1971: *Gentlemen Merchants: the merchant community in Leeds 1700–1830*, New York.

Woodward D. 1973: The Port Books of England and Wales. *Maritime History*, II.

Woolf S. J. 1984: Statistics, in J. C. Perrot and S. J. Woolf, *State and Statistics in France*, New York.

Wrigley E. A. and Schofield R. S. 1981: *The Population History of England 1541–1871*, Cambridge, Mass.

Zaninelli S. 1965: Una fonte per la storia dell'economia del Lombardo Veneto nella prima metà del secolo XIX: le Tafeln zur Statistik der Oesterreichischen Monarchie. *Archivio Economico dell'Unificazione Italiana*, 1st ser., XII.

Index